Harcourt
Health and Fitness

Harcourt

SCHOOL PUBLISHERS

Orlando • Austin • New York • San Diego • Toronto • London

Visit *The Learning Site!*
www.harcourtschool.com

CONSULTING AUTHORS

Lisa Bunting, M.Ed.
Physical Education Teacher
Katy Independent School District
Houston, Texas

Thomas M. Fleming, Ph.D.
Health and Physical Education
   Consultant
Austin, Texas

Charlie Gibbons, Ed.D.
Director, Youth and School Age
   Programs
Maxwell Air Force Base, Alabama
Former Adjunct Professor,
   Alabama State University
Health, Physical Education and
   Dance Department
Montgomery, Alabama

Jan Marie Ozias, Ph.D., R.N.
Director, Texas Diabetes Council;
   and Consultant, School Health
   Programs
Austin, Texas

Carl Anthony Stockton, Ph.D.
Dean, School of Education
The University of Texas at
   Brownsville and Texas
   Southmost College
Brownsville, Texas
Former Department Chair and
   Professor of Health Education
Department of Health and
   Applied Human Sciences
The University of North Carolina
   at Wilmington
Wilmington, North Carolina

Requests for permission to make copies of any part of the work should be addressed to School Permissions and Copyrights, Harcourt, Inc., 6277 Sea Harbor Drive, Orlando, Florida 32887-6777. Fax: 407-345-2418.

HARCOURT and the Harcourt Logo are trademarks of Harcourt, Inc., registered in the United States of America and/or other jurisdictions.

Grateful acknowledgment is made to the Partnership for Food Safety Education for permission to reprint Fight BAC! information graphic. Copyright 2003 by Partnership for Food Safety Education.

Printed in the United States of America

ISBN 0-15-337527-2

3 4 5 6 7 8 9 10   032   13 12 11 10 09 08 07 06 05

Chapters

Contents

Why should you learn about health?

You can do many things to help yourself stay healthy and fit. Just as importantly, you can avoid doing things that will harm you. If you know ways to stay safe and healthy and do these things, you can help yourself have good health throughout your life.

Keeping clean

Eating right

Getting enough rest

Staying active

Having good relationships with family and friends

Avoiding alcohol, tobacco, and other drugs

Dealing with emotions in positive ways

Why should you learn about life skills?

Being healthy and fit doesn't come from just knowing facts. You also have to think about these facts and know how to use them every day.

These are some important life skills for you to have:

Communicating

Sharing ideas, needs, and feelings with others

Making Responsible Decisions

Deciding the most responsible thing to do to avoid taking risks

Managing Stress

Finding ways to avoid and relieve negative feelings and emotions

Refusing

Saying *no* to doing things that are risky and dangerous

Setting Goals

Deciding on specific ways to make improvements to your health and fitness

Resolving Conflicts

Finding solutions to problems in ways that let both sides win

Whenever you see ![LIFE SKILLS] in this book, you can learn more about using life skills.

Building Good Character

Why should you learn about good character?

Having good character is also an important part of having good health. When you have good character, you have good relationships with others and can make responsible decisions about your health and fitness.

These are some important character traits:

Caring
Showing kindness and concern for friends, family, and others

Citizenship
Having pride in your school and community and obeying rules and laws

Fairness
Treating others equally, playing by the rules, and being a good sport

Respect

Showing consideration for yourself and others

Responsibility

Doing what you are supposed to do, practicing self-control, and completing tasks

Trustworthiness

Being honest, dependable, and loyal

Whenever you see **Building Good Character** in this book, you can learn more about building good character.

What are ways to be a successful reader?

Students need good reading skills to do well in school. Here are some tips to help you understand, remember, and use information you read.

Reading Tip

These sections can help you know what to look for as you read.

Reading Tip

Vocabulary words are listed at the beginning of the lesson so you can preview them. They are also highlighted and defined when they are first used.

LESSON 3

Staying Safe in a Conflict

Lesson Focus
You can resolve conflicts without fighting. You can learn skills to avoid getting hurt as a result of violence.

Why Learn This?
When you practice these skills, you reduce your risk of injury.

Vocabulary
bully
gang
weapon

Resolving Conflict

Conflict among people is normal. There are ways to resolve conflicts without fighting. Here are some suggestions:

- Stay calm. Keep your voice even and quiet.
- Speak respectfully. Do not call the other person names. Say "Please," "Thank you," and "I'm sorry."
- Agree that there is a problem. Listen to the other side. Try to see things the way others see them.
- Identify choices to end the conflict. Each person should compromise, or give a little.
- Leave if another person threatens you.

 DRAW CONCLUSIONS Why is it important to resolve conflicts peacefully?

Quick **Activity**

Resolving a Problem Look at the picture. Write how you would go about resolving the conflict these students are having.

148

Check your understanding by answering these questions at the end of each section. These questions also help you practice reading skills. You will see six reading focus skills:

► Compare and Contrast
► Draw Conclusions
► Identify Cause and Effect
► Identify Main Idea and Details
► Sequence
► Summarize

Whenever you see (Focus Skill) in this book, you can learn more about using reading skills.

Reading Tip

Use this section to summarize what you have read, review vocabulary and concepts, and practice writing skills.

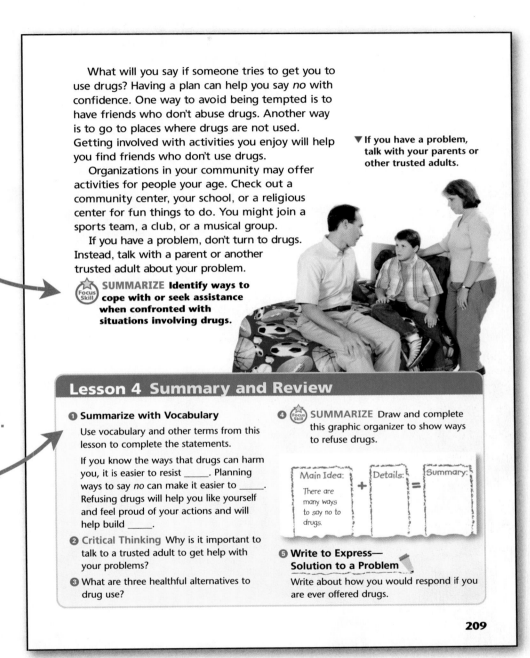

What will you say if someone tries to get you to use drugs? Having a plan can help you say *no* with confidence. One way to avoid being tempted is to have friends who don't abuse drugs. Another way is to go to places where drugs are not used. Getting involved with activities you enjoy will help you find friends who don't use drugs.

Organizations in your community may offer activities for people your age. Check out a community center, your school, or a religious center for fun things to do. You might join a sports team, a club, or a musical group.

If you have a problem, don't turn to drugs. Instead, talk with a parent or another trusted adult about your problem.

(Focus Skill) **SUMMARIZE Identify ways to cope with or seek assistance when confronted with situations involving drugs.**

▼ If you have a problem, talk with your parents or other trusted adults.

Lesson 4 Summary and Review

❶ **Summarize with Vocabulary**

Use vocabulary and other terms from this lesson to complete the statements.

If you know the ways that drugs can harm you, it is easier to resist _____. Planning ways to say *no* can make it easier to _____. Refusing drugs will help you like yourself and feel proud of your actions and will help build _____.

❷ **Critical Thinking** Why is it important to talk to a trusted adult to get help with your problems?

❸ What are three healthful alternatives to drug use?

❹ (Focus Skill) **SUMMARIZE** Draw and complete this graphic organizer to show ways to refuse drugs.

Main Idea: + Details: = Summary:
There are many ways to say no to drugs.

❺ **Write to Express— Solution to a Problem** ✏️
Write about how you would respond if you are ever offered drugs.

209

Throughout **Harcourt Health and Fitness**, you will have many opportunities to learn new ideas and skills that will lead to good health.

CHAPTER 1

Body Systems at Work

SEQUENCE When you sequence, you show the order in which things occur. Use the Reading in Health Handbook on pages 338–339 and this graphic organizer to help you read the health facts in this chapter.

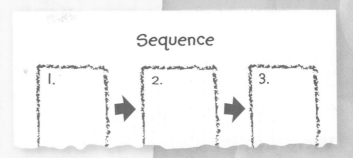

Sequence

1. → 2. → 3.

Health Graph

INTERPRET DATA The human body is about two-thirds water. Muscles are three-fourths water, and bones are about one-fourth water. In a 150-pound man, about how much more do the muscles weigh than the bones?

Weight of Organs
(150-Pound Man)

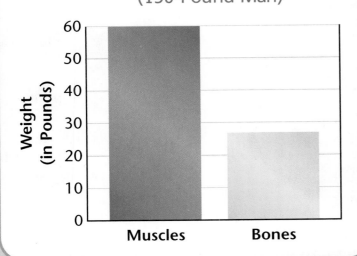

Daily Physical Activity

You should exercise to keep all of your body systems healthy.

 Be Active!
Use the selection Track 1, **Saucy Salsa**, to get your whole body moving.

You Are Growing

Lesson Focus
As you grow, your body will change.

Why Learn This?
As you learn what causes growth, you will understand the changes in your own body.

Vocabulary

trait
cell
nucleus
tissue
organs
system

Traits

Think of some physical qualities that describe you. You may have red hair like your mother's. Your nose may look like your father's. These qualities are examples of traits. A **trait** (TRAYT) is a characteristic, or quality, that you have. You may also have blue eyes like your grandmother's. She may have passed that trait on to your father, who passed it on to you. Characteristics passed on to you from your parents in this way are called *inherited* (in•HEHR•uh•tuhd) *traits*.

The instructions for your inherited traits are contained within each of your body cells. A **cell** is the smallest working part of your body. Some inherited traits affect the way your body works. Other traits affect how you look.

▲ What physical traits did this mother and father pass on to their daughter?

Some traits are not inherited. Your *acquired* (uh•KWYRD) *traits* are characteristics you develop as a result of your life experiences. For example, you might like to take care of dogs. Your parents might like dogs, too. But this trait was not passed to you through your parents' cells. You developed an interest in dogs after you were born. You might enjoy skateboarding, reading, or belonging to a club. Acquired traits may change as your interests change. Inherited traits do not change simply because your interests change.

Some traits may be both inherited and acquired. For example, you might be good at playing a musical instrument. You inherited a musical ability. You have become a skilled player because you have practiced. You practiced because you acquired the interest.

No two people are exactly alike. Together, your interests, skills, and talents make you a unique person.

SEQUENCE Describe how you might have ended up with an inherited trait from your grandmother.

Did You Know?

Identical twins have the same inherited traits. They look exactly alike and are either both boys or both girls. Fraternal twins do not have the same inherited traits. They do not look exactly alike. They can both be boys, both be girls, or a boy and a girl.

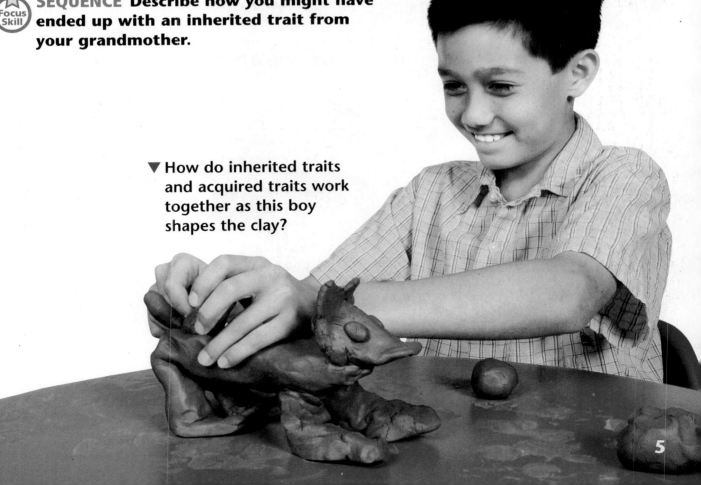

▼ How do inherited traits and acquired traits work together as this boy shapes the clay?

5

Activities of Cells

All living things are made up of cells. Cells take in food and get rid of waste. They grow, multiply, and die. The cells that make up your body come in many different shapes and sizes.

You grew from a single cell, which divided to make two cells. This process has continued, and now your body has trillions of cells. Your body's cells will continue to divide, making you grow and replacing worn-out cells. You can see some parts of a cell in the diagram below.

Different types of cells do different types of work. Red blood cells carry oxygen to all parts of the body. Nerve cells carry messages.

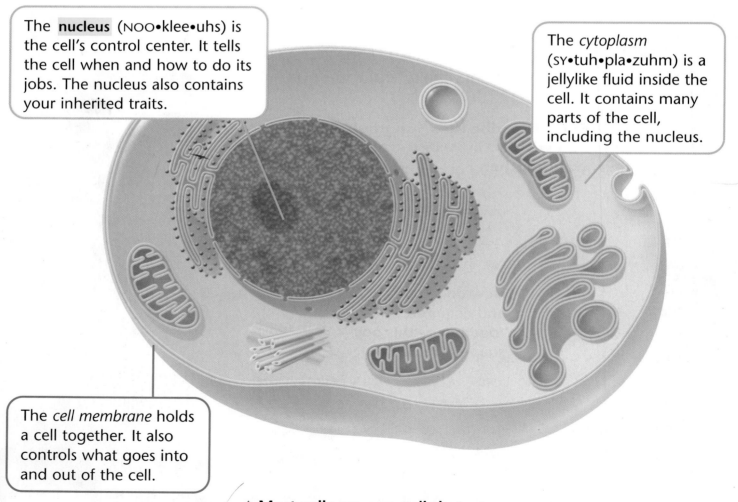

The **nucleus** (NOO•klee•uhs) is the cell's control center. It tells the cell when and how to do its jobs. The nucleus also contains your inherited traits.

The *cytoplasm* (SY•tuh•pla•zuhm) is a jellylike fluid inside the cell. It contains many parts of the cell, including the nucleus.

The *cell membrane* holds a cell together. It also controls what goes into and out of the cell.

▲ Most cells are so small that you can see them only through a microscope.

Types of Tissue

Tissue	Function
Muscle Tissue	Muscle cells are long and narrow. Muscle tissue contracts and relaxes to make your body parts move.
Epithelial Tissue	Epithelial cells are wide and flat. These tissues line surfaces inside your body and make up the outer layer of your skin.
Connective Tissue	Connective tissue holds up your body and connects all its parts. Bone is one kind of connective tissue.
Nerve Tissue	Nerve cells are long, and they branch through your body. Nerve tissue carries messages.

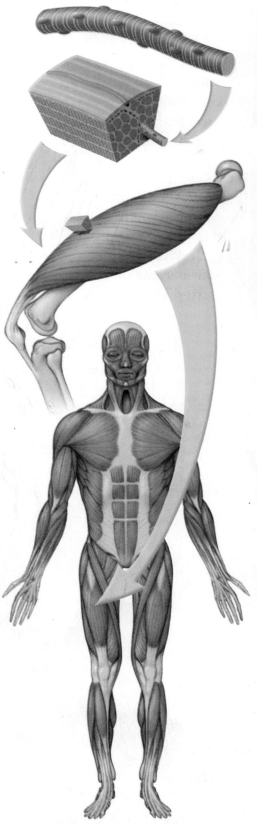

▲ Tell how cells join together to make up the muscular system.

A group of cells that work together to do a job in the body is called **tissue**. Groups of tissues join together to form **organs**. Each organ has a job to do. For example, your heart is an organ made mostly of muscle tissue. It pumps blood through your body. Other organs include your stomach, lungs, and brain.

Sometimes several organs work together to do a job. Groups of organs that work together are called a **system**. Your brain, nerves, and spinal cord make up your nervous system. Together, they send and receive messages throughout your body.

COMPARE AND CONTRAST Tell how organs are alike and different.

Real-Life Situation
Suppose you are
concerned about the
growth changes your
body is going
through.
Real-Life Plan
Write how you can
go about discussing
this concern or other
critical issues with
your parents or other
trusted adults.

Growing and Changing

When you get ready for school every year, do you notice that your old clothes no longer fit? That is because your body is growing. Between the ages of two and eleven, you grow about 2 or 3 inches each year. After age ten, girls have a growth spurt. They grow faster than boys for about two years. Then boys have a growth spurt.

This period of rapid growth is called *adolescence* (a•duhl•EH•suhnts). The physical changes you experience during adolescence are called *puberty*. Ask your parents or another trusted adult about these growth changes.

Everyone grows at his or her own rate. As a teenager, you will grow rapidly. Your looks will change in many ways. The different parts of your body will grow at different times and rates. For a time, it may be awkward for you to move or perform well in sports. This is normal. You will grow at your own rate until you reach adulthood.

▼ No two people are the same. Your size and shape differ from many other people your age.

Taking care of your body will help you reach your full height and size. Here are some healthful behaviors that can help:

- Eat healthfully. Choose fruits, vegetables, and low-fat meat and poultry. Limit sugary and high-fat snacks. Cells need the right nutrients to work best.

- Get enough physical activity—about one hour every day. Go for a walk, play on a sports team, or ride a bike. Being active helps deliver oxygen and nutrients to your cells and can also strengthen your heart.

- Get enough sleep. If you are tired, rest. People your age need about nine hours of sleep every night.

CAUSE AND EFFECT Why does your body change during adolescence?

Consumer Activity

Access Valid Health Information Find out more about how bones grow. Do adults and children have the same number of bones? What minerals are found in bones? Use the guidelines on pages 52–54. Write down the information you find.

Lesson 1 Summary and Review

❶ Summarize with Vocabulary

Use vocabulary and other terms from this lesson to complete these statements.

A trait passed on to you from your parents is an _____. The _____ is the control center of a _____. Groups of _____ join together to form _____, which work together as a _____.

❷ How are inherited traits and acquired traits alike? How are they different?

❸ Critical Thinking Describe how the activities and functions of a cell are like a house with a fence around it.

❹ SEQUENCE Fill in this graphic organizer to show the sequence of growth from child to adult.

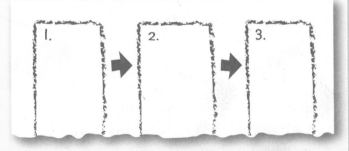

❺ Write to Inform—Description

Write a paragraph describing how you have grown since first grade.

Manage Stress
As You Grow

It can be hard to deal with changes in your body as you grow. Sometimes you might feel clumsy. You might trip over your own feet or drop a ball. Use the steps for **Managing Stress** to help you handle the stress of your changing body.

Lately, LaToya has grown taller and thinner. She is having a hard time coordinating her hands and arms. How can LaToya handle the stress she feels when she plays softball?

1 **Know what stress feels like and what causes it.**

2 **Try to determine the cause of the stress.**

Just before softball games, LaToya gets a headache and sweaty palms.

LaToya feels stressed because she doesn't want to let the team down or be made fun of.

3 Prepare to handle a stressful situation.

LaToya decides to practice with her father.

4 Think positively rather than negatively.

LaToya imagines herself catching the ball. She gives her full attention to what she is doing and tries her best.

Problem Solving

Miguel is getting ready to go to a party. He puts on his favorite jacket, but it doesn't fit. The sleeves are too short. Miguel is upset that he can't wear the jacket. Miguel has outgrown a lot of his clothes lately. Use the steps for **Managing Stress** to help Miguel manage his feelings about outgrowing his clothes. If you were Miguel's friend, what might you do to show caring in helping him to deal with his feelings?

The Brain and Nervous System

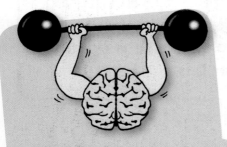

Your Nervous System

Your **nervous system** coordinates all your body's activities. You might think of the nervous system as a communications system.

The nervous system has two main parts. One part is the central nervous system, made up of the brain and the spinal cord. The **brain** is an organ that controls the nervous system. The spinal cord is a long column of nerve tissue. It links the brain with other parts of your body and helps send and receive messages. The other part of the nervous system is made up of nerves. **Nerves** are bundles of fibers that carry messages.

Identify the parts of the nervous system. What messages are being communicated in this person's body?▲

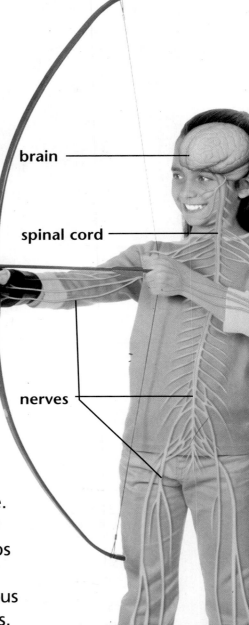

brain

spinal cord

nerves

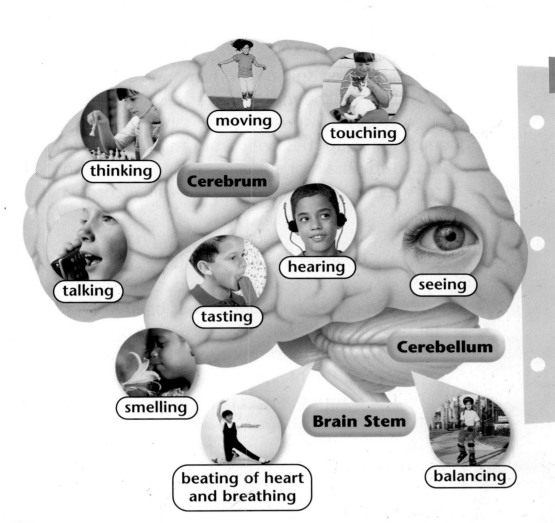

moving

touching

thinking

Cerebrum

talking

hearing

tasting

seeing

Cerebellum

smelling

Brain Stem

balancing

beating of heart and breathing

PERSONAL HEALTH PLAN ▶

Real-Life Situation
Your brain sends messages to parts of your body to help it function correctly. Suppose you want to help your brain do its job.

Real-Life Plan
Using the tips below, pick two behaviors that can help you take care of your brain. Write how you will plan to practice these behaviors.

The brain has three main parts. Each part has different jobs. Locate the parts in the diagram above.

The *cerebrum* (suh•REE•bruhm) controls thinking, memories, movement, and the five senses.

The *cerebellum* (sehr•uh•BEH•luhm) helps you keep your balance.

The *brain stem* controls your breathing and your heart rate.

SUMMARIZE How do the parts of the nervous system work together?

Caring for Your Nervous System

- Get enough sleep.

- Eat healthfully. Your brain needs protein and energy from foods.

- Avoid using tobacco, alcohol, and other harmful drugs.

- Wear a safety belt in vehicles.

- Wear a helmet for certain sports and physical activities.

Messages to and from Your Brain

Explain how this person's eyes, nerves, brain, and muscles work together to let her know when it is safe to cross the street. ▼

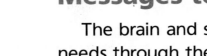

The brain and spinal cord respond to your body's needs through the messages carried by millions of nerve cells, or *neurons* (NOO•rahnz). Sensory neurons pick up messages from the body and send them to the brain or spinal cord. Motor neurons carry messages from the brain or spinal cord to muscles.

Suppose you are walking home and a stranger in a car pulls up beside you. Sensory neurons from your eyes carry the image to your brain. Your brain interprets the image and sends the message "Run!" to motor neurons in your spinal cord, which send the message to your leg muscles.

DRAW CONCLUSIONS Use what you read about neurons to describe what might happen when someone tosses you a ball.

Lesson 2 Summary and Review

❶ Summarize with Vocabulary

Use vocabulary and other terms from this lesson to complete these statements.

Your _____ is made up of the brain, spinal cord, and nerves. The _____ controls the nervous system. _____ carry messages. The part of the brain that controls breathing is the _____. Another name for nerve cells is _____.

❷ Explain how the nervous system is like a communications system.

❸ Critical Thinking How might the tips on page 13 help your nervous system?

❹ (Focus Skill) SEQUENCE Suppose you hear a strange noise in the middle of the night. Describe how messages move through your nervous system.

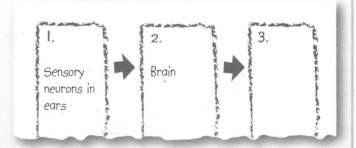

❺ Write to Inform—Narration

Write about a day in the life of your brain. Tell all the ways that your brain took care of your body and why its work was important.

Respect

Accepting Individual Differences

People have different shapes and are different sizes. They also have different physical and mental abilities. Every person, regardless of ability, deserves to be treated with respect. Here are ways to show respect for individual differences:

- **Avoid using put-downs. Don't call someone names.**
- **Think about how the other person feels. Put yourself in that person's place.**
- **Apologize if you hurt someone's feelings.**
- **Avoid talking unkindly about someone just because of his or her looks.**
- **Encourage others to try their best, regardless of their abilities.**
- **Try not to exclude others from your clubs or games. Give everyone a fair chance.**
- **If you see a person bullying someone else, tell your teacher or another trusted adult.**
- **Appreciate what is special about yourself and others.**

Activity

During physical education or one of your other classes, encourage one of your classmates to do his or her best. Make a list of the ways that you can show respect toward others. Share your list with your classmates.

The Digestive System

Lesson Focus

Your digestive system helps your body get energy from food.

Why Learn This?

Learning about your digestive system will help you take better care of it.

Vocabulary

esophagus
stomach
small intestine
large intestine
nutrients

Your Digestive System

Your body needs food. Food gives you energy to think, move, and grow. Your body needs energy for everything it does. The system that breaks down food is the digestive system.

The diagram shows your digestive system. It has several different parts. The mouth contains teeth, which break down food into smaller pieces. The **esophagus** (ih•SAH•fuh•guhs) is a tubelike organ that pushes food from your mouth to your stomach. The **stomach** is an organ that churns and mixes digestive juices with food.

The **small intestine** is another tubelike organ. It is just below your stomach. Food goes from the stomach to the small intestine. Another organ involved with digestion is the *liver*. The liver sends bile to the small intestine. Bile is a substance that breaks down fats into smaller particles that can be digested more easily.

The walls of the small intestine are lined with many small, finger-shaped bumps. Tiny blood vessels here absorb nutrients from digested food. From the small intestine, food goes to the **large intestine**, the last major organ of the digestive system. This tubelike organ handles solid wastes.

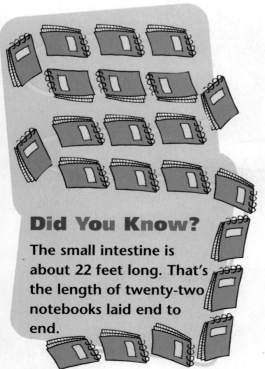

Did You Know?

The small intestine is about 22 feet long. That's the length of twenty-two notebooks laid end to end.

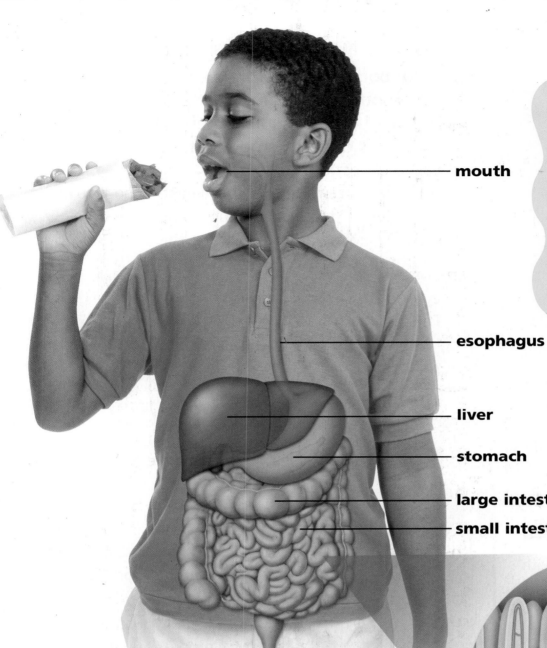

mouth

esophagus

liver

stomach

large intestine

small intestine

Quick Activity

Small Intestine Model
Fold a $\frac{1}{2}$-inch-wide strip of newspaper like an accordion. Lay it on a flat sheet of notebook paper. Add more until you cover the flat paper. The folded strips are like the bumps that line the small intestine.

▲ The wall lining of the small intestine.

 SEQUENCE List in order starting with the mouth the organs that make up your digestive system.

17

Digestion of Food

Your body can't use food in the form that you eat it. Food must be broken down into **nutrients** (NOO·tree·uhnts), or substances the body can use. This process of breaking down food into nutrients is called *digestion*.

In the diagram below, you can see the path that food takes as it travels through your digestive system. Use your finger to trace the path as you read about each step.

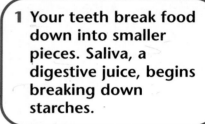

1 Your teeth break food down into smaller pieces. Saliva, a digestive juice, begins breaking down starches.

2 Muscles in the esophagus push food from the mouth to the stomach.

3 In the stomach, more digestive juices mix with the food. The food gets churned, broken down into nutrients, and pushed out of your stomach as a thick liquid.

4 Most digestion takes place in the small intestine, where digestive juices finish breaking down food. Nutrients are absorbed here into your blood and carried throughout your body to your cells. Your cells use the nutrients for energy and growth.

5 The leftover material that can't be used by the body is pushed into the large intestine. There, water in the material is absorbed.

6 Solid wastes pass into the *rectum*, the last part of the large intestine, and then out of the body.

Many foods contain an important substance called fiber. *Fiber* comes from plants. Your body cells don't need fiber. However, your digestive system needs it to help move food and wastes through the system. Oatmeal, brown rice, and beans are good sources of fiber. So are fruits such as oranges, apples, and pears. Vegetables such as broccoli, corn, and peas have a lot of fiber, too.

Drinking plenty of water and doing physical activity also help move food and wastes through your digestive system. A good way to protect your digestive system is to avoid tobacco and alcohol. These substances can cause diseases in digestive organs.

SUMMARIZE Why does your body need fiber?

▼ **Which of these high-fiber foods are a part of your diet?**

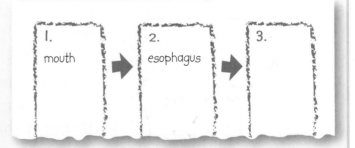

Lesson 3 Summary and Review

1 Summarize with Vocabulary

Use vocabulary and other terms from this lesson to complete these statements.

The _____ pushes food from your mouth to your _____. Food spends time in the _____ before going to the _____, where water and solid wastes are removed. The _____ makes bile to help digest fats.

2 In what organ of the digestive system does most digestion of food take place?

3 Critical Thinking How can being ill affect your digestive process?

4 (Focus Skill) SEQUENCE Draw and complete this graphic organizer to show how food moves through the digestive system.

1. mouth	→	2. esophagus	→	3.

5 Write to Inform—Explanation

Write a paragraph explaining how to take care of your digestive system. How can your behavior help?

The Respiratory and Circulatory Systems

Your Respiratory System

You've probably seen someone choke because food "went down the wrong way." Instead of going into the digestive system, the food went into the respiratory system.

Your respiratory system moves air into and out of the body. All your body's cells need oxygen from the air to live. When you breathe in, air from your mouth or nose goes into your **trachea** (TRAY•kee•uh), an organ that carries air into the lungs. The trachea branches into two smaller tubes called **bronchi** (BRAHNG•ky).

The trachea and bronchi are coated with mucus. Mucus is a sticky substance that traps germs and dust. Tiny hairs line the trachea and bronchi. These hairs constantly sweep the mucus up and out. This keeps dirt and germs out of your lungs. Smoking and breathing in tobacco smoke harm these small hairs. Tobacco smoke destroys lung tissue. It also decreases the amount of oxygen that can get into blood cells.

The **lungs** are organs that allow oxygen to pass into your body. Inside the lungs, oxygen passes through the thin walls of tiny air sacs. There, the oxygen moves into the blood and is carried to all parts of the body. Carbon dioxide from all parts of the body is carried by your blood into the lungs. Carbon dioxide is a waste gas. It goes out of your body when you exhale.

Breathing is made possible by the **diaphragm** (DY•uh•fram), a muscle beneath your lungs. When this muscle moves, air is moved into or out of your lungs.

 SEQUENCE Follow the path of oxygen from your mouth or nose into your blood vessels.

Quick Activity

Graph Your Breathing Record the number of breaths you take while sitting, walking, and running at different speeds. Then graph and interpret the data you collect.

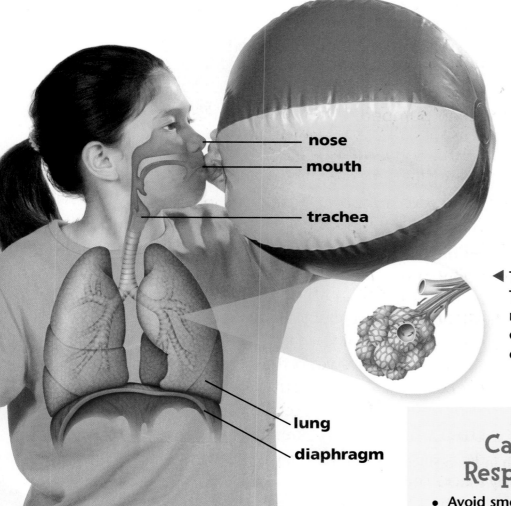

- nose
- mouth
- trachea
- lung
- diaphragm

◀ The lungs contain tiny air sacs. The walls of these air sacs have many blood vessels, where oxygen enters the blood and carbon dioxide leaves it.

Caring for Your Respiratory System

- Avoid smoking and breathing in tobacco smoke.

- Add active exercise to your daily activity.

- If you have asthma, a breathing disorder, follow your doctor's directions and take your medicines.

- Exercise indoors on days of high air pollution.

Your Circulatory System

How are nutrients and oxygen carried all through your body? That's the job of the circulatory system. Your circulatory system is made up of your heart, blood, and *blood vessels*, which are tubes through which blood flows. Think of the blood as a train and blood vessels as tracks. The blood delivers oxygen and nutrients to cells like a train dropping off passengers at different stations.

The **heart** is an organ that pumps blood. From the heart, blood goes through vessels to the lungs, where it gives up carbon dioxide and picks up oxygen. Next, the blood moves through vessels back to the heart. The blood is then pumped into other vessels that go all through the body. **Arteries** are blood vessels that carry blood away from the heart. Arteries branch into **capillaries**, tiny blood vessels that deliver blood to tissues. From the capillaries, blood flows to **veins**, blood vessels that carry blood back toward the heart.

▼ Trace the flow of blood from the heart to one of the feet and back to the heart.

heart

artery

vein

Caring for Your Circulatory System

- Eat foods low in fat and high in fiber. Fiber can help take away substances that may lead to fatty buildup in blood vessels.

- Eat foods high in iron to help your red blood cells carry oxygen.

- Avoid contact with another person's blood.

- Get plenty of physical activity to make your heart strong.

- Avoid tobacco use and tobacco smoke.

Blood is made up of several parts. Over half of your blood is a liquid called *plasma*. The rest is made of cells. Red blood cells carry oxygen to all parts of your body. White blood cells attack and kill invading germs. Platelets help clot your blood and stop the bleeding from a cut or a wound.

MAIN IDEA AND DETAILS
List the three types of blood vessels, and tell what each type does.

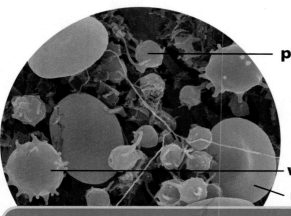
— platelet

— white blood cell
— red blood cell

Heartbeats

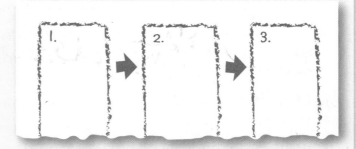

Beats per minute

whale	human adult	dog	human child	cat

The hearts of some living things beat faster than others. For example, the heart of a hummingbird beats 700 times per minute. How much faster is that than a human child's heart?

Lesson 4 Summary and Review

1 Summarize with Vocabulary

Use vocabulary from this lesson to complete these statements.

Air moves from your nose or mouth to the _____. When you breathe, your _____ moves air in and out of your lungs. Blood flows from your heart through _____ and returns through _____.

2 Critical Thinking What behaviors can harm your lungs and heart? What behaviors can help them?

3 How do your respiratory and circulatory systems work together?

4 SEQUENCE Draw and complete this graphic organizer to show how air moves through the respiratory system.

1.	→	2.	→	3.

5 Write to Entertain—Short Story

Imagine you are a red blood cell. Write a story that describes your journey through the circulatory system.

23

The Skeletal and Muscular Systems

Lesson Focus
Your skeletal and muscular systems support your body, protect your organs, and help you move.

Why Learn This?
When you know how your skeletal and muscular systems work, you will understand why it's important to take care of them.

Vocabulary
skull
skeletal system
spine
muscle
muscular system

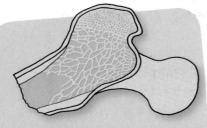

Myth and Fact
Myth: **Bones are solid.**
Fact: The outsides of bones have canals through which blood vessels pass. The insides of bones look like honeycombs and contain bone marrow, fat cells, and blood vessels.

Your Skeletal System

The bones in your head, called the **skull**, protect your brain. Bones make up the **skeletal system**, a body system that supports your body, protects your organs, and helps you move.

Your **spine**, or backbone, is made up of small bones that protect your spinal cord. Each of these bones has a hole in the center, as in a tire. These bones fit together, one on top of the other. Your spinal cord runs from your brain down your back inside your spine.

Your spine, pelvis, and leg bones work together to let you stand up straight, twist, turn, bend, and walk.

 SEQUENCE List the order of bones from the skull to the hips.

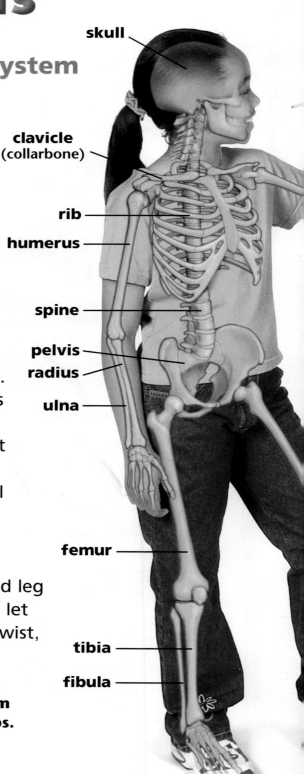

skull
clavicle (collarbone)
rib
humerus
spine
pelvis
radius
ulna
femur
tibia
fibula

Muscles and Bones
Make a list of the muscles labeled below. Name a bone or bones shown on page 24 that each muscle could move.

Your Muscular System

Bend one arm at the elbow while placing your other hand over the inside of that arm just above the elbow. Then unbend the arm. Can you feel the muscle bulging and then returning to its former position?

A **muscle** is an organ that contracts and relaxes to produce movement. Muscles make up the **muscular system**, a body system that enables your body to move.

Muscles move your arms, legs, face, head, and body. Some muscles work with other body systems. For example, your heart muscle pumps blood, your diaphragm relaxes and contracts, and your stomach churns food.

deltoid

biceps

abdominal

quadriceps

flexors

triceps

flexors

Helping People with Limited Movement
The EyeGaze System helps people who have limited movement of their body to type, speak through a device, control lights, and operate a phone or TV by using their eyes. The person looks at control keys on a special computer screen. The device can tell on which key the eyes are focused.

◀ Study these two diagrams, and place your hand on your body where each bone or muscle is located.

Caring for Your Skeletal and Muscular Systems

- Eat food with plenty of calcium for strong bones.

- Get plenty of physical activity for strong bones and muscles.

- Wear protective equipment during certain physical activities.

- Warm up your muscles by stretching before strenuous physical activity.

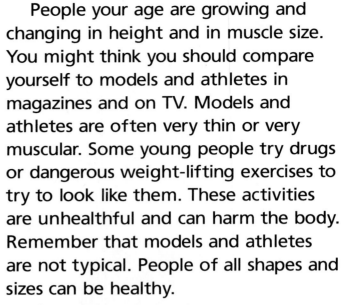

People your age are growing and changing in height and in muscle size. You might think you should compare yourself to models and athletes in magazines and on TV. Models and athletes are often very thin or very muscular. Some young people try drugs or dangerous weight-lifting exercises to try to look like them. These activities are unhealthful and can harm the body. Remember that models and athletes are not typical. People of all shapes and sizes can be healthy.

COMPARE AND CONTRAST How are your muscular and skeletal systems alike and different?

◀ Stretching and working your muscles are good physical activities for your body.

Lesson 5 Summary and Review

❶ Summarize with Vocabulary

Use vocabulary from this lesson to complete these statements.

Your _____ is made up of bones, and your _____ is made up of muscles. The bones called your _____ protect your brain. Your _____ protects your spinal cord. A _____ contracts and relaxes to produce movement.

❷ How do muscles work with bones to allow you to move?

❸ Critical Thinking What behaviors help you have strong bones and muscles?

❹ (Focus Skill) SEQUENCE Draw and complete this graphic organizer to show how muscle movements enable you to walk.

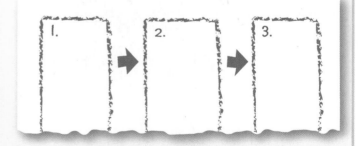

❺ Write to Express—Idea

Write a paragraph to share an idea of your own about the appearance of people shown in product advertising.

ACTIVITIES

Physical Education

Check Your Pulse Learn from your teacher how to take your pulse. Run in place for a minute, and then retake your pulse. Explain the increase in your pulse rate.

Science

Compare Blood Cells Use reference materials to find pictures and descriptions of blood cells. Draw a picture of what a drop of blood might look like under a microscope.

Technology Project

Review the chapter and list the main ideas of each lesson. Make an outline of ways to take care of your body systems. Use a computer to make a presentation. If a computer is not available, make a colorful poster or some slides to display your outline.

GO ONLINE For more activities, visit The Learning Site. www.harcourtschool.com/health

Home & Community

Appreciating Family Members Tell family members what you learned about the importance of appreciating individual differences. Let each person in your family know what you appreciate about him or her. Give each family member a chance to do the same thing.

Career Link

Medical Doctor A medical doctor is a physician who can treat a number of body system problems. Suppose you are a medical doctor. You have a patient who broke her arm because she was skateboarding too fast and went out of control. What would you tell your patient about following safety rules? What other ways would you tell her to protect her nervous, skeletal, and muscular systems?

27

Reading Skill

SEQUENCE

Draw and then use this graphic organizer to answer questions 1 and 2.

1. Show the path of nutrients from the mouth to body cells.
2. Show how blood flows from a vein in the leg to an artery in the arm.

Use Vocabulary

Match each term in Column B with its meaning in Column A.

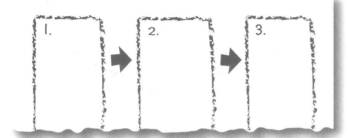

Column A	Column B
3 Characteristic	A cell
4 The smallest working part of your body	B heart
5 The brain, spinal cord, and nerves	C nervous system
6 Organ that churns to break down food	D skeletal system
7 Organ that carries air into the lungs	E stomach
8 Organ that pumps blood	F trachea
9 Body system that protects organs	G trait

Check Understanding

10. Which of the following tells cells when and how to do their job? (p. 6)
    A cytoplasm   C tissue
    B nucleus   D cell membrane

11. Suppose you touch a hot stove. Your nervous system works with your _____ system to make your hand draw back. (p. 25)
    F circulatory   H digestive
    G respiratory   J muscular

12. The _____ at the base of your brain controls your breathing and heart rate. (p. 13)
    A heart
    B cerebrum
    C brain stem
    D cerebellum

13. Which belongs in the skeletal system? (p. 24)
    F heart   H clavicle

    G biceps   J stomach

14 Which of the following is the missing term needed to complete the graphic organizer? (p. 7)

  A Tissue Systems
  B Communication Systems
  C Body Systems
  D Cell Systems

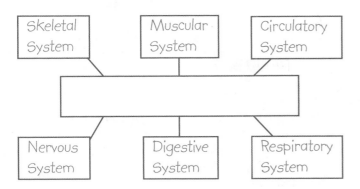

15 Which of the following does the skeletal system NOT do? (p. 24)

  F protect your organs
  G support your body
  H move messages to the brain
  J help you move

Think Critically

16 A person has a disease in which the small intestine does not absorb nutrients well. What might be the effects of that disease? Explain your answer.

17 Many people who smoke get lung infections and cough more than people who do not smoke. Why do you think this is true?

Apply Skills

18 **BUILDING GOOD CHARACTER** **Responsibility** When you ride in a car with your older sister, she never puts on her safety belt. Applying what you know about taking care of the nervous system, what could you do to be a positive role model for your sister?

19 **LIFE SKILLS** **Set Goals** You want to make your heart and muscles stronger through physical activity. List five activities that you enjoy, such as skateboarding or jumping rope. Set a goal to fit at least one of those activities from your list into your schedule every day.

Write About Health

20 **Write to Inform—Explanation** Explain how getting plenty of physical activity helps all of your body systems.

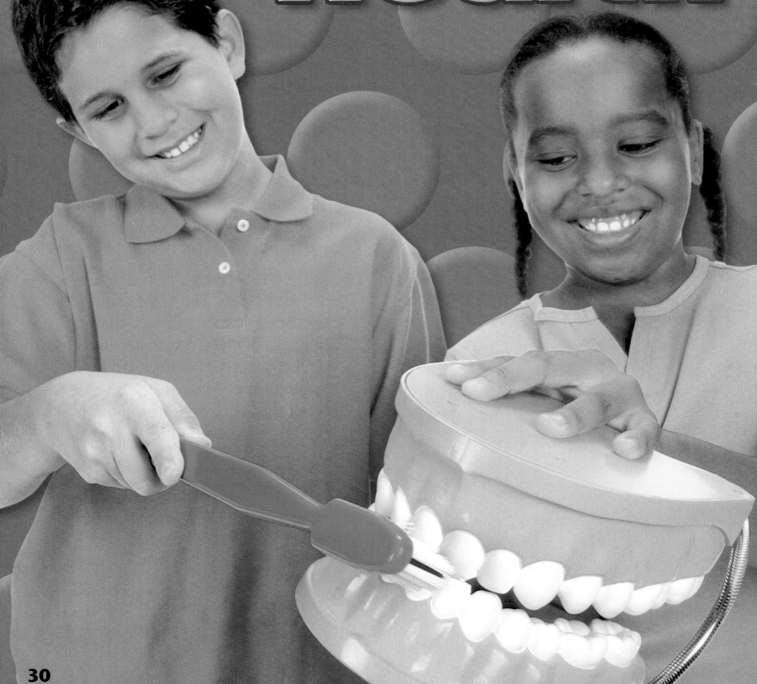

CHAPTER 2 Personal Health

30

IDENTIFY MAIN IDEA AND DETAILS
The main idea is the most important thought in a passage. Details tell about the main idea and help you understand it. Use the Reading in Health Handbook on pages 336–337 and this graphic organizer to help you read the health facts in this chapter.

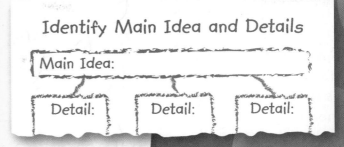

Identify Main Idea and Details

Main Idea:

Detail: Detail: Detail:

Health Graph

INTERPRET DATA The United States Department of Health and Human Services' Healthy People 2010 program has set some goals for cavity prevention. Compare the two graphs. How are they alike, and how are they different? How many more children without cavities per 100 is the goal?

Cavities

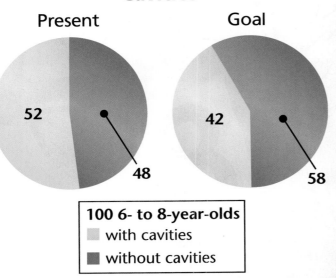

Present   Goal

52   42

48   58

| 100 6- to 8-year-olds |
| with cavities |
| without cavities |

Daily Physical Activity

Take an active role maintaining your personal health. Exercise for your health.

Be Active!
Use the selection Track 2, **Locomotion**, to take care of your muscles and bones.

31

Your Skin and Its Care

Lesson Focus

Taking care of your skin is important for your health.

Why Learn This?

Understanding how your skin protects you can help you make good choices about caring for it.

Vocabulary

epidermis
dermis

Your Skin

Look at your skin. Do you know what an important organ it is? Throughout your life, your skin protects you in many ways. Taking care of your skin helps it take care of you.

Your skin has two main layers—the epidermis and the dermis. You can see both layers and their parts in the picture on the next page.

The top layer of your skin is the **epidermis** (ep•uh•DER•mis). Its outermost part is made of dead skin cells. These cells keep moisture in your body and keep germs out. If the epidermis is broken, germs can enter the body. That's why washing cuts and keeping them clean until they heal is important.

Did You Know?

A three-quarter-inch square patch of skin that is about one-twentieth of an inch thick contains

- 9 feet of blood vessels
- 13 yards of nerves
- 600 pain receptors
- 300 sweat glands
- 4 oil glands
- 30 hairs

◀ It is healthful for you to sweat.

Epidermis
The dead skin cells that make up the top layer of the epidermis are constantly flaking off. New cells grow to replace them.

Pores are openings in the skin's surface, from which sweat is released.

Hair is a long, narrow stack of dead skin cells piled one on top of the other.

Each year up to nine pounds of your skin wear away as dead cells flake off. Cells in the bottom part of the epidermis make new cells to replace the dead ones. ▶

Sweat glands
Sweat produced in the sweat glands helps rid your body of wastes and helps keep you cool.

Dermis The thick bottom layer of skin, the dermis contains blood vessels and nerves.

Oil glands make oil that helps soften your skin.

Your skin has another important job. It keeps your body at the right temperature. It does this by producing sweat. Sweat is the salty liquid that forms on your skin when you are hot. Sweat is made by *sweat glands* in your skin. When your body gets hot, sweat glands become more active. Sweat helps cool your body.

Sweat reaches the skin's surface through *pores*. There, sweat changes from a liquid to a gas. This process is called *evaporation*. During evaporation, your body uses its heat energy to change the liquid sweat into a gas. As a result, your body loses heat and cools down.

Focus Skill **MAIN IDEA AND DETAILS What is the importance of your skin?**

Information Alert

Artificial Skin
Scientists are learning how to make skin that can be used to treat people who have been seriously burned.

GO ONLINE **For the most up-to-date information, visit The Learning Site. www.harcourtschool.com/ health**

Care of Your Skin

If your hands or face are dirty, germs can enter the body when you touch your eyes, nose, or mouth. Wash your face at least twice a day. Use soap, warm water, and a clean washcloth. When you wash your hands, rub them all over with soap and warm water. Squeeze the suds between your fingers. Scrub your knuckles and fingernails carefully. Germs often collect there. Rinse your hands well and dry them. Apply lotion if your skin feels tight or rough.

If you are very active, take a bath or shower every day. Wash your hair with shampoo when it begins to look or feel dirty.

Wash Your Hands

After
- blowing your nose
- sneezing or coughing
- going to the bathroom
- handling anything dirty
- touching an animal

Before
- handling food
- eating

Washing keeps your body clean. Deodorant can help prevent body odor. ▶

Too much sunlight can harm your skin. It can cause the skin to burn, dry out, and wrinkle. Over time, too much sun can also cause a serious disease called *skin cancer*.

You can protect your skin from the sun in several ways. If possible, stay out of the sun when it is strongest—between 10:00 A.M. and 4:00 P.M. Whenever you are in the sun, use sunscreen. *Sunscreen* is lotion that helps block some of the sun's harmful rays. Read the sunscreen label to see its sun protection factor (SPF). The higher the number, the more protection you get. Use a sunscreen that has an SPF of 30 or more. For additional protection, wear a hat and cover your skin with loose, light-colored clothes that are lightweight.

CAUSE AND EFFECT What is the effect of too much sun exposure?

▼ You can get sunburn in winter. When in the sun, be sure to use sunscreen. Also, wear a hat and cover your skin with clothing.

Lesson 1 Summary and Review

❶ Summarize with Vocabulary

Use vocabulary and other terms from this lesson to complete these statements.

The top layer of skin is the _____. Under it lies the _____. _____ helps keep your skin soft. _____ helps keep your body cool. Oil and sweat reach the top layer of your skin through _____. To help protect your skin from sunlight, you should use _____.

❷ What SPF should you use to protect your skin from the sun?

❸ Critical Thinking Why is your skin important to your health?

❹ (Focus Skill) MAIN IDEA AND DETAILS Draw and complete this graphic organizer to show the parts that make up the dermis.

Main Idea:		
Detail:	Detail:	Detail:

❺ Write to Inform—How-To

Write the steps you should use to thoroughly wash your hands.

Your Teeth and Their Care

Lesson Focus

Taking care of your teeth and gums is important for your health.

Why Learn This?

Knowing about your teeth and gums will help you make good choices about caring for them.

Vocabulary

plaque
cavities

ACTIVITY

Building Good Character

Responsibility Josh is going on a weekend camping trip with a friend's family. As he is leaving, his mother reminds him to continue caring for his teeth while he is away. What are two ways that Josh can show responsible behavior for his teeth?

Your Teeth

Your teeth do more than chew your food. They make your smile look nice. They also help you talk. They even help shape your face. Teeth are most important, though, for chewing. Your teeth grind the food you eat into smaller pieces. Your digestive system can more easily digest smaller pieces of food.

As you eat, however, leftover bits of food and bacteria can stick to your teeth. The bacteria are part of a sticky, natural film on the teeth called **plaque** (PLAK). Bacteria in plaque break down sugars in food to form acids. The acids can make holes, called **cavities** (KAV•uh•teez), in the outer layers of your teeth.

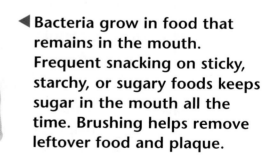

◀ Bacteria grow in food that remains in the mouth. Frequent snacking on sticky, starchy, or sugary foods keeps sugar in the mouth all the time. Brushing helps remove leftover food and plaque.

Cavities can get larger and larger until they reach deep inside a tooth. The process of forming cavities is called tooth decay. *Decay* means "to rot." If the cavity reaches the dentin layer, bacteria can travel through it into the tooth's pulp. Nerves in the pulp may swell with infection, causing pain. If the tooth is not treated in time, it can die.

Plaque can cause problems for your gums, too. If plaque is left on teeth, it hardens and becomes tartar. Tartar rubs against gums and can make them bleed. This can lead to infection that destroys the bone that holds teeth in place. Serious gum disease can cause even healthy teeth to fall out.

SEQUENCE **List in order the events that can result in the loss of a healthy tooth.**

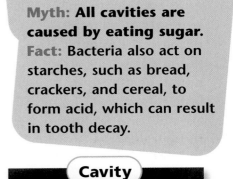

Myth and Fact

Myth: All cavities are caused by eating sugar.
Fact: Bacteria also act on starches, such as bread, crackers, and cereal, to form acid, which can result in tooth decay.

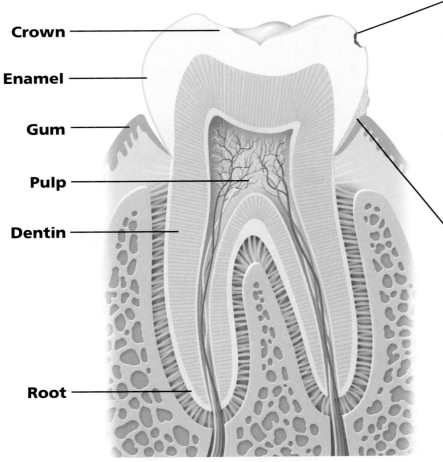

Crown

Enamel

Gum

Pulp

Dentin

Root

▲ Although your teeth have different shapes, they all have these same parts.

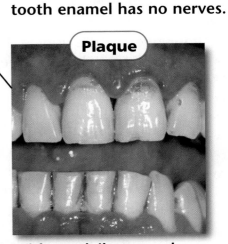

Cavity

▲ A cavity first forms on a tooth's enamel. At first, you can't feel a cavity because tooth enamel has no nerves.

Plaque

▲ Without daily care, plaque can build up on your teeth and along the gum line.

Did You Know?

Bottled drinking water is often advertised as "pure" or as containing only small amounts of minerals. Because the mineral fluoride is so important to dental health, some bottled-water companies are now adding fluoride to their water.

Preventing Tooth Problems

With proper care, your teeth can last a lifetime. Keep your teeth and gums healthy by practicing these healthful habits.

► Avoid sugary and sticky snacks. Milk products and fruits help build strong teeth. These foods are a good choice if you can brush soon after eating. Crunchy vegetables are the best choice if you can't brush right away.

► Floss once a day. Brush your teeth at least twice a day. Rinse your mouth with water after meals when you can't brush.

► Visit a dentist often. The dentist or dental hygienist will remove any tartar and check for problems. He or she may also apply sealants to protect the teeth or fluoride to strengthen them. *Flouride* (FLAWR•yd) is a mineral that helps prevent cavities.

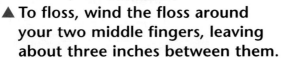

▲ To floss, wind the floss around your two middle fingers, leaving about three inches between them.

At the gum line, curve the floss around one side of a tooth. Gently rub the floss against the lower edge of that tooth. Do the same to the other tooth. Repeat, using clean floss for each of your teeth. ►

38

You can help prevent tooth decay and gum disease. Remember to floss and brush. Your toothbrush will remove plaque and bits of food scattered by flossing. When you brush, use a toothpaste that contains fluoride.

It's important to floss and brush properly. You can find out about the proper way to floss and brush by looking at the photos and reading the captions on these two pages.

DRAW CONCLUSIONS Why is tooth care important, and how should you take care of your teeth?

Tips for Proper Brushing

① Place the toothbrush at a 45° angle against the gums.

② Move the brush gently back and forth in short strokes.

③ Brush the outer, inner, and chewing surfaces of the teeth.

④ Use the end of the brush to clean the inside surfaces of front teeth.

⑤ Brush your tongue to remove bacteria and freshen your breath.

Your dentist can work with you to keep your teeth and gums healthy. ▼

Consumer Activity

Make Buying Decisions
Miranda is buying toothpaste for herself. As she stands in the aisle, she sees many different brands. Make a list of things she should consider before choosing.

When shopping for dental products, you'll find many different choices. Knowing how to choose dental products is important.

Any dental product with the American Dental Association (ADA) seal of approval is a good choice. Look for it on the product label. When you choose a toothpaste, look on the label for the word *fluoride*. Any toothpaste—paste or gel—with the ADA seal has fluoride. Some toothpastes have ingredients that kill bacteria in the mouth. If you use one of these, you still need to floss.

Dental floss can be waxed or unwaxed, flavored or unflavored. Waxed floss may be easier to use if your teeth are very close together.

▼ If you are unsure which dental products to use, ask a parent or a dental hygienist to help you choose.

Toothpaste
• contains fluoride; ADA seal
Dental Floss
• waxed or unwaxed; ADA seal
Toothbrush
• soft bristles, comfortable size, ADA seal

Choose a toothbrush with soft bristles. Soft bristles will remove plaque without hurting your gums. The toothbrush should fit comfortably in your mouth. It should have a shape that will help you get to hard-to-reach teeth. Your toothbrush can be manual or battery powered. Replace your toothbrush every three months and after an illness.

DRAW CONCLUSIONS **What should you look for on the label of any dental product?**

Quick Activity

Choosing Dental Products Which of the products pictured on this page would you use? Write a sentence explaining your reasoning for each of your choices.

▲ Many good dental-care products are available. Often your choices will depend on your own likes or dislikes, such as a favorite color or flavor.

Lesson 2 Summary and Review

❶ Summarize with Vocabulary

Use vocabulary and other terms from this lesson to complete these statements.

Bacteria in _____ form acid that can cause tooth _____. This can result in holes in the teeth called _____. Using toothpaste with _____ can help prevent dental problems.

❷ What is tartar, and what problem can result from its buildup?

❸ Critical Thinking If you are unable to brush after a meal, what is the next-best thing you can do?

❹ (Focus Skill) MAIN IDEA AND DETAILS Draw and complete this graphic organizer to show ways to care for your teeth.

Main Idea: _____

Detail: Brushing   Detail: Detail:

❺ Write to Inform—Explanation

Identify two healthful snacks for which you should brush afterward and two healthful snacks for which brushing is not needed.

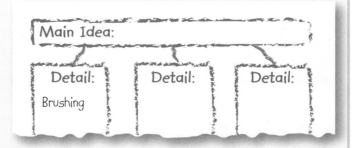

Your Vision and Hearing

How the Eye Works

The parts of your eye work together to help you gather information about the world around you. Light enters your eye through an opening called the **pupil**. The light passes through a clear, curved **lens**. The lens bends the light to form an image on the back part of your eye, the retina. The **retina** passes the image through nerve signals to the brain. Your brain uses the nerve signals to form a picture in your mind. The diagram shows the parts of the eye and how they work together.

For people with normal vision, the lens focuses images clearly on the retina. But not everyone has normal vision. Sometimes images do not focus correctly on the retina. As you can see from the diagram, a person may be nearsighted or farsighted. Both problems can be corrected by using corrective lenses—glasses or contact lenses. These lenses focus images correctly on the retinas.

CAUSE AND EFFECT
What causes many people to need corrective lenses?

Your eyes adjust to the light. Your pupils get bigger to let in more light when it is dark. Your lenses change shape to help you focus on objects both near and far.▶

Information Alert!

Braces for Your Eyes
Special contact lenses can be used to correct vision while you sleep. As you wear the lenses, the eye is reshaped. In the morning, you remove the lenses, and you can see without glasses or contacts.

GO ONLINE
For the most up-to-date information, visit The Learning Site. www.harcourtschool.com/health

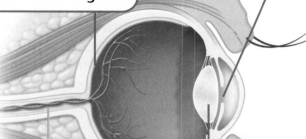

The **retina** contains nerves that change light into nerve signals.

Light enters the eye through the **pupil**.

Nerves carry the image from the retina to the brain.

The **lens** bends light to form an image on the retina.

Caring for Your Eyes

- Keep sharp objects away from your eyes.

- Wear safety goggles when using hammers and other tools.

- Wear sunglasses to protect your eyes from sunlight.

- You should get an eye exam every two years. If you have an eye or vision problem or a family history of vision problems, you need exams more often.

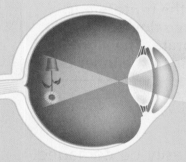 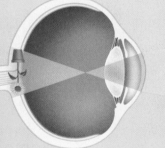 

▲ People who are *nearsighted* can see objects that are near, but faraway things look blurry. Their eyes focus images in front of the retinas.

▲ People who are *farsighted* can see faraway things clearly, but close-up things are blurry. Their eyes focus images behind the retinas.

How the Ear Works

When an object makes a sound, the sound travels as sound waves. Some of these waves enter your ear. The diagram shows the path that sound takes through the ear.

3. The **eardrum** vibrates when sound waves hit it. The vibrations pass to the middle ear.

5. In the **inner ear**, vibrations are changed into nerve signals that move to the brain.

1. Sound enters through your **outer ear**.

2. It moves through the ear canal to the eardrum.

4. In the **middle ear**, three tiny bones vibrate. The vibrations pass to the inner ear.

Did You Know?

A person with hearing loss in one ear often has a hard time knowing where certain sounds come from. That is because the brain needs information from both ears to tell the direction of sound.

Some parts of the ear can easily be damaged. Your inner ear can be permanently damaged by loud sounds. If you're in a noisy place where you must shout to be heard by others, the noise may be harmful. If your ears ring when a loud noise stops, you may have damage. Listening to loud sounds again and again will cause hearing loss. *Hearing loss* is the inability to hear sounds you once were able to hear. Following a few simple tips can help you protect your ears.

Avoid loud sounds. Keep the volume down when using a stereo or headphones. Stay away from noisy places or wear earplugs. Keep objects, including cotton swabs, out of your ears. Wear a helmet with ear protection when you play sports. See a doctor if you develop a problem with your ears or hearing.

 MAIN IDEA AND DETAILS **List some ways that you can protect your ears from harm.**

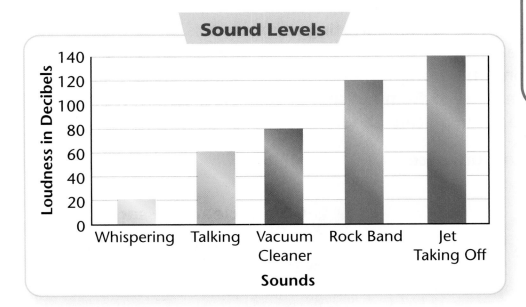

Sound Levels

ACTIVITY

Life Skills
Manage Stress
Your friend is playing his stereo so loudly that the sound is stressing you. How can you deal with this situation and manage your stress? Use the steps to **Manage Stress** on pp.10–11 to write a paragraph that describes how you might deal with your stress.

◀ Sounds are measured in decibels (DES•uh•belz). The louder the sound, the greater the number in decibels. Your hearing can be damaged after just one hour of listening to noise of 100 decibels. How can you prevent injury from these noises?

Lesson 3 Summary and Review

1 **Summarize with Vocabulary**

Use vocabulary and other terms from this lesson to complete these statements.

Light enters the eye through the _____. The _____ then bends the light and focuses it on the _____. For people who are _____, faraway objects appear blurry. For people who are _____, close-up objects are blurry.

2 List three ways to protect your vision.

3 **Critical Thinking** Your friends say that you don't hear them sometimes when they talk to you. What can you do?

4 **MAIN IDEA AND DETAILS** Draw and complete this graphic organizer to show what the parts of the ear do.

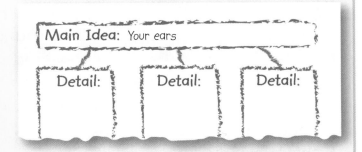

Main Idea: Your ears

Detail: Detail: Detail:

5 **Write to Inform—Explanation**

Explain how decibels and hearing loss are related.

45

Communicate
About a Health Need

Communication is important to your health. Sharing your feelings with your parents or other health providers and talking about any problems you are experiencing enables them to help. Using the steps for **Communicating** can make this task easier.

Tonya has noticed that she has difficulty seeing the chalkboard from her seat in class. How can Tonya communicate about her vision problem?

1 Understand your audience.

Tonya knows that she needs to talk to her parents or her teacher about the problem she has seeing things clearly.

2 Give a clear message.

Tonya tells her parents that faraway things look blurry.

3 Listen carefully and answer any questions.

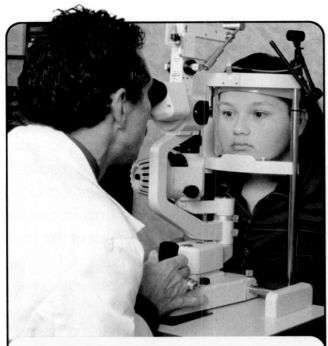

At the eye doctor's office, Tonya follows the instructions given her. She tells the doctor when things appear clear.

4 Gather feedback.

After talking with the doctor, Tonya realizes that using corrective lenses can solve her vision problem.

Problem Solving

Alex fell from a swing while on the playground. He landed awkwardly and hit his mouth. It hurt, but he didn't think much about it and continued to play. Once in class, however, he found that he had loosened a tooth. Use the steps for **Communicating** to explain how Alex can get help for his injury. Also explain how Alex's going to someone about his problem shows that he is responsible.

Being a Health Consumer

Analyze Media Messages

You don't have to look far to see **advertising** (AD•ver•tyz•ing), a method businesses use to give people information about their products. You can find advertising along roadsides, on television, radio, and computers, in magazines, and in ballparks and stadiums. Businesses hope their advertisements will get people to buy their products.

Advertising can be helpful. It makes you aware that a product is for sale.

It also may offer some important information about how a product is used or what it is made from. A **consumer** (kuhn•SOOM•er) is someone who buys products. As a consumer you should be aware that some ads use tricks to get you to buy the product.

Advertisements are also called ads. ▶

Have you ever seen an ad that only said bad things about another product? If so, did the ad give any useful information about its own product? Often, companies that advertise in this way do not want you to know the truth—that the other product may be just as good as or better than their own! When you see ads, form your own opinions about the product. Look at the product label to learn facts about it. You can see some other ways of advertising here and on page 48.

SUMMARIZE Why is it important to form your own opinions about products and not just believe everything that is advertised?

He's read the advertisements on page 48.

Quick Activity

Analyze Ads The boy in the picture is trying to decide on a pair of sunglasses. He's read the advertisements on page 48. Help him make a decision by writing a reply to each advertisement.

THE REAL YOU
Trick: People who use this product become more popular.
Truth: A product can't make someone more popular.

FEEL THE QUALITY
Trick: Your favorite sports or music star tells you to buy the product.
Truth: The star cannot know whether the product is right for you. Something else may be better.

THE LATEST RAGE
Trick: Everyone is using this product, and you'll be left out if you don't.
Truth: Everyone cannot be using the same product. Buy only things that you need.

Tips for Analyzing Ads and Media Messages

- Find out who is giving the message and why.

- Watch for tricks to make you notice or agree with the ad.

- Notice the values and points of view shown.

- Learn whether important information has been left out.

Make Wise Buying Decisions

Advertisements shouldn't be the only information you use to make buying decisions. Here are some other steps to help you.

1. Decide whether your choice is based on a true need for the item or a want for the item.
2. Compare several brands of the same item.
3. Choose the best item for the lowest price.
4. Think about the result of your decision.

SEQUENCE What should you do before you buy a product?

Lesson 4 Summary and Review

1 Summarize with Vocabulary

Use vocabulary and other terms from this lesson to complete these statements.

_____ is a method businesses use to tell people about a product. A person who buys a product is a _____. When making a buying decision, compare several _____ of the same item.

2 Critical Thinking In what two ways can an ad be helpful in your buying decisions?

3 List three tips for analyzing ads.

4 MAIN IDEA AND DETAILS Draw and complete this graphic organizer to show the types of tricks used in advertising.

Main Idea:

Detail: | Detail: | Detail:

5 Write to Inform—How-To

Write a sign that tells consumers how to make good buying decisions. Use your own words.

Trustworthiness

Be Truthful About Personal Care

You are becoming more and more responsible for your personal care. However, your parents or other adult family members may still remind you to brush your teeth well. They might even check to see if you do. They do this because they are responsible for you. When they ask questions about your personal care, they rely on you to be truthful. Here are some simple guidelines for being trustworthy.

- **Answer your parents' or other adult family members' questions about your personal-care habits honestly.**
- **Don't exaggerate to make yourself appear better.**
- **Inform your parents or other adult family members if you have a health problem.**
- **Don't try new health products without permission.**
- **Practice good personal-care habits without being told.**
- **Wear earplugs when you are around loud noises.**

Activity

With another student, role-play a parent questioning a child about practicing a certain personal-care habit. Show how to use honest answers to communicate with one another. Switch roles several times, and cover several personal-care habits.

Getting Health Information

Lesson Focus
Getting reliable health information can be important to your health.

Why Learn This?
Learning about where to find reliable health information will be helpful when you have health questions or problems.

Using Reliable Sources

If you want health information, where do you go? Television, newspapers, magazines, and books are just a few sources of health information. You can also find a lot of health information on the Internet.

Not everything you see and read about health is true, however. Some information is based on opinions, not facts. Some information is meant to get you to buy a product. Other information is wrong because the person who wrote it just didn't know the facts. Knowing where you can find reliable health facts is important.

▼ Have a parent or teacher help you look for information on the Internet.

Quick Activity

Accessing Information The sources listed on page 53 are not the only places to find good health information. List at least three other reliable sources of health information.

Suppose you had a problem with your bike. You probably would ask a bike expert, not a baker, how to fix it. The same is true for health information. The best information comes from people who are health experts.

Among the best sources of health information are health professionals. Nurses, doctors, and pharmacists are good examples. Such people are more likely to give you trustworthy information. They have studied health and deal with health problems every day.

For most other sources, especially the Internet, you should think about which person or group has given out the information. If the source is not one of the kinds mentioned in this lesson, it may not be one you should trust.

DRAW CONCLUSIONS For health information, why is a doctor a more reliable source than what you already know?

Reliable Sources

- College and university websites, which end in .edu

- Science and health journals

- Major national newspapers

- National health magazines

- National health organizations and their websites, which end in .org

- Government health organizations and their websites, which end in .gov

▼ Many government health departments, as well as health organizations such as the American Red Cross and the American Cancer Society, write reports and pamphlets that have reliable health information.

Access Valid Health Information

- Find out who is responsible for the information.
- Decide if the information is reasonable.
- Check the information against other reliable sources. Keep a questioning attitude.
- Discuss the information with a parent or a health expert.

Evaluate Health Websites

It's important to remember that almost anyone can put information on the Internet. Follow these guidelines when you are looking at health websites.

► Be sure the website is a reliable source, such as a college or a government agency.

► Look for initials of a college degree after the writer's name.

► Find out if the website is selling anything. Websites that sell something may tell you only what sounds good.

► Look for sites that show evidence from health research.

► Always check with more than one source.

SUMMARIZE Why would a website selling a product probably not be a good source of reliable information?

Lesson 5 Summary and Review

① Summarize with Vocabulary

Use terms from this lesson to complete these statements.

It is very important for health information to be trustworthy, or _____. Nurses and doctors can give good information because they are health _____. Science journals and health magazines usually are reliable _____.

② Critical Thinking Why isn't all health information reliable?

③ What are three things you should consider when evaluating health websites?

④ (Focus Skill) MAIN IDEA AND DETAILS Draw and complete this graphic organizer to show three reliable sources of health information.

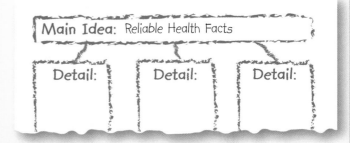

Main Idea: Reliable Health Facts

Detail: Detail: Detail:

⑤ Write to Inform—Explanation

Your friend plans to eat only raw vegetables because of an ad. Write about why this may not be a good idea.

Math

Count Hairs Cut a one-inch-square hole in a sheet of paper. Hold the sheet of paper on top of your forearm. Use a hand lens to count the hairs on your arm that are visible inside the square. Then measure your whole arm. Use the count to estimate how many hairs are on your arm.

Home & Community

Communicate Create an advertisement for a health product, using one or more of the techniques discussed in this chapter. Include some important information about the product. Apply labels to your ad that identify advertising techniques and useful information. Show your ad to your family to help them become more alert to advertising tricks.

Art

Protection Poster With a partner, make a poster that shows ways to protect the eyes or ears. Draw pictures, and write one or more slogans. Share your poster with younger students.

Career Link

Dental Hygienist A dental hygienist cares for the basic dental needs of patients, such as dental cleaning and X rays. Suppose you are a dental hygienist. A new patient arrives for her first visit. Describe what you would tell your patient about what to expect during her visit. Explain the importance of each step in her treatment.

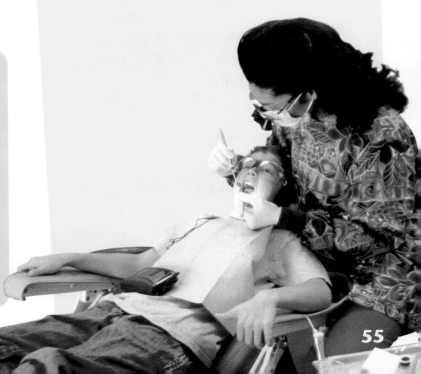

Technology Project

Use the main ideas that you learned in this chapter to make lists of ways to care for your skin, teeth, eyes, and ears. Use a camera to take pictures of your classmates as they demonstrate the care tips. Use the pictures to make a personal health collage.

GO ONLINE For more activities, visit The Learning Site. www.harcourtschool.com/health

Reading Skill

MAIN IDEA AND DETAILS

Draw and then use this graphic organizer to answer questions 1 and 2.

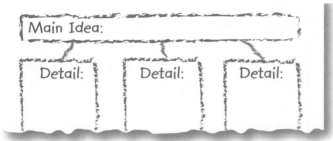

Main Idea:

Detail: Detail: Detail:

1 What is most important when getting health information?

2 Name three sources for health information.

ABC **Use Vocabulary**

Match each term in Column B with its meaning in Column A.

Column A	Column B
3 The top, thinner layer of skin	**A** cavities
4 The thick, bottom layer of skin	**B** consumer
	C dermis
5 Sticky material on teeth that contains bacteria	**D** epidermis
	E plaque
6 Holes in the surfaces of teeth	**F** pupil
7 The hole where light enters the eye	
8 Someone who buys products	

? **Check Understanding**

9 Sweat reaches the surface of skin through _____. (p. 33)

  A evaporation   **C** oil glands

  B sweat glands   **D** pores

10 Toothpaste containing _____ helps strengthen teeth and prevent decay. (pp. 38–39)

  F milk   **H** fluoride

  G mint flavoring   **J** gel

11 If nearby objects appear blurry but faraway objects are clear, you are _____. (p. 43)

  A normal   **C** farsighted

  B blind   **D** nearsighted

12 Which of these does **NOT** help prevent hearing loss? (p. 45)

F    **H**

G    **J**

13 What part of the ear is missing from the graphic organizer? (p. 44)

A pupil **C** tartar
B lens **D** eardrum

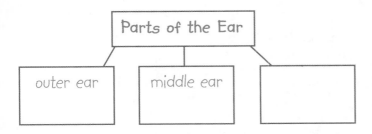

14 Advertising offers some important _____. (p. 48)

F sales **H** notes
G tips **J** information

15 Before believing information about health, you should make sure it _____. (pp. 52–54)

A is well written
B is funny
C is reliable
D is written by someone you know

 Think Critically

16 You are spending the day at the pool. What should you do to help protect your skin from sunlight each time you get out of the pool?

17 You have found information about dental floss from two different sources that disagree. What should you do?

 Apply Skills

18 **BUILDING GOOD CHARACTER**
Trustworthiness You need to start finding information for a report that is due tomorrow. Your parents, who are at a neighbor's house, have told you not to use the computer unless they are home. What could you do to show that you are trustworthy?

19 **LIFE SKILLS**
Communication You are at school, and an earache is really bothering you. Use the steps for Communicating to explain your problem to the school nurse.

 Write About Health

20 **Write to Inform—Explanation** Explain why learning to analyze advertising helps you to be a wise consumer.

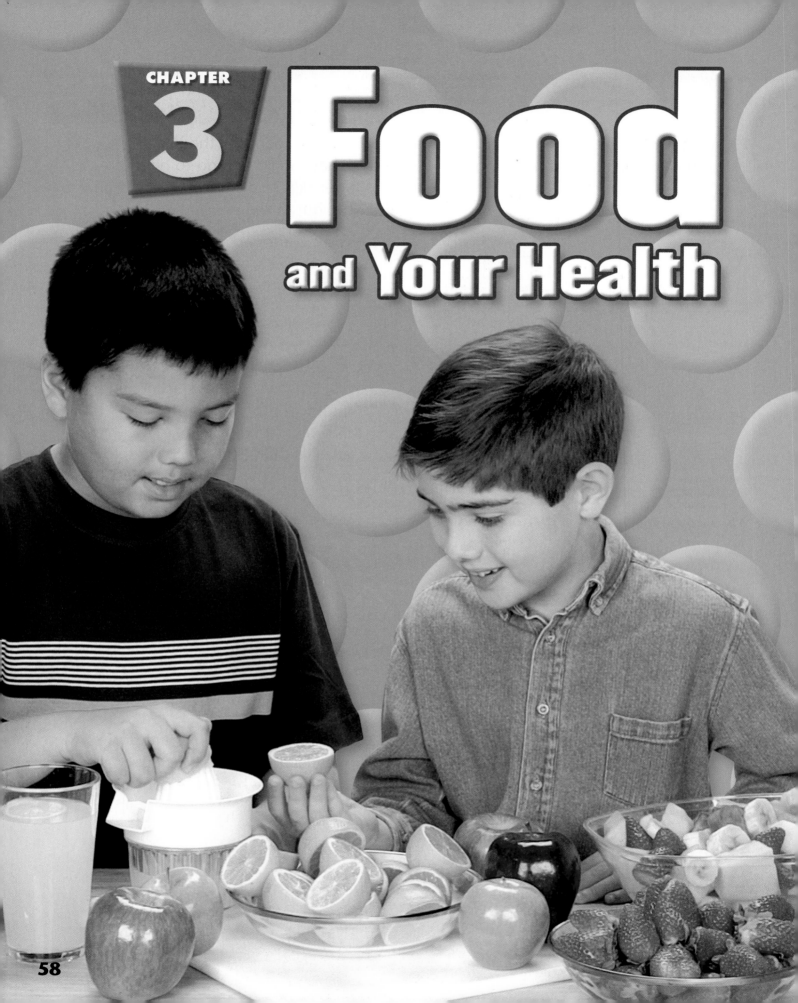

3 Food
and Your Health

Reading Skill

COMPARE AND CONTRAST When you compare, you tell how two or more things are alike. When you contrast, you tell how they are different. Use the Reading in Health Handbook on pages 330–331 and this graphic organizer to help you read the health facts in this chapter.

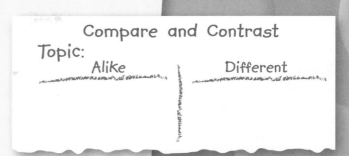

Compare and Contrast

Topic:

Alike   Different

Health Graph

INTERPRET DATA Some food products have added sugar. If you are a person trying to limit the amount of sugar in the foods you eat, which of the following foods would you pick?

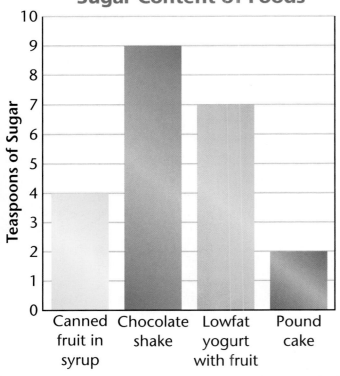

Sugar Content of Foods

Teaspoons of Sugar

- Canned fruit in syrup: 4
- Chocolate shake: 9
- Lowfat yogurt with fruit: 7
- Pound cake: 2

Daily Physical Activity

You should eat the right amounts of healthful foods every day. Exercise should also be a part of your day.

🎵 *Be Active!* Use the selection Track 3, **Late for Supper** to use some food energy.

Nutrients for Your Body

Energy Nutrients

In Chapter 1, you learned that nutrients are the substances in food that you need for growth, energy, and good health. Foods contain six important kinds of nutrients: carbohydrates, fats, proteins, vitamins, minerals, and water. You must eat a variety of foods to get all the nutrients you need to stay healthy.

Carbohydrates (kar•boh•HY•drayts) are starches and sugars. They are your body's main source of energy. Most carbohydrates come from plants.

You can get starches from breads, potatoes, cereals, beans, carrots, peas, and corn. Sugars are found in fruits and sweets such as cookies and pies. Sugars are used quickly by the body. Starches are used more slowly.

◄ What provides this skater with energy?

Fats give your body more energy than any other kind of nutrient. Fats come from some plant and animal products. Your body stores extra fat when you don't use all the food you take in. You use this energy from stored fats when you don't get enough energy from carbohydrates. Oils, butter, meat, cheese, milk, and nuts all have fats. Many fast foods are high in fat.

Proteins (PROH•teenz) are another kind of nutrient that give you energy. They help build and repair your cells. Without protein your body would not grow or get better if you were ill. You can get protein by eating eggs, meat, poultry, fish, and peanut butter. Some vegetables, seeds, grains, and beans also have some protein.

 **COMPARE AND CONTRAST** **How are carbohydrates and fats alike and different?**

Quick **Activity**

Identify Energy Nutrients Look at the foods shown on these pages. Name three foods for each of the energy nutrients.

61

Vitamins, Minerals, and Water

Not all nutrients give you energy. **Vitamins** (VYT•uh•minz) are nutrients that help your body do certain jobs. You need only small amounts of each vitamin. Vitamins can be made by living things, like plants and animals.

Each vitamin does one or more jobs in the body. Vitamin A keeps your skin and eyes healthy. You need vitamin C for healthy gums and teeth. Vitamin D keeps bones and teeth strong. Vitamin E slows down cell damage. Your body uses vitamin K to control blood clotting.

Minerals (MIN•er•uhlz) are nutrients that help your body grow and work. Like vitamins, minerals are needed in only small amounts. However, minerals are not made by living things. One way we can get minerals is from plants. The plants take in minerals from the soil. When we eat certain plants we take in minerals.

▼ Some vitamins are found in many foods.

Vitamins in Foods

Vitamin	Food
A	carrots, tomatoes, asparagus, spinach, red and yellow vegetables, sweet potatoes
C	oranges, strawberries, tomatoes, broccoli, potatoes
D	eggs, milk, fish, fortified cereals
E	parsley, fish, sunflower seeds, spinach, asparagus, plant oils
K	cheese, spinach, broccoli, liver

Minerals for Good Health

Mineral	Source	Role in the Body
Calcium	milk, cheese, yogurt, dark green leafy vegetables	Builds strong bones and teeth, helps muscles and nerves work, helps blood clot
Iron	dark green leafy vegetables, peas, beans, meat, enriched grain products	Helps blood carry oxygen, helps cells use energy, protects against infection
Phosphorus	meat, peas, beans, whole grains, dairy products	Builds strong bones and teeth, helps cells function
Potassium	potatoes, lima beans, oranges, bananas	Helps nerves and muscles work, helps cells use energy
Zinc	eggs, seafood, grains, nuts, beef, liver, whole grains	Helps the body grow, helps heal wounds, maintains the senses of smell and taste

Did You Know?

Water makes up more than half of your body. Your body needs 48 to 64 ounces of water every day. That's equal to six to eight 8-ounce glasses.

Some minerals are added to prepared foods. For example, sodium is part of table salt. Salt is added to many foods as a preservative or for flavor. Since many foods contain added salt, eating too much salt can become a problem.

Water is a nutrient necessary for life. You could live only a few days without water. Foods such as lettuce, melons, apples, celery, and raw carrots have a lot of water. But actually drinking water is the best way to get the water your body needs. Water helps the body use vitamins and minerals. It carries digested nutrients to your cells. It also carries away wastes.

CAUSE AND EFFECT **What is the effect of eating the right amount of vitamins and minerals?**

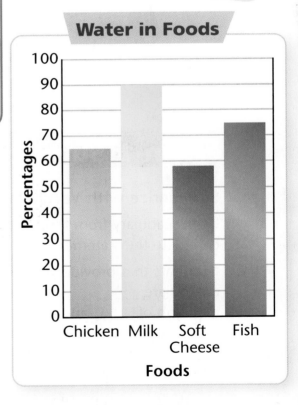

Water in Foods

Some foods contain more water than others. Which of these foods contains the most water? Which vitamins and minerals are also in these foods?

The fork you use at meals is a fairly new arrival to America. Until the introduction of forks from Europe and acceptance of their use in the mid-1700s, most people used only a knife and spoon for most of their eating.

Mealtime Is Important

People often come together for meals. Families try to meet for breakfast and dinner. Many people eat lunch at work or at school.

Families and friends also use mealtime as a time to communicate. During meals people often talk with and listen to one another. Children may talk about their day at school. Adults may talk about how their day has been. Mealtime can be a time of sharing that allows family members to talk about their feelings and thoughts.

Meals can also be shared for special occasions. People use meals as a way to celebrate birthdays, anniversaries, and holidays. Families sometimes use mealtimes to celebrate customs or traditions.

DRAW CONCLUSIONS Why is it important for people to have mealtimes?

Lesson 1 Summary and Review

1 Summarize with Vocabulary

Use vocabulary from this lesson to complete the statements.

Nutrients that provide your body with energy are _____, _____, and _____. The main job of _____ and _____ is to help your body grow and work. Breaking down foods and helping the body use vitamins and minerals is a job for _____.

2 Identify the benefits of the six major nutrients contained in foods.

3 Critical Thinking How can mealtime affect your relationships at school?

4 COMPARE AND CONTRAST Draw and complete this graphic organizer to show how vitamins and minerals are alike and different.

Topic: Vitamins and Minerals

Alike	Different

5 Write to Inform—Explanation

Explain why good nutrition is important for good health.

Respect

Using Good Table Manners

Good table manners are ways to act that help make mealtimes enjoyable for everyone. Using good table manners shows the people you eat with that you have respect for them. Here are some simple rules for good table manners.

- **Wait to start eating until everyone is served.**
- **Ask for food to be passed to you instead of reaching for it.**
- **Cut food into small pieces.**
- **Chew with your mouth closed.**
- **Swallow your food before you talk.**
- **Eat with your fingers only if the food was meant to be eaten that way. Follow the example of adults at the table.**
- **Use a napkin during your meal.**
- **At a friend's house, eat the way your hosts do.**
- **If you don't like the food, don't complain or make a face. Just leave it on the plate.**
- **Remember to say "Please" and "Thank you."**

Activity

Play a good-manners game with your family. Make a chart that shows each person's name. At mealtime, watch and listen for examples of good manners. Each time you notice one, give the person who used good manners a point. At the end of the meal, the person with the most points wins the game. Be sure to take turns keeping score!

Food and the Nutrients It Contains

Lesson Focus
Foods are divided into six groups based on the nutrients they contain.

Why Learn This?
A food guide pyramid can help you achieve a balanced diet.

Vocabulary

food guide pyramid
serving
balanced diet
portion

Food Groups

A healthful diet includes a variety of healthful foods in the right amounts. Foods are divided into six groups based on the nutrients they contain. The most healthful diet includes foods from several groups at each meal or snack.

Fats, Oils, and Sweets

Doughnuts, chocolate bars, cookies, cakes, butter, oil, and chips are just a few of the foods in this group. These foods give you very few nutrients. They may also contain large amounts of salt, fat, and sugar.

Milk, Yogurt, and Cheese

Cottage cheese, yogurt, and hard cheeses are made from milk. Milk and foods made from milk are good sources of protein, vitamins, and minerals. Some of these foods are also high in fat.

Meats, Poultry, Fish, Dry Beans, Eggs, and Nuts

Nuts, dry beans, eggs, fish, poultry, and meat are all good protein sources. They contain vitamins and minerals. Many of these foods are high in fat.

Vegetables

Broccoli, cauliflower, carrots, corn, lettuce, and celery are in this group. Vegetables are rich in minerals, vitamins, and fiber. Many have small amounts of protein and very little or no fat.

Fruits

Fruits include peaches, strawberries, bananas, apples, oranges, and pineapples. These foods are rich in minerals, vitamins, carbohydrates, and fiber. They have little or no fat and protein.

Breads, Cereals, Rice, and Pasta

Foods in this group are grains or are made from grain. They include tortillas, cereals, rice, breads, pasta, and crackers. These foods contain carbohydrates, proteins, fiber, minerals, and vitamins. Most are low in fat.

To have a healthful, balanced diet, eat a combination of foods every day. Don't choose too many foods from only one group. Choose very few foods from the Fats, Oils, and Sweets Group. You get plenty of these nutrients from foods in the other groups.

SUMMARIZE Name the six food groups and at least two foods found in each group.

The USDA Food Guide Pyramid

Fats, Oils, and Sweets Group
Use sparingly; not every day.

Milk, Yogurt, and Cheese Group
You need 3 SERVINGS. One serving equals 8 ounces of milk or yogurt or $1\frac{1}{2}$ ounces of cheese.

Vegetable Group
You need 3–5 SERVINGS. One serving equals $\frac{1}{2}$ cup cooked vegetable or 1 cup salad.

Bread, Cereal, Rice, and Pasta Group
You need 6–9 SERVINGS. One serving equals 1 slice of bread, 1 corn tortilla, $\frac{1}{2}$ cup cooked cereal, 1 cup dry cereal, $\frac{1}{2}$ cup cooked pasta.

Meat, Poultry, Fish, Dry Beans, Eggs, and Nuts Group
You need 2–3 SERVINGS. A serving size is 2–3 ounces of cooked meat, chicken, or fish, $\frac{1}{2}$ cup cooked dry beans, 1 egg, or $\frac{1}{3}$ cup nuts.

Fruit Group
You need 2–4 SERVINGS. One serving equals 1 apple, 1 banana, 4 ounces of fruit juice, or 15 grapes.

The number of servings from each food group are suggested for children ages 7–12.

Getting the Nutrients You Need

The United States Department of Agriculture (USDA) is an agency involved with food production and safety. The USDA has developed a **food guide pyramid**, a tool to help you choose foods for a healthful diet. The USDA Food Guide Pyramid shows how many servings you should eat from each food group each day. A **serving** is the measured amount of a food recommended for a meal or snack.

The bottom of the pyramid is the largest part. This tells you that the foods from this group should form the largest part of your diet. These foods include pasta, rice, bread, and cereal. The foods from the top of the pyramid should be the smallest part of your diet. Eat these foods only in small amounts, and not every day.

The food guide pyramid shows you that no one food group gives you all the nutrients you need. It can help you choose a healthful variety of foods. It reminds you not to eat too many unhealthful foods. By using the USDA Food Guide Pyramid, you can be sure to get a balanced diet. A **balanced diet** is a diet made up of a healthful amount of foods from each of the food groups. Eating a balanced diet gives your body the nutrients it needs.

SEQUENCE If you listed the foods on the food guide pyramid from the greatest number of servings to the least, which food group would follow the vegetable group?

Use Serving Sizes to Control Portions

It is important to know the difference between servings and portions. You already know that a serving is the measured amount of a food you would probably eat during one meal or as a snack. A serving is not always the same as a portion.

A **portion** is the amount of food you want to eat or the amount you may be served. Sometimes you may be served one portion, but it might contain more than one serving. You can control your portions by using serving sizes. Some estimates of serving sizes are shown below.

Serving Size Estimates

▲ about the size of a 3-ounce serving of fish, chicken, or meat

▲ about one medium-sized fruit

▲ about equal to $1\frac{1}{2}$ ounces of cheese

▲ about the size of $\frac{1}{2}$ cup of cooked pasta or cooked cereal

▲ about one teaspoon of oil or butter

Do you choose the right portions for the foods you eat? If you eat portions that are too large, you may be overeating. This isn't healthful for you. When you are choosing foods to eat, remember the following:

- Use the USDA Food Guide Pyramid.
- Serving sizes are not always the same as a portion.
- Control the size of your food portions by using serving sizes.

In the next lesson, you will learn how to make good food choices from a menu and how to select healthful snacks.

DRAW CONCLUSIONS Why are food servings and portion amounts important when making meal choices?

Consumer Activity

Accessing Valid Health Information Use a computer to learn more about food servings and portion sizes. Write a paragraph explaining what you learned. Use the information on pages 52–54 for accessing valid health information.

Lesson 2 Summary and Review

1 Summarize with Vocabulary

Use vocabulary from this lesson to complete the statements.

A food guide _____ can help you achieve a _____. The measured amount of food recommended for a meal or snack is a _____. A _____ is the amount of food you are served.

2 How are foods grouped?

3 Critical Thinking Explain how the shape of a pyramid is related to the amount of food servings you should eat daily.

4 (Focus Skill) COMPARE AND CONTRAST Draw and complete this graphic organizer to show how food servings and portion sizes are alike and different.

Topic: Food Servings and Portion Sizes
Alike | Different

5 Write to Inform—How-To

Write a plan on how to achieve a balanced diet.

Using a Food Guide Pyramid

Choosing Foods from a Menu

Do you sometimes eat at a fast-food or another kind of restaurant? If so, you know that choosing a healthful meal is not always easy. A food guide pyramid can help you make a healthful choice.

Choosing foods wisely now will help you stay healthy all your life. It will help you form healthful eating habits. A **habit** is something you do so often that you don't even think about it.

The foods on the USDA Food Guide Pyramid are grouped according to type. But most of your meals contain more than one type of food. These are called *combination foods*. Some examples are stews, salads, pizza, sandwiches, and spaghetti with meatballs.

Healthful choices about meals can be made at a restaurant. ▶

The more often you choose healthful foods, the easier making healthful choices will become. You don't want to make a habit of eating too many foods from just one group. Eating this way wouldn't be a healthful habit.

Ramón is at a restaurant. He reads the menu. He wants to make choosing healthier foods a habit. He thinks about the food groups found in each of the menu choices. He asks himself, "Will I have a balanced diet if I choose that food? How many servings are in each portion?" Ramón wants to choose the food that will provide him with the nutrients he needs.

DRAW CONCLUSIONS Use the USDA Food Guide Pyramid to determine food groups in Ramón's menu choices.

Personal Health Plan ▶

Real-Life Situation
Suppose you are ordering lunch from a restaurant menu.
Real-Life Plan
Write a step-by-step plan for ordering a healthful, balanced meal.

Combination Pizza
Deep-dish delicacy topped with pepperoni, sausage, ground beef, and double-layered cheeses. Comes with buttered breadsticks.

Cheeseburger
Mouth-watering all-beef patty topped with cheese, lettuce, and tomato on a whole-wheat bun. Accompanied by your choice of French fries or salad.

Taco Salad
Mix of ground beef, shredded lettuce, chopped tomato, onions, and shredded cheese, topped with sour cream, nestled in a deep-fried shell.

Quick Activity

Analyze Menu Choices
Look at Ramón's menu choices. Decide for yourself which is the healthiest meal. Compare and contrast the amounts and balance of food groups represented in each selection.

Choosing Healthful Snacks

You're hungry. It's not yet dinnertime. What do you choose for a snack? Should you choose cookies or fruit? A glass of milk or a doughnut?

When you choose a snack, think of the USDA Food Guide Pyramid. Limit the amount of sugar, fat, or salt that you eat. Foods high in these substances don't give you the nutrients you need. Think about the servings you have already had today and what you will have for dinner. Remember, don't overeat.

How you are feeling can also affect what you want to eat. Do you want something warm? Cold? Crunchy? Soft? Smooth? There's a healthful snack for every mood.

A mix of unbuttered popcorn, unsalted pretzels, and sunflower seeds?

Peanut butter on whole-wheat bread?

Sliced cucumbers and celery dipped in plain yogurt?

A glass of low-fat milk and a granola bar?

Baked tortilla chips dipped in salsa?

◄ Keisha is deciding what snack she is in the mood for.

You can eat tasty foods that are also healthful. Be daring! Be creative! Try something new! Be sure to make a healthful choice. Here are some ideas to help you:

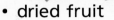
▼ Which of these foods might you choose for your next snack?

- fresh fruit
- raw vegetables
- nuts and seeds
- whole-grain cereal
- rice cakes

- plain granola bars
- low-fat yogurt
- cheese
- unbuttered and unsalted popcorn

- dried fruit
- animal crackers
- peanut butter on whole-wheat crackers

SUMMARIZE List some things to think about when you are choosing snacks.

Lesson 3 Summary and Review

1 Summarize with Vocabulary

Use vocabulary and other terms from this lesson to complete the statements.

Choosing healthful foods can form healthful eating _____. With practice you can choose healthful combination _____, or foods that contain more than one food group. Eating a healthful _____ can give you the energy you need until your next meal.

2 Critical Thinking How can you develop healthful eating habits?

3 List at least four different healthful snacks you enjoy or would be willing to try. Then name the food groups in which they are found.

4 (Focus Skill) COMPARE AND CONTRAST Draw and complete this graphic organizer to show how healthful and unhealthful snacks are alike and different.

Topic: Healthful and Unhealthful Snacks
Alike   Different

5 Write to Express—Idea

Suppose you want to know the nutritional value of foods in a fast-food restaurant. Write what you might say in a letter requesting the information.

Make Responsible Decisions

About Meals and Snacks

Every day you have to make decisions about meals and snacks. You must think through the decisions that you make. Using the steps for **Making Responsible Decisions** can help you make healthful choices.

Mai overslept this morning. She doesn't have time for her favorite breakfast of eggs, toast, and juice. What should Mai do?

1 Find out about the choices you could make.

Mai can skip breakfast or eat a candy bar, or she can prepare juice and toast with cheese.

2 Eliminate choices that are against your family rules.

Mai knows her mother would not approve of the candy bar. She eliminates that choice.

3 Ask yourself: What could happen with each choice? Does the choice show good character?

If Mai skips breakfast, she may be sleepy at school. If she eats breakfast, she may have more energy.

4 Make what seems to be the best choice.

Mai decides to eat breakfast so she will have the energy she needs. Her decision shows she is being responsible.

Problem Solving

After school Madeline is allowed to have a snack before doing her homework. On the counter Madeline sees cupcakes her dad baked for her little brother's birthday. She knows there are 25 students in her brother's class. She counts 28 cupcakes.

Use the steps for **Making Responsible Decisions** to help Madeline make the best decision. Explain how Madeline's decision shows trustworthiness.

Food Guidelines and Labels

Dietary Guidelines for Americans

There are guidelines that can help you make good food choices. The USDA provides a nutrition plan called the Dietary Guidelines for Americans. This plan suggests ways for you to be physically active, eat well, and make good choices.

Aim for Fitness

► Aim for a weight that is good for you. Find out your recommended weight range from a health professional. If you need to, set goals to reach a good weight.

► Be physically active each day. Get enough exercise to help balance the types and amount of foods you eat. In the next chapter, you can discover how the Activity Pyramid can help you plan each week's activities.

Build a Healthy Base

▶ Use a food guide pyramid to guide your food choices.

▶ Each day, choose a variety of grains such as wheat, oats, rice, and corn. Choose whole grains when you can.

▶ Each day, choose a variety of fruits and vegetables.

▶ Keep food safe to eat. (Follow the tips in Lesson 5 for safe preparation and storage of food.)

Choose Sensibly

▶ Choose a diet that is moderate in total fat and low in saturated fat and cholesterol.

▶ Choose foods and drinks that are low in sugar. Lower the amount of sugars you eat.

▶ Choose foods that are low in salt. When you prepare foods, use very little salt.

▶ Choose reasonable food portions. Eat servings that meet your nutritional needs based on the recommendations of the USDA Food Guide Pyramid.

Following these guidelines will help you make good choices about your health.

MAIN IDEA AND DETAILS **Write a sentence that states the main purpose of the Dietary Guidelines.**

Reading a Product Label

Trisha has been reading the label on a box of cereal. Product labels are provided on almost all packaged foods. The labels show how **nutritious** the food is, or how much nutritional value it has.

One part of a label tells how much protein, carbohydrate, and fat the food contains. It shows the amount of fiber. It also lists some vitamins and minerals in the food.

A product label also tells you the serving size. On Trisha's cereal box, a label states that a serving is one cup. The total calories, fats, proteins, and carbohydrates are given for one serving. What other things are listed?

Did You Know?

In some parts of the world, insects are a major source of protein, vitamins, and minerals. The ancient Greeks and Romans ate insects such as locust and beetle larvae. Today ants, grasshoppers, water bugs, and crickets are just a few of the many insects that are eaten by people. A caterpillar called the mopane worm is even packaged as a food product.

Product labels have information to help you make good eating choices.▼

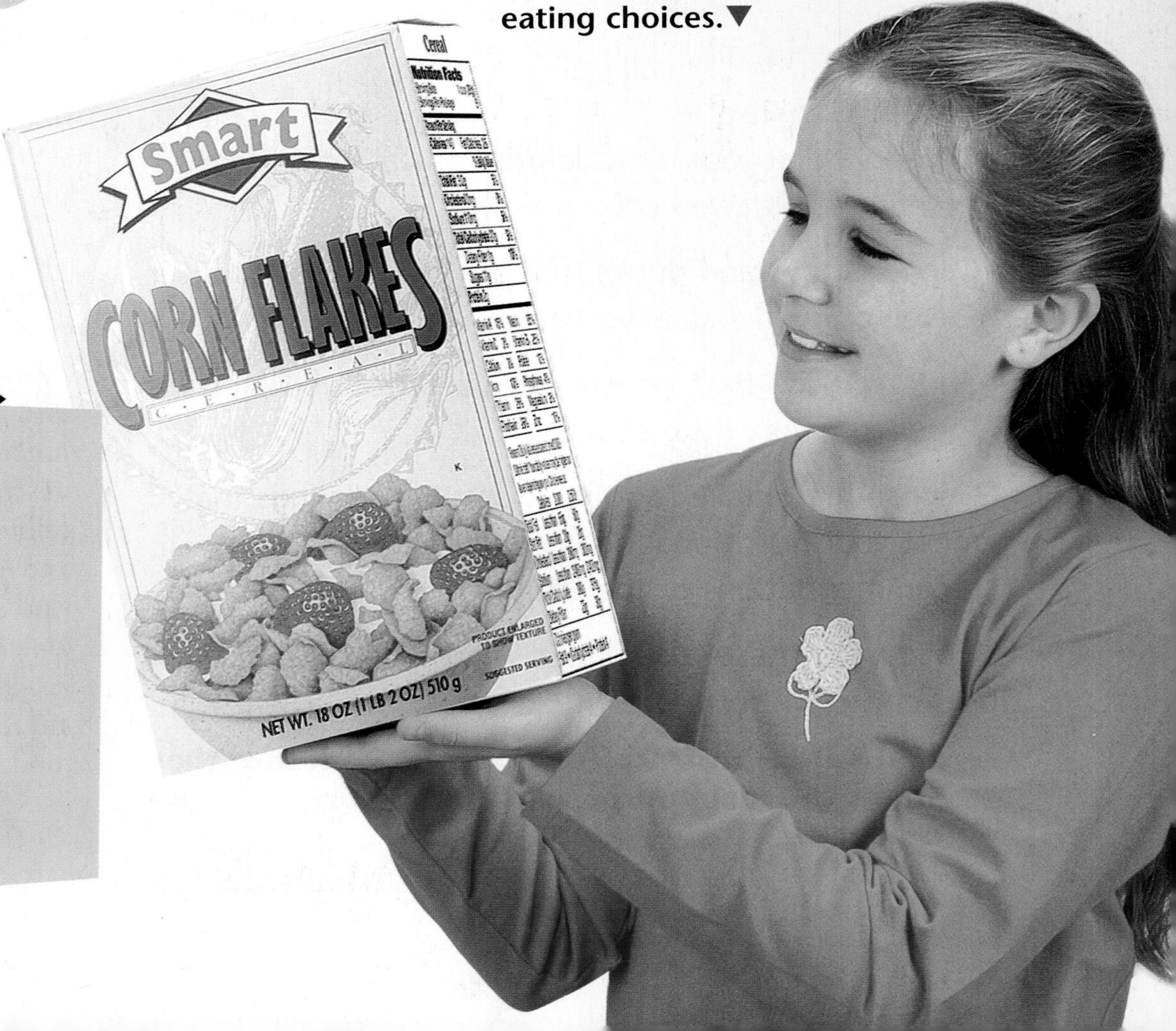

Smart
CORN FLAKES
CEREAL
NET WT. 18 OZ (1 LB 2 OZ) 510 g

Personal Health Plan ▶

Real-Life Situation
Suppose you want to control the portions in your daily diet better.

Real-Life Plan
Write a personal health goal listing ways you might use product labels to control better the amount of foods you eat.

Cereal

Nutrition Facts

Serving Size	1 cup (29g)
Servings Per Package	8

Amount Per Serving

Calories 140	Fat Calories 25

	% Daily Value
Total Fat 3.0g	5%
Cholesterol 0mg	0%
Sodium 110mg	5%
Total Carbohydrate 27g	9%
Dietary Fiber 1g	10%
Sugars 11g	
Protein 2g	

Vitamin A	15%	Niacin	25%
Vitamin C	0%	Vitamin B6	25%
Calcium	0%	Folate	10%
Iron	10%	Phosphorus	4%
Thiamin	25%	Magnesium	2%
Riboflavin	25%	Zinc	10%

*Percent Daily Values are based on a 2,000-Calorie diet. Your daily values may be higher or lower depending on your Calorie needs:

	Calories:	2,000	2,500
Total Fat	Less than	65g	80g
Sat. Fat	Less than	20g	25g
Cholesterol	Less than	300mg	300mg
Sodium	Less than	2,400mg	2,400mg
Total Carbohydrate		300g	375g
Dietary Fiber		25g	30g

Calories per gram
Fat 9 • Carbohydrate 4 • Protein 4

serving size, number of servings in the package

calories per serving

amounts of protein, fat, carbohydrate, sodium (salt), and dietary fiber

vitamins and minerals the food contains

the amounts of major nutrients you need each day

If Trisha ate two cups of cereal, the total calories as well as amounts of nutrients would double. So you see, it is important to check the serving size before you eat packaged foods and snacks.

Another part of a food label is the ingredients list. The **ingredients** are all the things used to make a food product. The ingredients are listed in order from greatest amount to least amount.

Trisha is surprised when she reads the list of ingredients in her cereal. There are so many things in it!

DRAW CONCLUSIONS Explain how a product label can help you make food choices.

Quick Activity

Analyze a Label Read the ingredients list below. Find the four main ingredients. Think about what you know about the USDA Food Guide Pyramid. Is this food a good nutritional choice? Why or why not?

INGREDIENTS: Cornmeal, rice flour, oat flour, wheat flour, sugar, salt, corn syrup, malt flavoring, baking soda.
VITAMINS AND MINERALS: Vitamin C, zinc, iron, Vitamin B6, Vitamin B2, Vitamin A, Vitamin B1, Vitamin B12, Vitamin D.

Comparing Product Labels

Product labels give you information about a food. Reading a product label can help you decide if a food is healthful.

Suppose you want to buy peanuts. You find jars labeled "PEANUTS" and "HONEY ROASTED PEANUTS." You want to know which nuts to choose, so you look at the ingredients list on each jar. What differences do you think you'll see?

When you buy a food such as peanuts, you might expect the jar to contain only peanuts. As you read the label on the "PEANUTS" jar, you learn the food has no oil, no salt, and no sugar. It has just one ingredient—peanuts.

When you look at the "HONEY ROASTED PEANUTS" label, you find that peanuts are the first ingredient. But sugar is the second; then there's salt!

When you look closely, you see that most of the other ingredients are sugars. Honey, corn syrup, and fructose are all forms of sugar.

Plain Peanuts

INGREDIENTS: PEANUTS

Honey Roasted Peanuts

INGREDIENTS: PEANUTS, SUGAR, SALT, HONEY, CORN SYRUP, FRUCTOSE, CORNSTARCH

You might not know some of the words on an ingredients list. Some ingredients are used to keep the food from spoiling. Other ingredients may be food coloring. Coloring is usually added to make the food look better.

The Dietary Guidelines for Americans suggest choosing foods low in sugars, fats, and salt. You put back the honey roasted peanuts and take the plain peanuts. You munch happily, knowing you are eating a healthful snack, not a snack full of sugar!

SUMMARIZE What information does an ingredients list on a label tell you?

Lesson 4 Summary and Review

❶ Summarize with Vocabulary

Use vocabulary and other terms from this lesson to complete these statements.

Using the Dietary _____ for_____ and product _____ can help you choose a healthful diet. Reading the _____ list on a product label can help you determine how _____ the food is.

❷ List three things a food label can tell you.

❸ Critical Thinking Which part of Dietary Guidelines for Americans is most important to you? Make sure to explain your choice.

❹ (Focus Skill) **COMPARE AND CONTRAST** Draw and complete this graphic organizer to show how the two parts of a product label are alike and different.

Topic: Product Labels
Alike   Different

❺ Write to Inform—Explanation

Write to someone to explain how following the Dietary Guidelines for Americans can benefit a person's health.

Keeping Foods Safe

Lesson Focus

You must handle food carefully in order to avoid illness.

Why Learn This?

You can use what you learn to help you handle and prepare foods safely.

Vocabulary

food poisoning

Preparing Foods Safely

You may have seen moldy bread or rotten fruit. But foods don't have to look or smell spoiled to be dangerous. Germs can come from many places. Some fresh foods, including eggs, raw meat, and raw poultry, carry germs. Even when you are healthy, your body carries germs that can get onto food.

Food poisoning is an illness caused by eating food that contains germs. Some kinds of food poisoning are mild and do not last long. Other kinds can be very serious and can even cause death. To avoid food poisoning, you need to handle food safely.

SUMMARIZE **Explain what food poisoning is.**

How to Tell if Food Has Spoiled

Sometimes it's easy to tell that a food has spoiled. Breads, fruits, and vegetables may be covered with white or gray fuzzy mold. Spoiled meat or sour milk may smell strange. Sometimes spoiled food doesn't smell or look spoiled. It's always best to play it safe. If you think there's a problem, throw out the food.

You can help prevent food spoilage. When you return from shopping, put fresh foods in the refrigerator right away. After you eat, wrap leftovers and store them in the refrigerator.

Handling Food Safely

- ☐ Wash your hands with soap and warm water before and after handling food.
- ☐ Use a cutting board when cutting raw chicken or meat.
- ☐ Wash all work surfaces and utensils with hot water and soap.
- ☐ Don't eat foods that are made with raw eggs.
- ☐ Cook eggs until the yolks are hard.
- ☐ Cook meat and chicken until no red or pink shows.
- ☐ Wash all fresh fruits and vegetables.
- ☐ Don't handle food when you are ill.
- ☐ Thaw food in the refrigerator or microwave, not at room temperature.
- ☐ Keep pets away from food.

Quick Activity

Identify What's Wrong Study the picture of the boy and his mother in the kitchen. What unhealthful practices can you find? Discuss what they should do instead.

Freeze bread and meat to keep them longer. Do not buy dented cans or cracked eggs. The dents or cracks may let germs get into the food. If the dents or the cracks happen at home later, throw the food away. The table below can help you store food safely.

Food Shelf Life

Food	Storage Life	Helpful Tips
Cereal	unopened 6–12 months; opened 2–3 months	Keep package free from air by tightly wrapping the liner.
Toaster Pastries	2–3 months	Keep in airtight container.
Ketchup	unopened 12 months; opened 1 month	Keep in refrigerator after opening.
Peanut Butter	unopened 6–9 months; opened 2 months	Will keep longer if refrigerated.
Lunch Meat	unopened 2 weeks; opened 3–5 days	Keep in refrigerator.

CAUSE AND EFFECT **What might be an effect of eating food from a dented can?**

Lesson 5 Summary and Review

❶ Summarize with Vocabulary

Use vocabulary and other terms from this lesson to complete the statements.

Preparing foods safely can help prevent an illness called _____. An important step in safe food preparation is _____ your hands with soap and _____ water.

❷ Name three ways you can help keep the foods you prepare safe.

❸ Critical Thinking Why is it a good idea to throw away any food that you might think is spoiled?

❹ (Focus Skill) **COMPARE AND CONTRAST** Show how safe and spoiled foods are alike and different.

Topic: Safe and Spoiled Foods

Alike   Different

❺ Write to Inform—Narration

Write a comical or serious story about a family that could use some food safety advice. Be sure to include introductory and concluding paragraphs.

ACTIVITIES

Math

Calculate Servings With a partner, plan a menu for a family of four for one day. Calculate how much of each food you'll need so that everyone will get enough servings from each food group.

Science

Observe Bacterial Growth Put about half a cup of milk in each of two clear containers that can be sealed tight. Put one container in the refrigerator and the other in a warm, dark place. After one day, look at the containers of milk side by side. Describe the appearance of the milk in each container. Check both containers and write about your observations every day for a week.

Your teacher will tell you how to dispose of the milk. ▲

Technology Project

Use a computer to make a slide presentation of at least four tips for eating healthful meals. Present your slide show to your family or classmates.

GO ONLINE **For more activities, visit The Learning Site.** www.harcourtschool.com/health

Home & Community

Communicating Make a poster encouraging people to use the USDA Food Guide Pyramid as a guideline. Display your poster in your classroom or cafeteria.

Career Link

Restaurant Manager Suppose that you are the manager of a restaurant. Write a note to your employees in which you explain the importance of cleanliness. Make sure that you tell the employees why they need to wash their hands often and keep the kitchen and dining room areas clean.

Reading Skill

COMPARE AND CONTRAST

Draw and then use this graphic organizer to answer questions 1 and 2.

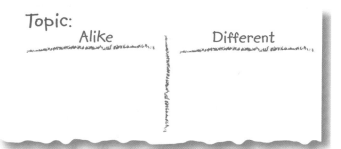

Topic:
Alike   Different

1 Write at least two ways nutrients and food groups are alike and different.

2 Write at least two ways vitamins and minerals are alike and different.

Use Vocabulary

Match each term in Column B with its meaning in Column A.

Column A	Column B
3 Energy nutrients	**A** balanced diet
4 A diet that has a healthful amount of foods from each group	**B** food poisoning
	C ingredients
5 Food that has nutritional value	**D** nutritious
	E proteins
6 Things used to make a food product	
7 An illness caused by eating food that has germs	

 Check Understanding

Choose the letter of the correct answer.

8 If you want to know how much vitamin C is in a food, where would you look to find out? (p. 80)
A food guide pyramid
B Dietary Guidelines for Americans
C product label
D Food Shelf Life table

9 Which of these foods is considered one serving? (pp. 68–69)
F 1 cup of nuts   **H** 2 eggs
G 1 slice of bread   **J** 10 crackers

10 On a food guide pyramid, the foods you should eat the smallest amount of are located at the _____ (p. 69)
A bottom of the pyramid
B middle of the pyramid
C top of the pyramid
D center of the pyramid

11 If you were trying to add calcium to your diet, which of these foods would be the BEST to choose? (p. 63)

F   **H**

G   **J**

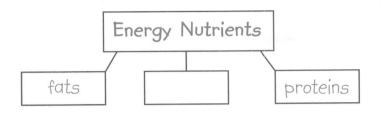

Energy Nutrients

fats   proteins

12 What nutrient is missing from the graphic organizer? (p. 60)
A carbohydrates   **C** vitamins
B minerals   **D** water

13 Which of these is a way to control portions? (p. 70)
F Eat everything on your plate.
G Eat three meals a day.
H Use recommended serving sizes.
J Wash your hands before eating.

14 Dents in cans or cracks in eggs are a way _____ can get into food. (p. 86)
A vitamins   **C** germs
B minerals   **D** proteins

15 The Dietary Guidelines for Americans suggest ways on how to eat well, make sensible choices, and _____. (p. 78)
F find the right amount of nutrients in a food
G be physically active
H read a product label
J figure out an expiration date

Think Critically

16 You buy raw chicken for tomorrow night's dinner. How would you safely store and handle the chicken before you cook it?

17 Study the ingredients list of the snack food label shown here. What does this information tell you about the healthfulness of the snack?

INGREDIENTS: flour, oats, molasses, corn syrup, vegetable oil, and salt

Apply Skills

18 **BUILDING GOOD CHARACTER**
Respect You have been invited to a friend's house for dinner. When the food is served, you notice a food that you don't like. Apply what you know about using good table manners to make a decision about what you should do.

19 **LIFE SKILLS**
Make Decisions You live in a cold area, and your family doesn't buy much fresh fruit. Make a healthful decision on how you might get the servings of food you need from the fruit group.

Write About Health

20 Write to Inform—Explanation
Explain why eating healthful foods now can help you when you are an adult.

4 Fitness and Activity

IDENTIFY CAUSE AND EFFECT
Effect is what happens. Cause is the reason, or why, it happens. Use the Reading in Health Handbook on pages 334–335 and this graphic organizer to help you read the health facts in this chapter.

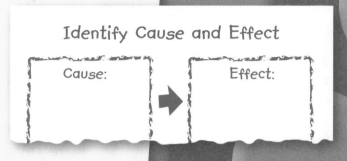

Identify Cause and Effect

| Cause: | | Effect: |

Health Graph

INTERPRET DATA Young people in the United States are becoming less fit and more overweight. One reason is that they spend more time watching television each week than they spend exercising. About how many hours per day do young people watch television?

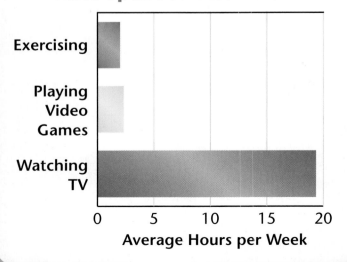

Time Spent on Activities

Exercising
Playing Video Games
Watching TV

0   5   10   15   20
Average Hours per Week

Daily Physical Activity

You need to be physically active. Stay active for your health.

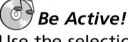 *Be Active!*
Use the selection Track 4, **Jam Jive**, to give your heart a workout.

Good Posture

Improve Your Form

Imagine that a string is gently pulling upward on the center of your head. Your ears, shoulders, and hips are in a straight line. Your chin is parallel to the floor. Your shoulders are level, and your knees are relaxed. This is good **posture** (PAHS•cher). It is holding your body in a balanced way when you stand, sit, and move. Good posture prevents problems with your bones, muscles, and joints. It also helps you feel good about yourself.

Many people suffer from aches and pains. You can help prevent pain by using good posture when you stand, when you sit, and when you lift and carry.

Lesson Focus

Good posture is important for your health and your self-image.

Why Learn This?

What you learn can help you have good posture, take pride in your appearance, and stay healthy.

Vocabulary

posture

Did You Know?

In the morning, when you first get up, you are taller than when you went to bed. Overnight the discs that separate the bones in your spine swell with water so that you become taller. During the day, gravity and exercise squeeze out this liquid and your height is lessened.

You show good posture when your ears, shoulders, and hips are in a straight line.

▼ Be sure to lift heavy objects properly.

Quick Activity

Identify What's Wrong
List ways each student can improve his or her posture.

Practice good posture when you sit. Always sit with your back straight. When you sit at a desk, pull your chair close. Rest your feet on the floor to prevent backaches. Do not lean over your work. Sit up straight.

Use good posture when you lift heavy things. It is important to let your legs do most of the work. This is because your leg muscles are stronger than your back muscles. Never bend over to lift something heavy. Instead, bend your knees and keep your back as straight as possible. Stand behind the object. Hold it close to your body, and slowly lift it as you straighten your knees. The picture on page 92 shows how to lift objects by using good posture.

 CAUSE AND EFFECT **What might be the effect of keeping your knees straight when you bend over to lift a heavy object?**

Good Posture Tips

1. Keep your back straight.
2. Stand up straight.
3. Keep your chin up, with your head centered over your shoulders.
4. Keep your feet apart a little less than your shoulders are wide.
5. Keep your knees slightly bent.
6. Ears, shoulders, and hips should line up.

93

This girl is wearing a backpack correctly. The boy is not. ▶

Wearing a Backpack

Your back and abdominal (ab•DAHM•uh•nuhl) muscles can support the weight of a backpack that is worn correctly. If your backpack is too heavy, or if you don't wear it correctly, you could harm your back. Carrying an overweight backpack can pull your body forward and force your spine to stretch or press together. That puts too much stress on your back. It can make your shoulders rounded and your upper back curved. This can cause shoulder, neck, and back pain.

SUMMARIZE What happens to your spine when you carry a backpack that is too heavy?

Using a Computer

Good posture is important when you sit at a computer. It will help you work or play safely without getting tired. Your chair should support your shoulders and back. The seat should be high enough so that the monitor is at eye level. Your feet should rest comfortably flat on the floor. The keyboard should be at wrist level. You should be able to type without having to reach up or bend forward. Keep your wrists straight when you type. Hold the mouse loosely to prevent cramps in your hand.

Your neck and shoulders should be relaxed.

Your shoulders should be in line with your ears and hips.

The top of your screen should be at or just below eye level.

Keep your wrists straight. Your arms need to be level with your keyboard, with your forearms horizontal.

Keep your feet flat on the floor.

Sitting at a computer can make you as tired as playing your favorite sport can. Your muscles can feel tired from lack of movement. Your back may start to ache. It is important to stand up and stretch to help your muscles relax. Your eyes may also get tired. To help your eyes feel better, blink them often to moisten them.

Every few minutes, look away from the screen. Looking into the distance lets your eyes rest and adjust. Work in a room that is well lighted, away from the glare of windows.

MAIN IDEA AND DETAILS What is the main idea about computer use? What details support this main idea?

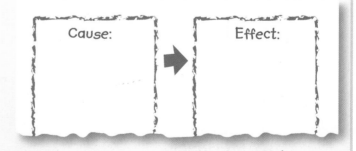

◄ Stretch at least once every half hour to help your muscles relax.

Lesson 1 Summary and Review

❶ Summarize with Vocabulary

Use vocabulary and other terms from this lesson to complete the statements.

Good _____ means holding your body in a balanced way. When you lift things, _____ your knees and keep your back as _____ as possible. Good posture is important when sitting and when working at a _____.

❷ Critical Thinking How could carrying a heavy backpack affect your riding a bike?

❸ What are three tips for preventing eyestrain when working at a computer?

❹ (Focus Skill) CAUSE AND EFFECT Complete this graphic organizer to show the effects of poor posture at a computer.

Cause:	Effect:

❺ Write to Inform—Description

Suppose you are going to make a poster about posture. You want to illustrate and describe five good posture tips and tell how each one helps your body. Write the tips for the poster.

Fairness

Working with Others

You can't always do what you want to do. Others may have ideas and activities that they would like to do. It is important that you listen to others to understand their needs and wants. This way you can show fairness.

- **Give your full attention to the speaker by facing or leaning toward him or her.**
- **Look for things to agree about.**
- **Wait your turn; don't interrupt.**
- **Summarize what you have heard.**
- **Try to understand how the other person feels.**
- **Allow others to comment or to ask questions.**
- **To be fair to everyone, suggest taking turns playing the games or doing the activities.**

Activity

Role-play the following scene with a small group. One student is very thirsty and wants a drink of water. He or she tries to cut into line at the drinking fountain. Why won't the other students let the first student cut into line? Listen to others. List reasons the other students may feel the first student is not being fair to everyone else. Suggest ways the first student can avoid making mistakes like this again.

Physical Fitness

What Your Body Needs

Do you like to jump rope, ride a bicycle, or swim? You might like these activities because they are fun. Physical activities such as these are what your body and mind need. They are forms of exercise. Exercise is any physical activity that makes your body work hard. Regular exercise can help you do better in school, sleep better, feel less tired, and be less stressed. Physical activities and team sports help you learn to interact and cooperate with others. You can meet new friends. Exercise can also help you feel good about yourself.

◀ Stretching is a good way to increase your flexibility.

Doing push-ups, sit-ups, and pull-ups can help your muscles get stronger. ▶

Exercise is good for you. You need to work your muscles. Exercise makes them strong. Doing regular exercise can help build your body and keep it healthy. It helps you do better in sports. Regular exercise can also help reduce your chances of injury.

 CAUSE AND EFFECT **What is the effect of having strong muscles?**

Did You Know?

You have 650 muscles in your body. They make up about one-half of your body weight. For example, if you weigh 80 pounds, about 40 pounds of you is muscle!

Three Basic Parts of Physical Fitness

1. **Endurance** (en•DUR•uhnts) Ability of your muscles to work hard for a long period of time without getting tired

2. **Muscle strength** Ability of your muscles to apply force. The more strength you have, the easier it is to do activities.

3. **Flexibility** (flek•suh•BIL•uh•tee) Ability to move joints and muscles through a full range of motion

Physical activity can be fun and help you stay healthy.▼

99

Personal Health Plan ▶

Real-Life Situation
Between school and after-school activities, you know you're not getting enough exercise.
Real-Life Plan
Make a plan to do ten minutes of aerobic exercise every day after school. Next week, increase your time to fifteen minutes.

Exercise Your Body

Different kinds of exercise are needed for strength, endurance, and flexibility.

Aerobic exercise (air•OH•bik) is exercise that causes you to breathe deeply and makes your heart beat faster. You should do an aerobic exercise for at least 30 minutes. Aerobic exercise also improves your cardiovascular system (kar•dee•oh•VAS•kyuh•ler), which includes your heart and blood vessels. Skating, fast walking, bike riding, and cross-country running are examples of aerobic exercise.

Anaerobic exercise (an•air•OH•bik) builds muscle strength. Anaerobic exercises are short, intense activities such as curl-ups, pull-ups, sprinting, and push-ups.

▲ Aerobic exercise helps build endurance.

Aerobic Activities

◀ Anaerobic exercise builds strong muscles. It can help your ability to jump, throw, twist, lift, push, and pull.

If doing your homework makes you tired and sleepy, take a quick activity break. Walk in place for a few minutes, or walk up and down stairs a few times. You'll feel better and be able to concentrate more. If you are having a bad day at school, go for a short walk during recess. Exercise helps take your mind off things that are bothering you and reduces stress. It also can help you let go of anger and other uncomfortable feelings. The physical activity of exercise can give you more energy and help you feel better.

COMPARE AND CONTRAST How are aerobic and anaerobic exercises the same and different?

Quick **Activity**

Evaluate Fitness Have a friend keep count while you do as many curl-ups as you can in one minute.

ACTIVITY

Life Skills
Manage Stress

Mark is feeling stress because he has a big test tomorrow. He knows he needs to relax and get a good night's sleep. Use what you have learned to suggest some healthful ways that Mark can deal with his stress and get a good night's sleep.

Rest and Sleep

After a busy day of school and other activities, your body needs **rest**. Rest gives your heart and other muscles a chance to slow down. Resting is also good for your mind. Quiet activities such as reading, drawing, and listening to music help you rest.

Sleep is another way your body rests. When you sleep, your heart rate and breathing rate slow down. Your body's muscles relax. Even your brain rests. Sleep is important and necessary for everyone. While you sleep, your body repairs damaged cells and makes new cells to help you grow. During sleep, your body stores energy from the food you have eaten.

▼ Activities such as quiet games help your body rest.

Avoid hard exercise within two hours before bedtime. Instead, try an activity that will help you relax, such as reading or taking a bath.

Your body needs about ten hours of sleep every night. When you don't get enough sleep or rest, you can become ill. Without enough sleep, you may have a hard time paying attention or following directions in school. If you don't get enough sleep one night, try to go to bed earlier the next night.

DRAW CONCLUSIONS
Why is it important to get enough sleep?

Consumer Activity

Access Valid Health Information Find out more about the importance of rest and sleep. How can rest and sleep affect your school performance? Use the steps to Access Valid Health Information on pages 52–54. Write down the information you find.

◀ Reading is another quiet activity that is good for your body and mind.

Lesson 2 Summary and Review

❶ Summarize with Vocabulary

Use vocabulary and other terms from this lesson to complete the statements.

The three parts of physical fitness are _____, _____, and _____. _____ exercise causes you to breathe deeply. _____ exercise builds muscle strength. The heart is part of your _____ system. You need _____ and at least ten hours of sleep each night.

❷ Critical Thinking How can aerobic exercise improve your endurance?

❸ Explain why you need anaerobic exercise.

❹ (Focus Skill) CAUSE AND EFFECT Draw and complete this graphic organizer to show the effects of not getting enough sleep.

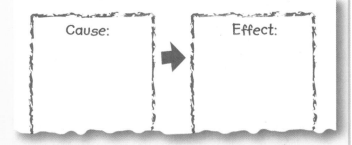

Cause: → Effect:

❺ Write to Inform—Explanation

Explain the effects of exercise on your body and mind. Suggest a variety of enjoyable physical activities that you can do regularly.

Set Goals
About Fitness

Exercise helps keep your body healthy, but you need to get enough rest to help your muscles rebuild after physical activity. Burt loves to play sports. Lately, he has not been getting enough rest. He feels tired a lot and has trouble staying awake in school. Use the steps for **Setting Goals** to help Burt get enough rest.

1 **Choose a goal.**

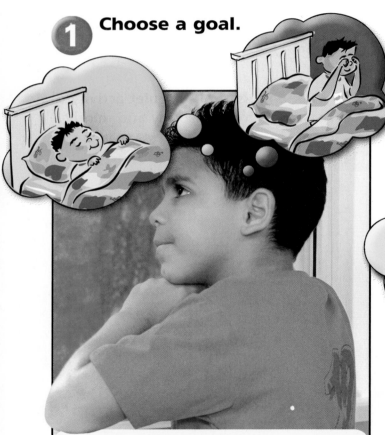

Burt decides to set a goal to get more hours of sleep each night.

2 **List steps to meet the goal. Determine how long it will take to meet the goal.**

Burt lists things he can do to relax. He plans his routine so that he can get to bed earlier for a better night's sleep.

3 Check your progress as you work toward your goal.

Each night Burt checks the time he goes to bed.

4 Reflect on and evaluate your progress toward the goal.

Burt finds that he is now getting more sleep. He feels good and is awake and alert in school.

Problem Solving

Anne knows she should do aerobic exercise at least three times a week for thirty minutes each time. She likes to run, but during much of the winter, it's dark by the time she gets home from school. Use the four steps for **Setting Goals** to help Anne solve her problem. How can she use the goal-setting steps to help her take responsibility for getting the aerobic exercise she needs?

Your Personal Fitness Plan

Be Physically Active

To improve your endurance, you need the exercise you get from doing activities. To help you choose activities that are right for you, use the **Activity Pyramid**, a guide to physical activity.

Sitting Still
Watching television, playing computer games
Small amounts of time

Light Exercise
Playtime, yardwork, softball
2–3 times a week

Regular Activities
Walking to school, taking the stairs, helping with housework
Every day

Like the USDA Food Guide Pyramid, you can use the Activity Pyramid when planning your personal fitness plan. Choose more activities from the base of the pyramid, fewer from the top.

A good fitness plan includes different kinds of exercise. Your plan should have exercises that help you develop aerobic fitness, muscle endurance, strength, and flexibility. Also include the three steps pictured here as part of your exercise program.

A warm-up of light activity, such as running in place, can help prepare your muscles for physical activity. Include slow gentle stretching, without bouncing. Doing stretches can help prevent muscle injury.

SEQUENCE List in order the steps for exercise: *workout, cool-down, warm-up*. Explain why they must occur in that order to avoid injury.

▲ *Warm up* for five to ten minutes to get your body ready for exercise. Good warm-up activities include jogging slowly, walking, and stretching.

▲ *Work out* after warming up, and exercise for at least thirty minutes.

Strength and Flexibility Exercises
Weight training, dancing, pull-ups
2–3 times a week

Aerobic Exercises
Biking, running, soccer, hiking
30-plus minutes, 2–3 times a week

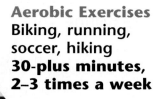

If you warm up and cool down, you are less likely to injure yourself during exercise. ▶

▲ *Cool down* after exercise for five to ten minutes, ending with stretching. Walking is a good cool-down activity.

After-school activities can be fun and great exercise. ▶

Work Your Heart and Lungs

At least three days a week, the main part of your fitness plan should include aerobic exercise. It strengthens your heart and lungs.

If you are exercising hard enough, you will begin to breathe heavily. If you feel pain, you should stop and tell an adult. Over time you will be able to exercise harder.

Also, do sets of exercises that strengthen your muscles. For example, you might do three sets of ten push-ups, two days a week. Remember to warm up and cool down.

DRAW CONCLUSIONS **Why should you do aerobic exercise for thirty minutes, three times a week?**

Keep Your Exercise Safe

Sometimes people hurt themselves when they exercise. You can lower your chances for injury by exercising safely. You can do this by wearing the proper safety gear and by using sports equipment correctly.

Safety gear is anything players wear to keep from getting hurt. Shin guards protect your legs from kicks while you play soccer. A helmet protects your head in case you fall off your bicycle. A mouth guard protects your mouth while you play hockey or volleyball. For skateboarding and inline skating, you need a helmet, wrist guards, elbow pads, and kneepads.

Many activities require safety gear, such as helmets, to protect the body from injury. ▼

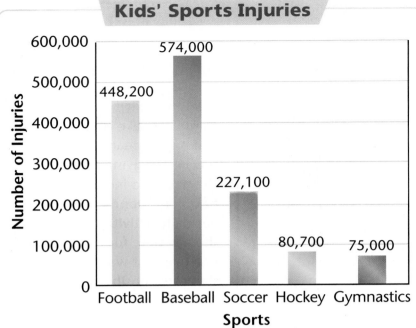

Kids' Sports Injuries

Number of Injuries vs Sports

- Football: 448,200
- Baseball: 574,000
- Soccer: 227,100
- Hockey: 80,700
- Gymnastics: 75,000

▲ This graph shows how many children were hurt playing five sports in one year. What kinds of safety gear might have helped avoid some of these injuries?

It is important to follow the rules of whatever sport or game you play. Rules help keep you safe and keep the game fair and fun for all. Following rules on the school playground and in PE class will keep you and your friends safer.

You can be physically active outside of school. You can enjoy public parks, playing fields, rinks, and pools. Wherever you exercise or play, be safe and have adult supervision.

 CAUSE AND EFFECT What is the effect of wearing a helmet when you ride your bike?

Lesson 3 Summary and Review

1 Summarize with Vocabulary

Use vocabulary and other terms from this lesson to complete the statements.

You can use the _____ to help you make a personal fitness plan. Before a _____, you need to _____. After you exercise, you need to _____. You should wear _____ and follow the _____ of the game.

2 Why is choosing an activity you like to do an important part of creating a personal fitness plan?

3 Critical Thinking How can following the rules of a game protect you and others from getting injured?

4 **CAUSE AND EFFECT** Draw and complete this graphic organizer to show the effect of cooling down after exercising.

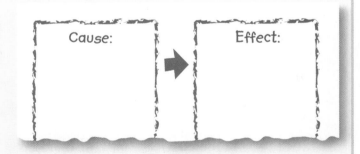

Cause: → Effect:

5 Write to Inform—Description

Write about three activities that you could do as part of your personal fitness plan. Use the Activity Pyramid to help you decide how long and how often you need to do each one.

Physical Education

Find a Fitness Role Model Choose a sport, and research a famous athlete from the United States or another country who has played that sport. Write a report that tells others about the athlete and the sport he or she plays and why he or she is fit.

Science

Exercise and Sleep Research shows that people who get regular exercise sleep better than those who don't. For one week, keep a record of how much exercise and sleep you get. Describe how you feel each morning when you get up. After one week, review your sleep and exercise patterns. How do you feel when you get enough exercise and sleep? How do you feel when you don't get enough?

Technology Project

List at least four tips for starting an activity plan. Use a computer to make a slide presentation of the tips. If a computer is not available, make colorful posters to display your tips.

 GO ONLINE **For more activities, visit The Learning Site.** www.harcourtschool.com/health

Home & Community

Communicating Make a poster encouraging others to use the Activity Pyramid to improve their fitness. Illustrate your poster with pictures of activities that are fun and healthful. Display your poster at home or in a hallway at school.

Career Link

Athletic Trainer An athletic trainer helps people exercise correctly. Suppose that you are an athletic trainer at a local gym. Your job is to get adults and children into better shape, or physically fit. Write a flier about the importance of creating a personal fitness plan. Tell people what to include in a personal fitness plan and why they need one. Decorate your flier with pictures of people exercising.

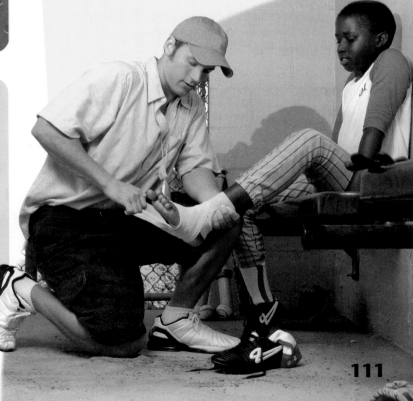

111

Reading Skill

CAUSE AND EFFECT
Draw and then use these graphic organizers to answer questions 1 and 2.

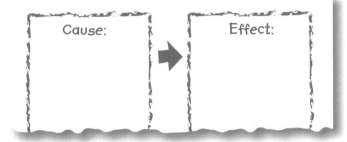

Cause: → Effect:

1 Write at least two effects of aerobic exercise.

2 Write at least two effects of warming up before exercising.

Use Vocabulary

Match each term in Column B with its meaning in Column A.

Column A	Column B
3 Holding your body in a balanced way	**A** safety gear
4 What you have when your muscles can work for a long time without getting tired	**B** flexibility **C** aerobic exercises
5 The ability to move joints and muscles through a full range of motion	**D** good posture
6 Something you wear to help prevent injury	**E** endurance
7 Exercises that use fast walking	

Check Understanding

Choose the letter of the correct answer.

8 What does aerobic exercise mostly increase? (p. 100)
A endurance **C** strength
B energy **D** power

9 Muscle strength is the ability of your muscles to apply _____. (p. 99)
F flexibility **H** force
G endurance **J** motion

10 When you lift heavy objects, you should use your _____, not your back. (p. 93)
A arms **C** hands
B spine **D** legs

11 The Activity Pyramid suggests that you should do which activity least often? (p. 106)

F  **H**

G  **J**

12 You can use the Activity Pyramid to create a _____. (pp. 106–107)
A work schedule
B sleep record
C personal fitness plan
D cardiovascular system

13 _____ should be a part of both warm-ups and cool-downs. (p. 107)

  F Endurance **H** Running

  G Lifting weights **J** Stretching

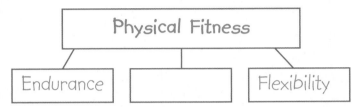

Physical Fitness

Endurance — [ ] — Flexibility

14 The graphic organizer shows the three parts of physical fitness. What is missing? (p. 99)

  A heart strength

  B muscle strength

  C cardiovascular fitness

  D lung strength

15 When you sleep, your body repairs damaged _____. (p. 102)

  F cells **H** blood

  G energy **J** eyes

16 Which of the following do you need most after a busy day? (p. 102)

  A workout **C** rest

  B cool-down **D** endurance

 Think Critically

17 You are going to play soccer with your friends. How would you safely warm up your body before playing?

 Apply Skills

18 **BUILDING GOOD CHARACTER**
Fairness You and your friend Tony decide to start working out together. But every time you are supposed to get together, Tony makes excuses for not coming to your house. His house is one mile away from yours. Apply what you know about being fair and communicating with others to make a decision about what you should do.

19 **LIFE SKILLS**
Set Goals You would like to try out for your school's track team this spring. In order to make the team, you need to be able to run a mile in seven minutes. Use what you know to help you set a goal to make the team.

Write About Health

20 **Write to Inform—Explanation** Explain why exercising now can help you when you are an adult.

Safe at Home

Reading Skill

SEQUENCE To sequence is to place in order the events that take place. It is also the order of the steps for doing a task. Use the Reading in Health Handbook on pages 338–339 and this graphic organizer to help you read the health facts in this chapter.

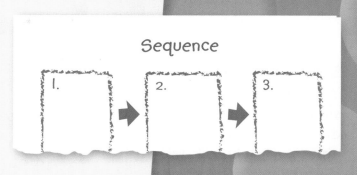

Sequence

1. → 2. → 3.

Health Graph

INTERPRET DATA Every year, hundreds of thousands of children go to emergency rooms for treatment of injuries. Of the causes shown in the graph, which results in the greatest number of injuries? How many more injuries are there from falls than from burns? From falls than from poisonings?

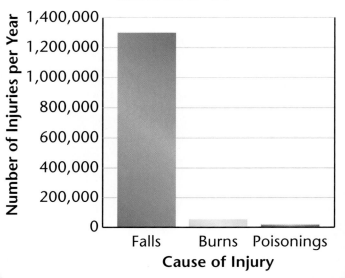

Unintentional Injuries
Children 5–14

Daily Physical Activity

Enjoy being active. Keep your activities safe.

 Be Active!
Use the selection Track 5, **Flexercise**, to practice safe warm-ups and exercises.

Responding to Emergencies

Lesson Focus

You can prepare for some emergencies or disasters. In an emergency, you can take steps to get help.

Why Learn This?

You can use what you learn to help yourself and others stay safe during a disaster.

Vocabulary

emergency
family emergency plan

Make an Emergency Phone Call

You see a house on fire in your neighborhood. This is an emergency. An **emergency** (ee·MER·juhn·see) is a situation in which help is needed right away. Other examples of emergencies are severe burns, severe bleeding, stopped breathing or stopped heartbeat, poisoning, drowning, and broken bones.

In an emergency, you must act quickly. The first thing to do is to tell an adult. If an adult isn't around, you must call for help.

For Emergencies

• Write down your name, your home address, your parents' or guardians' names, and their phone numbers at work.

• Post this list by a telephone in your home.

◀ When you tell the 911 operator what the emergency is, the operator will contact the right kind of help and send it to you.

Communication skills are very important when you talk with a 911 operator. Remember to do the following:

- Stay calm.
- Speak slowly and clearly.
- Tell the 911 operator your name, the problem, the phone number you are calling from, and the address.
- Answer the operator's questions as completely as possible. If you are at home, you can read your *For Emergencies* list by your phone.
- Stay on the phone until the operator tells you to hang up.

SEQUENCE **What is the first thing you should do in an emergency?**

ACTIVITY

Life Skills
Communicate
Rena decides to practice giving information to an emergency operator. She knows that she needs to speak clearly. What else does Rena need to do? Use the steps for **Communicating About a Health Need** on pages 46–47.

117

Make an Emergency Plan

An emergency can happen without warning. If there is a fire, you might need to leave your home quickly. If there is a storm, your electricity might be out for a long time. You can prepare for such situations by making a **family emergency plan**, a list of steps your family will take to stay safe during an emergency.

Know What Could Happen

Find out what kinds of natural disasters can happen where you live. Learn how to prepare for them and what to do if they happen. Know your community's warning signals and what you should do when they are given.

Decide on Escape Routes

If there is a fire in your home, you need to get out quickly. Your family emergency plan should have a drawing of each room in your house. Include two ways to escape from each room.

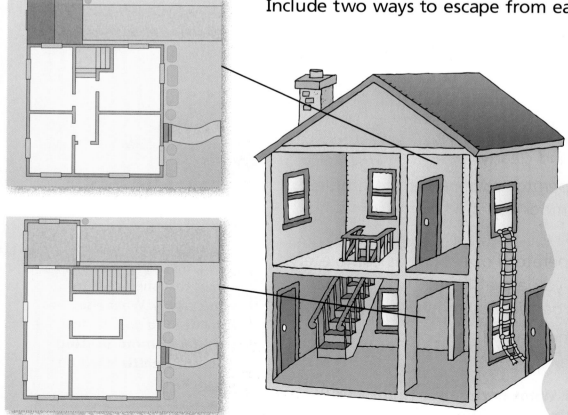

Quick Activity

Plan an Escape Sketch your bedroom, including the windows and doors. Write two ways you could escape from the room, and show these escape exits on your sketch. Decide whether you would need a ladder.

118

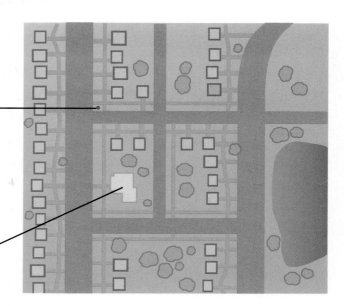

Know Your Family Contact

For a family contact, choose someone who lives in another city. Write down the person's name, address, and phone number. If a disaster happens and you become separated from your family, you should call this person to let him or her know where you are. If you are with your family, call to say the family is OK.

Learn How to Turn Off Utilities

Water, gas, and electricity are utilities. These may be damaged in an emergency and become dangerous. Ask a parent or another adult to show you how to shut them off.

Choose Two Meeting Places

All members of your family should meet in the same place. One place should be near your home. Another place should be away from your neighborhood in case you can't return home.

MAIN IDEA AND DETAILS **What is a family emergency plan? What are five things the plan should include?**

119

Make an Emergency Supply Kit

If an emergency happens, your family might be without electricity or running water. Plan for emergencies by keeping an emergency supply kit. Always keep it in the same place. Include the following supplies in your kit:

- canned fruits, vegetables, meats, and soups, plus a manual can opener
- plastic cups, plates, and eating utensils
- bottled water
- flashlight, battery-operated radio, and batteries
- clothes, shoes, and bedding
- first-aid kit and medicines

DRAW CONCLUSIONS **Why is it important to have a family emergency supply kit?**

Lesson 1 Summary and Review

❶ Summarize with Vocabulary

Use vocabulary and other terms from this lesson to complete the statements.

An _____ is a situation in which help is needed right away. If someone is hurt, tell an _____ or call the number _____. Your family can follow a _____ in an emergency to help stay safe. Gas, water, and electricity are examples of _____.

❷ Name five items that belong in an emergency supply kit.

❸ Critical Thinking Why do you need to know two ways to escape from each room if a fire happens in your home?

❹ (Focus Skill) SEQUENCE Draw and complete this graphic organizer to show what happens from the time you see an emergency until help arrives.

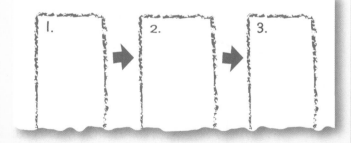

❺ Write to Express—Idea

Write a paragraph to tell why being prepared for an emergency is important. Include examples from this lesson or from what you already know.

Citizenship

Respecting Authority

In an emergency, an adult who has authority decides what to do. An adult in charge, such as a police officer or firefighter, may wear a uniform. But he or she also can be your parent, a teacher, or another adult. Being a good citizen means that you respect people who have authority. You cooperate and do what they say, to protect yourself and others from harm. Here are ways you can show respect for authority during an emergency drill or a real emergency:

- **Follow the instructions given by the adult in charge.**
- **Listen carefully. Don't interrupt when the person is talking. Ask questions if you don't understand what to do.**
- **Do what you are asked to do. Don't talk back to the person in authority.**
- **Don't fool around or make jokes. An emergency or even a drill is a serious situation.**
- **Help others obey authority. Don't ask them to break rules or laws.**

Activity

In small groups, think of an emergency situation. It might be a tornado, a loss of electric power for several days, or an injury to a person. Write a skit that shows how people should respect authority in that situation. Choose one member to act the role of the person in authority. Perform your skit for the class.

Staying Safe at Home

Prevent Injuries in the Home

You might be surprised to learn that many injuries are caused by accidents in the home. Using injury prevention can help. *Injury prevention* (IN•juh•ree prih•VEN•shuhn) means "keeping injuries from happening."

One way to prevent injuries is to practice *safety measures*, actions you take to stay safe. One safety measure is to get rid of or be careful around hazards. A **hazard** (HAZ•erd) is an object or condition that makes a situation unsafe. For example, electricity can be a hazard when it's not used properly.

Falls are the most common cause of home injuries. People fall in bathtubs, out of windows, and on stairs. Floors can be dangerous when they are wet or slippery.

Fires also cause many injuries in the home. Here are tips to prevent injuries from fire:

- Get permission before using an electrical or cooking appliance. Make sure you know how to use it.
- Know where fire extinguishers are.
- Make sure there are smoke detectors on every level of the house and in sleeping areas.

DRAW CONCLUSIONS What can you do to prevent injuries?

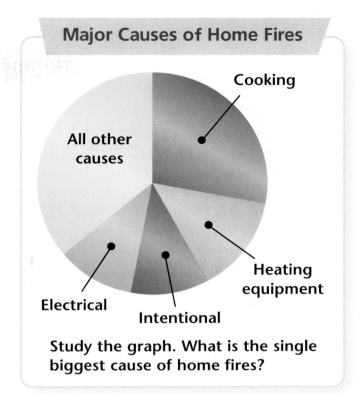

Major Causes of Home Fires

Cooking

All other causes

Heating equipment

Electrical

Intentional

Study the graph. What is the single biggest cause of home fires?

Quick Activity

Look for Hazards
Look at the picture on these two pages. What safety hazards can you find? Make a list of safety rules you might use at home to prevent injury from some of these hazards.

Stay Safe in a Fire

Fires are a major cause of injuries, loss of life, and property loss. Your family needs a plan to escape from your home in the event of a fire. Have a family fire drill every six months. Practice getting out quickly. Doing so can mean the difference between safety and danger. Here's what to do in a fire:

- Follow your escape route. If it's blocked, use your second route. Test any door you come to. If it's hot, leave it shut. Find a different way out.
- Crawl low, under the smoke. Hold a wet cloth over your nose and mouth.
- Meet outside at your family meeting place. DO NOT go back inside your house.
- Use a neighbor's phone to call 911.

DRAW CONCLUSIONS **Why is it important for your family to have a fire drill every six months?**

Myth and Fact

Myth: You have several minutes to get out of a house if a fire starts.

Fact: A fire can double in size every minute. After a fire starts, you have two to three minutes to either put it out or get out of the house.

▲ If your clothing catches on fire, STOP. Running fans the flames. Shout for help, but don't run.

◀ DROP to the floor or ground. Cover your face.

▼ ROLL back and forth slowly to put out the flames.

Prevent Poisoning

Poisons are substances that cause harm when they enter the body. A poison can also be deadly. Poisons can be swallowed or breathed in, or they can get into your body through the skin. Cleaning products that are usually safe when used properly can be poisonous. Medicines taken improperly can be poisonous. Some plants are also poisonous if they are eaten. For these reasons, extra care should be taken to prevent injury. Follow these safety guidelines to prevent poisoning:

- Never take medicine unless a parent or another trusted adult says it's safe.

- Use arts and crafts supplies that are labeled *nontoxic*, meaning "not poisonous."

- Do not use insect sprays, bleach, paints, or other household products without an adult.

MAIN IDEA AND DETAILS What is the main idea of this section?

Lesson 2 Summary and Review

❶ Summarize with Vocabulary

Use vocabulary and other terms from this lesson to complete the statements.

Being careful around a _____ is an example of a safety measure. When you keep injuries from happening, you are practicing _____. _____ are the most common cause of injuries in the home. Substances that cause harm when they enter the body are called _____.

❷ Critical Thinking Why should your home have a fire extinguisher in the kitchen?

❸ What are ways to prevent falls?

❹ SEQUENCE Draw and complete this graphic organizer to show the steps you should take if a fire breaks out in your home.

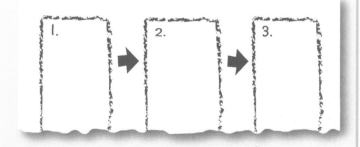

❺ Write to Inform—How-To

Write a list of safety rules to prevent poisonings. Post the rules in your home.

LIFE SKILLS

Make Responsible Decisions
About Staying Safe

Sometimes you are home alone and you need to make a decision. You can use the steps for **Making Responsible Decisions** to help you make healthful decisions about staying safe.

Ken's mother is next door when Ken's new friend, Eddie, calls. Eddie asks Ken to come to his house to swim. Eddie's parents aren't at home either. What should Ken do?

1 **Find out about the choices you could make.**

Ken could go swimming without asking his mother's permission, or he could tell Eddie they shouldn't swim without an adult present. They could also plan to go swimming at Eddie's when it's OK with their parents.

2 **Eliminate choices that are against your family rules.**

Ken knows that swimming without adult supervision is against his family's rules. It is also dangerous. He eliminates that choice.

3 Ask yourself: What is the possible result of each choice? Does the choice show good character?

If Ken goes swimming without first asking permission, his parents will be upset. If he talks to his parents, he and Eddie may be able to plan for a day that both his and Eddie's parents say is OK.

4 Make what seems to be the best choice.

Ken decides to talk to his parents. He'll plan a day when both he and Eddie can have permission to go swimming and there will be supervision. Eddie thinks that's a good idea.

Problem Solving

Nora is playing at Carmen's house. Carmen wants to use her older sister's electric hair-curling iron. Nora asks, "Do you have permission to use it?" Carmen says, "No, but I've watched my sister. I think I can do it." Use the steps for **Making Responsible Decisions** to help Nora. Come up with a response that Nora can give to Carmen that will demonstrate responsible decision making and also show Carmen how to respect her sister's belongings.

Staying Safe near Water

Lesson Focus

When you practice safety habits while swimming and boating, you help prevent injuries and death by drowning.

Why Learn This?

What you learn can help keep you and others safe around water.

Vocabulary

lifeguard

Stay Safe While Swimming

There's nothing like having fun in a swimming pool, a lake, or the ocean. However, people can be injured in or around water. Practicing water safety can help prevent injury. When you are at a swimming pool, follow these safety rules:

- Obey the **lifeguard**, a person who has special training to keep people safe in and around water.
- Don't run or push near the pool. Wet decks are slippery and hard.
- Don't bob underwater at the edge of the pool. Someone might come in on top of you.
- Don't jump in the pool backward.

If someone in the water needs help, yell for help. Find an adult. Do NOT get into the water. If the person is close enough, REACH—hold something long and strong out to the person. Hold on to something secure, such as a dock pole or a tree branch. ▶

REACH

If the person is too far away for you to reach, attach a rope to something that floats. Attach the other end to something secure. THROW the object to the person. ▶

THROW

Diving can result in serious injuries. Follow these safety rules when diving into water:

- Dive only in water 9 feet deep or more.
- Never dive into an above-ground pool.
- Dive only from the end of the diving board.
- Don't dive from the side of a pool.

 SEQUENCE **What is the first thing you should do if you see storm clouds or hear thunder while swimming?**

Personal Health Plan ▶

Real-Life Situation
Suppose you are planning to go to a public swimming pool.
Real-Life Plan
List three behaviors that you can practice to help you and others stay safe while swimming.

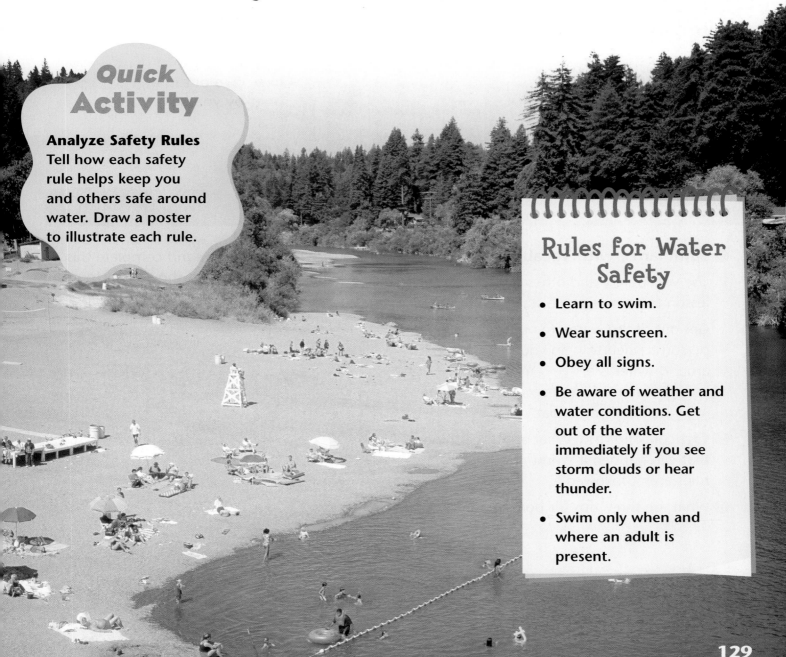

Quick Activity

Analyze Safety Rules
Tell how each safety rule helps keep you and others safe around water. Draw a poster to illustrate each rule.

Rules for Water Safety

- Learn to swim.
- Wear sunscreen.
- Obey all signs.
- Be aware of weather and water conditions. Get out of the water immediately if you see storm clouds or hear thunder.
- Swim only when and where an adult is present.

Be Safe While Boating

More than 70 million people enjoy boating each year. Follow these safety rules while boating:

- Wear a life jacket. It will keep you afloat if you fall in the water.
- Don't make sudden movements or stand up. If you fall in the water, hold on to the boat.
- Make sure someone on shore knows where you are and when you plan to return.

CAUSE AND EFFECT **What is an effect of wearing a life jacket on a boat?**

◀ Never go out in a boat by yourself.

Lesson 3 Summary and Review

❶ Summarize with Vocabulary

Use vocabulary and other terms from this lesson to complete the statements.

Get out of the water if you hear _____. A person trained to help you be safe in or around water is a _____. You should _____ only in water 9 feet deep or more. Wear a _____ to keep you afloat.

❷ Critical Thinking What are three things that can happen if swimming-pool safety rules aren't followed?

❸ What are three tips for boating safety?

❹ (Focus Skill) SEQUENCE Draw and complete this graphic organizer to show what to do if someone in the water needs help and is close to you.

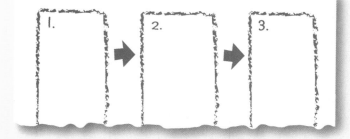

❺ Write to Entertain—Short Story

Write a story about a boy who goes swimming but doesn't know the safety rules. Have his friends tell him the rules so that no one gets hurt.

ACTIVITIES

Math

Calculate the Number of Fires Fire departments respond to a lot of home fires. If just twenty fire departments responded to one home fire every hour, how many home fires would that be in one day?

Science

Out of the Pool Predict the swimming conditions for your area or for another region of the country. Use weather forecasts in sources provided by your teacher to predict if the weather conditions will be safe for swimming. Use the same sources to check your predictions for a week.

Technology Project

Many electrical outlets have a device called a GFCI (ground-fault circuit-interrupter), which helps prevent shocks. Use the Internet to research how a GFCI works. Identify some types of appliances that have built-in shock protectors. Then use a computer to make a slide show to inform others about these devices.

GO ONLINE **For more activities**, visit **The Learning Site.** www.harcourtschool.com/health

Home & Community

Practice Fire Drills Organize a family fire drill, using your family emergency plan. Each person should start in a different room and use one of the room's escape exits. The whole family should meet at the chosen location outdoors. Then discuss the drill, and decide how the family might improve its plan.

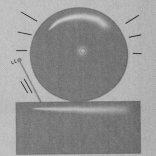

Career Link

The Coast Guard The Coast Guard is one of the armed forces in the United States. One of its goals is to enforce safety rules for people who boat for fun. Suppose you are a Coast Guard officer. Some people tell you that they don't understand why it's important to wear a life jacket if they know how to swim. What will you tell them?

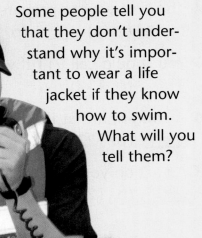

131

Reading Skill

SEQUENCE

Copy this graphic organizer, and then use it to answer questions 1 and 2.

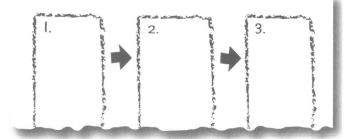

1 What steps should you take if your clothes catch fire?

2 What should you do in an emergency?

 Use Vocabulary

Fill in the blanks with the correct terms to complete the sentences.

3 _____ means "keeping injuries from happening." (p. 122)

4 The best way to prepare for a disaster is to make a(n) _____. (p. 118)

5 You should call 911 if you see a(n) _____. (p. 117)

6 A condition that is NOT safe is a(n) _____. (p. 122)

7 An action you take to stay safe is a(n) _____. (p. 122)

Check Understanding

Choose the letter of the correct answer.

8 What is the first thing you should try to do in an emergency? (p. 116)
  A Write down your phone number.
  B Speak slowly and clearly.
  C Tell an adult.
  D Call the nearest hospital.

9 Which of the following can be a hazard when you are swimming? (p. 128)

F   **H**

G  **J**

10 Which of the following is **NOT** an important part of a family emergency plan? (pp. 118–119)
  A having two ways to escape from each room
  B knowing the phone number of the nearest fire department
  C having two meeting places outside
  D knowing your family contact

11 A _____ can alert you if a fire breaks out. (p. 123)
  F 911 operator   **H** fire extinguisher
  G hazard   **J** smoke detector

12 Becca is planning foods to put in her emergency supply kit. Tell what's missing under "Supplies." (p. 120)

Emergency Supply Kit

Food canned tuna, peanut butter, crackers

Supplies for Food plates, forks and spoons, cups

A salt   C napkins
B jelly   D can opener

13 If your clothing catches on fire, which of the following should you do? (p. 124)

F shout, drop, roll   H jump, drop, roll
G run, shout, roll   J stop, drop, roll

14 What does a 911 operator need to know if you call about an emergency? (p. 117)

A that you are worried
B the name of your school
C what the problem is
D the location of your emergency supply kit

15 Which of the following rules can help keep you safe while swimming? (p. 128)

F Jump in the pool backward.
G Don't run or push near the pool.
H At the edge of the pool, bob underwater.
J If a storm is coming, stay in the water until you see lightning.

16 Your older brother is using paint thinner. He pours what is left over into an empty juice bottle. Why is this action unsafe?

17 When you're in a boat, why is it important to wear a life jacket even if you know how to swim?

Apply Skills

18 **BUILDING GOOD CHARACTER**
Citizenship You see someone throwing rocks at bottles floating in the swimming area of the lake where you swim. Later you see a boy and a girl getting ready to go for a swim there. What can you do to be a good citizen and to show caring for others?

19 **LIFE SKILLS**
Make Decisions Your sister comes home from school and rushes upstairs. She drops her backpack on the stairs. When you mention it, she says, "I'll pick it up later." Use the steps for Making Responsible Decisions to explain to her how her behavior can harm your family or keep it safe.

Write About Health

20 **Write to Inform—Explanation** Write about a time when you or someone you know had an accident. Explain how the accident could have been prevented. Describe what you can do in the future to prevent that type of accident.

CHAPTER

6 Safe
Away from Home

DRAW CONCLUSIONS Sometimes when you read a lesson, not all of the information is provided. You have to use information from the passage plus what you already know to draw a conclusion. Use the Reading in Health Handbook on pages 332–333 and this graphic organizer to help you.

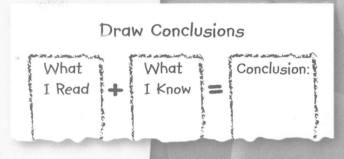

Health Graph

INTERPRET DATA Thunderstorms are the most frequent type of dangerous storm in the United States. The danger comes from lightning.

1. How many more thunderstorms does Florida have than Texas? Than Indiana? Than California?
2. Why is a person at higher risk of getting struck by lightning in Florida than in the other states shown?

Number of Thunderstorms in Some States

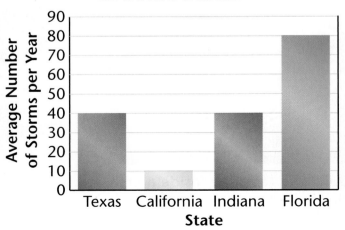

Daily Physical Activity

You can be active and safe outdoors. Help your body stay healthy.

 Be Active!
Use the selection Track 6, **Muscle Mambo**, to move your heart and other muscles toward good health.

Staying Safe Outdoors

Lesson Focus
You can practice safety measures while spending time outdoors.

Why Learn This?
You can protect yourself and others from injuries when you are outdoors.

Vocabulary
flood
lightning
hurricane
tornado

Camping and Hiking

Spending time outdoors can be fun, but you need to stay safe. The last thing you want when you go camping or hiking is to become injured or ill. The pictures on these two pages give some tips for staying safe while camping. Here are other tips to follow when you are outdoors:

- Wear sunscreen, even on cold or cloudy days.
- Don't go hiking by yourself. If you get lost, stay where you are. Wear a whistle and use it.
- Take along a first-aid kit.

Quick Activity

Identify Precautions
What safety precautions can you identify in this picture?

Don't wear loose, flowing clothing that can easily catch fire.

Make sure an adult is present when a campfire is burning.

Keep a bucket of water nearby to put out your campfire.

Build the campfire inside a fire ring. Clear away all dead wood and leaves from the ring.

Make sure the tent is secure and waterproof.

Use a cooler with ice or ice packs to store foods that can spoil.

Look for dangers on the ground, such as broken glass, thorns, or fallen branches.

Do not go near wild animals.

▲ poison ivy

▲ poison oak

▲ poison sumac

Most wild animals are usually afraid of people. But if you get too close, a wild animal may bite you. Going near a young animal can also be dangerous. The mother might be nearby and could attack you to protect her young.

Ticks and insects, such as mosquitoes, can carry germs that cause diseases. Use a repellent and keep your skin covered. Wear long pants and shirts with long sleeves. If you get a tick on you, ask an adult to remove it. Watch for stinging insects.

Some people react to posion ivy, posion oak, or posion sumac. These plants can cause skin redness, itching, and a rash. Avoid touching any plant with leaves in groups of three. If you do touch one of these plants, wash your skin with plenty of soap and water.

 DRAW CONCLUSIONS **How can you stay safe when camping?**

Focus Skill

Information Alert!

West Nile Virus West Nile virus is spread by mosquitoes. It first appeared in the U.S. in 1999, reaching Texas in 2002. Find out the number of cases in your state.

 For the most up-to-date information, visit The Learning Site. www.harcourtschool.com/ health

GO ONLINE

Head coverings or earmuffs protect your ears from frostbite.

Your head and neck lose heat more quickly than other parts of your body.

Wearing several layers of clothing helps keep in your body heat.

An outer waterproof layer keeps moisture away from your body. The middle layer lets air pass through and pulls wetness away from your body. The lining helps hold in heat.

Mittens allow your fingers to warm each other.

Waterproof shoes or boots keep your feet dry.

Tips for Winter Safety

- ☐ Never skate, sled, or ski alone or after dark.
- ☐ Wear brightly colored clothing.
- ☐ Stay out of the paths of others.
- ☐ Don't sled or ski in areas that have trees, fences, rocks, poles, traffic, or roads.
- ☐ Avoid skiing or sledding on icy, steep, or bumpy hills.

Hot and Cold Weather

Summer can be a great time to have fun. But be careful of the heat. If you get too hot, you can become faint or dizzy or feel sick to your stomach. In very hot weather, wear light, loose-fitting clothing. Rest often in the shade. Drink plenty of water. Be sure to wear sunscreen to protect your skin.

You can have fun in cold weather too, but your body can lose a lot of heat. It may not be able to keep itself warm. Getting too cold can be dangerous. Dress in layers to keep warm. Very cold weather can damage your skin. Be sure to stay covered up. You should wear sunscreen.

COMPARE AND CONTRAST How are safety rules for hot and cold weather alike and different?

Weather Emergencies

Storms are dangerous because high winds, lightning, and floods can occur. A **flood** is an overflow of water onto normally dry land. Floods can sweep away people and property.

CAUSE AND EFFECT **Tell what can happen as a result of storms.**

Thunderstorms can bring strong winds, heavy rain, lightning, and flash floods. **Lightning** is a large release of electricity. It can injure or kill people, cause fires, and damage property.

A **hurricane** is a storm that forms over an ocean and covers a large area. It brings strong winds, heavy rain, and floods.

A **tornado** is an extremely strong windstorm. Its winds spin in a funnel-shaped cloud. Tornadoes can flatten houses and other buildings and lift cars and trucks.

Safety in Bad Weather

The best way to stay safe in bad weather is to be prepared. If bad weather occurs, follow your family emergency plan. Listen to TV and radio reports.

SEQUENCE What can you do before a thunderstorm to help keep safe?

Did You Know?

Lightning strikes Earth about one hundred times each second. A lightning bolt can have a temperature of more than 60,000 degrees Fahrenheit. That's hotter than the surface of the sun!

What to Do in Bad Weather

Type of Weather	What You Should Do
Blizzard	Dress in layers of wool or silk to keep in body heat. If you are in a car, do not leave it.
Hurricane	Bring toys and bicycles indoors. Move inland away from the coast, if you are told to do so.
Thunderstorm	Quickly get inside a building or motor vehicle. If you are outdoors, crouch down. Don't lie flat.
Tornado	Stay away from windows. Go to a basement, a closet, or a bathroom without windows.

Lesson 1 Summary and Review

1 **Summarize with Vocabulary**

Use vocabulary from this lesson to complete the statements.

_____ from a thunderstorm can cause fires. A storm called a _____ can pick up a truck. A _____ forms over an ocean. It can bring a _____, which can sweep away people and property.

2 How can you prevent a campfire from getting out of control?

3 **Critical Thinking** While hiking, your friend sees a baby porcupine and wants to get closer. What would you tell her?

4 **DRAW CONCLUSIONS** Draw and complete this graphic organizer to show why some storms are dangerous.

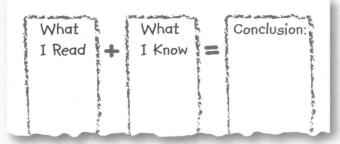

| What I Read | + | What I Know | = | Conclusion: |

5 **Writing to Inform—How-To**

Suppose your family is going on vacation in a very cold climate. Write about what you and your family can do to stay safe when you are outdoors on your vacation.

Responsibility

Being a Positive Role Model

Positive role models set good examples for others. They behave in responsible ways that keep themselves and others safe. Below are tips on how you can be a positive role model, especially during outdoor activities. Notice that the first letters of the tips combine to spell **MODEL.**

- **Mind laws, rules, and people in authority.** If the lifeguard tells you to leave the pool, do it. Others will follow your example because they know you are responsible.
- **Observe unsafe situations and take action.** While on a picnic, you notice lightning in the distance. Tell your family so that all of you can pack up and leave the area.
- **Decide to resist pressure to take wrong actions.** A friend wants you to sneak out of your campsite with him while others are sleeping. Be a positive role model by refusing to go.
- **Examine your behavior to see how it helps or harms others.** When you skate, make sure you do not get in the way of others.
- **Look out for the safety of others.** On a hike, you discover a friend has forgotten her sunscreen. You share yours.

Activity

By sharing ideas, your class can learn ways to be positive role models. For one school week, choose one tip to follow each day, and write down what you did. At the end of the week, share your descriptions with your class.

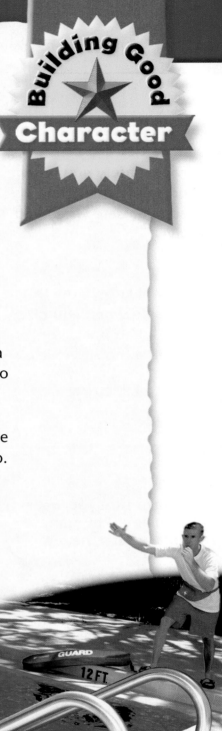

Staying Safe on the Road

Biking

Riding your bike is a great way to travel. Following these safety rules can reduce your risk when you ride:

- Ride in a street, road, or bike path. Don't ride alone.
- Ride in a straight line near the right-hand side of the road. Pass on the left.
- Follow traffic signs and safety laws.
- Use the proper hand signals for stops and turns.
- Slow down around people on foot.
- Watch out for doors opening from parked cars.
- Don't ride at night.

CAUSE AND EFFECT What is an effect of wearing bright or light-colored clothing when biking?

Make sure you wear a helmet. In many places, it's the law.

Wear bright or light-colored clothing. Make yourself easy to see.

Use a basket, not a backpack.

Sound a horn or bell to help others hear you coming.

Wear closed-toe shoes to avoid foot injuries. Do not wear loose clothing that may catch in the chain or wheels.

Skating and Skateboarding

Skating and skateboarding can be fun. They give you a chance to play with your friends. The exercise can help you stay healthy and fit. However, your experience is fun only if you don't get hurt. To stay safe, wear the proper safety gear. Also stay safe by following these rules:

- Skate on the sidewalk or paths for skating—not in the street. Watch out for rocks, bumps, and holes.

- If you lose your balance, crouch down so that you won't have far to fall. Relax and try to roll.

DRAW CONCLUSIONS **Why is it important to follow safety rules when you skate?**

Quick Activity

Identify Safety Gear
Identify the safety gear this person is wearing. How does it keep a skater safe?

Mouth guards protect your teeth and tongue if you fall.

A helmet will protect your head in case there is a collision or fall.

Wrist guards help prevent bones in your arms and wrists from breaking if you fall.

Knee and elbow pads protect you from bruises and broken bones.

Closed, nonslip shoes keep you from slipping.

Personal Health Plan

Real-Life Situation
Suppose you are going to ride on a bike trail.
Real-Life Plan
Make a list of safety gear you have for biking. What additional gear do you need in order to be safe?

Riding in a Motor Vehicle

Safety belts can save lives. You should always wear one when you ride in a motor vehicle. Know how to wear a safety belt correctly.

- Fasten the lap belt snugly across your hips, not across your stomach.
- Use a booster seat if you are less than 4 feet 9 inches tall and weigh less than 80 pounds. The lap belt should not cross your face or neck.
- Don't share your safety belt with anyone else.
- Don't distract the driver. Always speak softly to other passengers.
- Don't play with the windows or seats.
- Don't play with sharp objects or drink from a bottle, can, or cup while the vehicle is moving.

An **air bag** is a device in a motor vehicle that inflates, or blows up like a balloon, during a crash. Air bags protect people in the front seats but not people in the back seats. Air bags inflate quickly, and the force can injure a child in the front seat. For this reason, you should always ride in the back seat.

Follow these safety rules for riding a bus:

- Stand at least 6 feet away from the curb while you are waiting to get on.
- Cross the street at least 10 feet in front of the bus.
- Make sure the driver sees you. Never walk behind the bus.
- Use the handrails to avoid falls.
- Stay seated at all times.
- Keep your head and arms inside the bus.
- Don't distract the bus driver.

SUMMARIZE Explain how to correctly wear a safety belt.

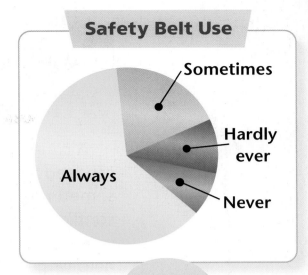

Safety Belt Use

Sometimes

Hardly ever

Always

Never

Quick Activity

Interpret Graphs
How does the amount of people who always use safety belts compare to the amount who never use them?

Lesson 2 Summary and Review

❶ **Summarize with Vocabulary**

Use vocabulary and other terms from this lesson to complete the statements.

When you skate or bike, wear a _____ to protect your head from injury. Don't bike at _____. Always wear your _____ when you ride in a car. Ride in the back seat to avoid injury from an _____ if it inflates. Use the _____ on the bus to avoid falls.

❷ What should you do if you start to fall when you are skating or skateboarding?

❸ **Critical Thinking** List the safety gear to wear when biking. Which is the most important?

❹ (Focus Skill) **DRAW CONCLUSIONS** Draw and complete this graphic organizer to show details about following safety rules on a bus.

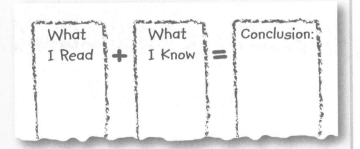

What I Read + What I Know = Conclusion:

❺ **Write to Inform—Explanation**
Write a paragraph telling why everyone should wear safety belts.

Resolve Conflicts
With Friends

A conflict is a disagreement. Sometimes conflicts can lead to unsafe situations. Even friends disagree sometimes. It's important to resolve, or work out, conflicts if you want to remain friends and stay safe. You can use the steps to **Resolve Conflicts** to help you work out conflicts without fighting or getting angry.

Tamara doesn't think April is playing fair because she doesn't pass the ball. April thinks Tamara hogs the ball. How can Tamara and April resolve this conflict peacefully?

1 **Use "I" messages to tell how you feel.**

2 **Listen to the other person. Consider that person's point of view.**

Tamara tells April, "I get upset when the ball is not passed to me."

April says she's angry with Tamara for not sharing the ball so other players can have chances to make goals.

146

③ Negotiate.

April says maybe they should play on different teams. Tamara says they could try to pass the ball more.

④ Compromise on a solution.

Tamara and April agree that they can each give up the ball more often. Players in scoring positions will have chances to make goals, and the team will do better.

Problem Solving

Victor and his brother Jerome are at the playground. Jerome is crawling on top of the horizontal ladder. He knows this is unsafe. Victor tries to persuade Jerome to stop. Jerome tells Victor to mind his own business. There are other children under the ladder. How can Victor and Jerome use the steps to **Resolve Conflicts** to resolve their conflict? Explain how their solution can also demonstrate responsibility for the safety of the other children playing there.

Staying Safe in a Conflict

Resolving Conflict

Conflict among people is normal. There are ways to resolve conflicts without fighting. Here are some suggestions:

- Stay calm. Keep your voice even and quiet.
- Speak respectfully. Do not call the other person names. Say "Please," "Thank you," and "I'm sorry."
- Agree that there is a problem. Listen to the other side. Try to see things the way others see them.
- Identify choices to end the conflict. Each person should compromise, or give a little.
- Leave if another person threatens you.

 DRAW CONCLUSIONS Why is it important to resolve conflicts peacefully?

Quick Activity

Resolving a Problem Look at the picture. Write how you would go about resolving the conflict these students are having.

▲ A bully may tease others in a mean way, call them names, shove them, or trip them.

Dealing with Bullies

Your friends tease you in a friendly way. Someone else starts teasing you in a mean way. This bully continues to pick on you. A **bully** is a person who hurts or frightens others. Bullies usually try to bother people who are different or alone. Being picked on by a bully is no fun. Here are some ways to help keep a bully from hurting or frightening you:

- Don't react or say anything. Keep your cool.

- Don't push, kick, or hit the bully.

- Laugh at yourself. Bullies often leave people alone who don't get angry.

- Refuse if a bully pressures you to do something.

- Walk away and ignore the bully.

- Get help from an adult if a bully threatens you or keeps bothering you.

COMPARE AND CONTRAST What is the difference between teasing from a friend and teasing from a bully?

ACTIVITY

Life Skills

Refuse Tyler tells Takai to steal a calculator from someone's backpack. He says Takai is "chicken" if he doesn't do it. How can Takai use refusal skills in this situation?

149

Avoid fights by following these guidelines.

Fights

- **Walk away if you see a fight.**

- **Avoid fighting. Instead, talk things out.**

- **Keep it light. No problem is worth fighting about.**

- **Get away if a person tries to harm you.**

Consumer Activity

Analyze Media Messages Many TV shows, video games, and movies show people fighting to resolve conflicts. Write a paragraph explaining a better, more positive message about resolving conflicts.

Avoiding Violence

Most conflicts don't end in a fight. If a conflict does get out of control, it may lead to physical force, or *violence*. The use of physical force can result in harm to someone. If you are trying to resolve a conflict, carefully observe the other person. Watch for signs that the person is becoming angry or may become violent. Some signs are a clenched fist or jaw, a red face, and a shaking body. If you see any of these signs, back off. If you are near a fight, don't try to stop it. You might get injured. Get away. Find an adult to help.

Another way to avoid violence is to stay away from gangs. A **gang** is a group of people who often use violence. They often commit crimes, use drugs, and carry weapons.

150

Gangs

- Avoid being alone.
- Stay away from gang members.
- Stay away from places where gang members hang out.
- Tell an adult if someone asks you to join a gang.

Weapons

- Never touch a gun, even if you think it is a toy.
- Stay away from people who carry weapons.
- Tell an adult if you see a person with a weapon.

A **weapon** is an object that is used to injure or threaten someone. A weapon can be a gun, a knife, or even a baseball bat. Police officers carry weapons as part of their job. Some adults keep weapons in their homes for protection against attackers. Others use weapons for hunting and for target shooting.

Weapons also may be used by terrorists. *Terrorism* is the use of violence to promote a cause. You don't always know where or when a terrorist attack might occur. However, you'll be safer if you stay calm. Do as your family, your teacher, or another person in charge tells you.

MAIN IDEA AND DETAILS **What's the most important action you can take to avoid violence? Name several ways to do this.**

ACTIVITY

Building Good Character

Citizenship Schools do not allow weapons. Good citizens obey rules and laws. Suppose you know that a classmate has brought a knife to school in his or her backpack. What should you do?

Staying Safe Online

You can use the Internet for many things. It can be helpful for schoolwork. You may be allowed to play games on it. You can use it to stay in touch with friends. The Internet is like a city you can visit without leaving your home. Just as in a real city, there are places you don't want to visit. There are also people you don't want to meet. To stay safe online, you should follow some safety rules.

SUMMARIZE List rules for being safe online.

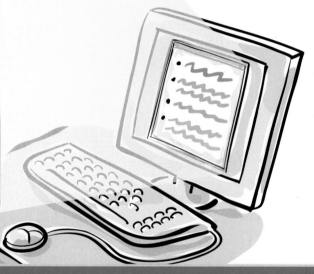

STAYING SAFE ONLINE

- Follow family rules for going online.
- Don't give out personal information, such as your name, address, school, telephone number, or picture.
- Tell your parents or guardian if you come across information or get a message that makes you uncomfortable.
- Never agree to meet in person someone you've only met online.

Lesson 3 Summary and Review

1 Summarize with Vocabulary

Use vocabulary and other terms from this lesson to complete the statements.

A person who trips someone on purpose is a _____. A gun is one type of _____. Members of a _____ may hurt people and commit crimes. The use of physical force to harm someone is _____.

2 Critical Thinking Suppose you ignore or try to avoid a bully, but he or she keeps bothering you. What can you do?

3 What are ways to stay safe from weapons?

4 (Focus Skill) DRAW CONCLUSIONS Draw and complete the graphic organizer to show how to resolve conflicts.

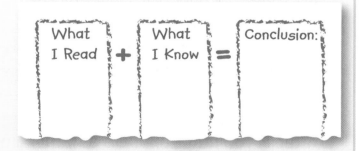

What I Read + What I Know = Conclusion:

5 Write to Inform—How-To

Write a paragraph that tells students in your school how to avoid gangs.

ACTIVITIES

Language Arts

Weapon Safety Poster

With a small group, write tips on weapon safety. Draw pictures to go with your tips. Display your posters in hallways or on bulletin boards where other students can see them.

Physical Education

Teamwork Games

Make up some games that are good for relieving stress brought about by conflict situations. Ask the physical education teacher to suggest types of activities that are physically active. In your games, include activities that require teamwork.

Technology Project

Weather radios broadcast information from the National Weather Service 24 hours a day. Announcers alert people about dangerous weather so they can be prepared. With a partner, find out what a thunderstorm watch and warning are. Then create your own broadcast telling listeners about an approaching storm. Provide safety guidelines. "Broadcast" your message to your class.

GO ONLINE For more activities, visit **The Learning Site.** www.harcourtschool.com/health

 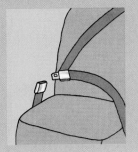

Home & Community

Promote Safety Belt Use

Make posters urging people to wear safety belts. With permission, hang the posters in stores and meeting places in your community.

Career Link

FEMA Worker

FEMA is the short name for the Federal Emergency Management Agency. FEMA workers help people before and after weather emergencies or other disasters. Suppose you are a FEMA worker. How would you help people get ready for a hurricane?

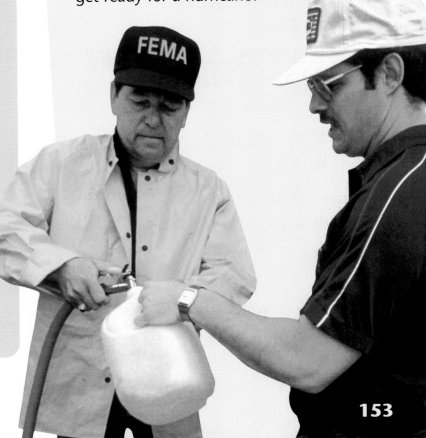

Focus Skill ## Reading Skill

DRAW CONCLUSIONS

Draw and then use this graphic organizer to answer questions 1 and 2.

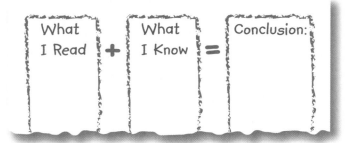

What I Read + What I Know = Conclusion:

1 Why might it be a good idea to walk away if you suspect someone is a gang member?

2 What is the purpose of a fire ring, and why do you suppose it works to prevent fires from spreading?

 ## Use Vocabulary

Match each term in Column B with its meaning in Column A.

Column A	Column B
3 It inflates during a car crash	**A** air bag
4 Funnel–shaped cloud	**B** bully
5 One who hurts others	**C** flood
6 Large release of electricity	**D** lightning
7 Violence to promote a cause	**E** terrorism
8 Overflow of water	**F** tornado
9 Object used to injure someone	**G** weapon

 ## Check Understanding

Choose the letter of the correct answer.

10 Suppose a bully trips you in the hallway. What should you do? (p. 149)
A Yell at the bully.
B Walk away and ignore the bully.
C Trip the bully.
D Laugh at the bully.

11 Which piece of safety gear should you wear when you skate, skateboard, and bike? (pp. 142–143)

F

H

G

J

12 You can stay safe from gangs if you _____. (p. 150)

A keep silent if asked to join a gang
B go places by yourself
C hang out where they hang out
D tell an adult if asked to join a gang

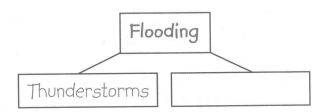

13 Which is another cause of flooding? (p. 139)

F lightning   H tornado
G hurricane   J blizzard

14 If you find a gun, what should you do? (p. 151)

A Keep it a secret.
B Show it to your friends.
C Look at it closely to see if it is a toy.
D Tell an adult.

15 You are camping and notice people doing the following. Which is unsafe? (p. 137)

F applying bug repellent
G sitting on plants with three leaves
H putting out the campfire
J watching some squirrels from several feet away

Think Critically

16 You are online when a person you do not know e-mails you. He says he has a really cool video game you can play if you meet him after school. What should you do?

17 What should you always wear outdoors in any kind of temperature and for any activity?

Apply Skills

18 **BUILDING GOOD CHARACTER**
Responsibility You have just learned to skateboard. Your friends are more skilled than you. They are pushing you to go faster and do tricks you are not ready for. What do you say to your friends? Apply what you know about being responsible to keep yourself and others safe.

19 **LIFE SKILLS**
Resolve Conflicts You are trying to resolve a conflict with a classmate. Suddenly his face turns red, he clenches his fist, and he begins yelling. Use what you know about resolving conflicts to tell what you should do next.

Write About Health

20 **Write to Inform—Description** Write a paragraph explaining what can happen if a person gets overheated in hot weather. Describe safety rules that can help for hot weather.

Guarding Against Disease

FIGHT DISEASE

STAY HEALTHY

COMPARE AND CONTRAST When you compare, you tell how two or more things are alike. When you contrast, you tell how they are different. Use the Reading in Health Handbook on pages 330–331 and this graphic organizer to help you read the health facts in this chapter.

Compare and Contrast

Topic:

Alike   Different

Health Graph

INTERPRET DATA Public health in the United States improved greatly in the twentieth century. Cleaner water for personal use was one main reason for this. Another reason was the development of vaccines (vak•SEENZ). Describe how the number of whooping cough (pertussis) cases changed from the 1940s to the 1970s.

Whooping Cough

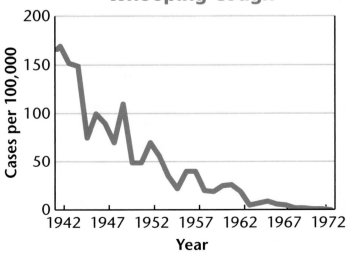

Cases per 100,000 (y-axis: 0, 50, 100, 150, 200)

Year (x-axis: 1942, 1947, 1952, 1957, 1962, 1967, 1972)

Daily Physical Activity

Protect yourself and others from disease. Stay fit and healthy.

 **Be Active!** Use the selection Track 7, **Movin' and Groovin'**, to beef up your body's protection.

Why People Become Ill

Everybody Gets Ill

Jeff felt sick, so he told his mother. His mother felt Jeff's head, and it felt warm. Together, they went to see the doctor.

Like Jeff, everyone gets ill from disease sometimes. A **disease** (dih•ZEEZ) is a condition that damages or weakens part of the body. When you have a disease, your body doesn't work as it should.

Jeff had the flu, a communicable disease. A **communicable** (kuh•MYOO•nih•kuh•buhl) **disease** is an illness that can spread from person to person. Someone in Jeff's class had the flu. The flu spread to Jeff. Then Jeff spread the flu to his mother. Colds, flu, pinkeye, and strep throat are also communicable diseases.

An illness that does not spread from one person to another is a **noncommunicable** (nahn•kuh•MYOO•nih•kuh•buhl) **disease**. *Asthma*, *allergies*, and *cancer* are types of noncommunicable diseases. So are heart disease and diabetes.

Noncommunicable diseases have many causes. Some, such as diabetes, are more common in some families than in others. Things that pollute air and water can cause other diseases, including cancer. Sometimes unhealthful habits, such as eating a lot of high-fat foods, can cause noncommunicable diseases. Also, people who use tobacco have a much greater chance than nonsmokers of getting cancer and heart disease.

 COMPARE AND CONTRAST How are communicable and noncommunicable diseases alike and different?

Information Alert!

Influenza, or flu, is a major cause of illness. Each year in the United States, flu causes about 36,000 deaths and sends 114,000 people to the hospital. Find out how you can help protect yourself against flu.

GO ONLINE For the most up-to-date information, visit The Learning Site. www.harcourtschool.com/health

Trace the spread of flu from Jeff to his mother. How do you think the disease was spread? What do you think Jeff's mother could have done to avoid catching flu?▶

159

Real-Life Situation
Suppose that you have a cold and need to take care of yourself.
Real-Life Plan
Write a paragraph describing some things you would do to take care of yourself. Also include some healthful behaviors that you should practice all the time.

When Getting Well Takes Time

Most communicable diseases are acute diseases. An *acute* (uh•KYOOT) disease lasts only a short time. Colds and flu are examples of acute diseases.

Chronic (KRAH•nik) diseases last a long time, sometimes months or even years. An allergy is an example of a chronic disease.

⭐ **COMPARE AND CONTRAST**
How are acute and chronic illnesses alike and different?

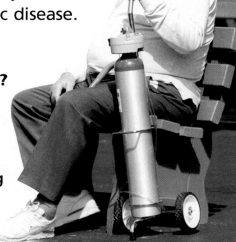

Mr. Kelly gets oxygen from a portable tank to help him breathe. He has a chronic lung disease called emphysema. ▶

Lesson 1 Summary and Review

❶ Summarize with Vocabulary

Use vocabulary and other terms from this lesson to complete the statements.

_____ is another name for *illness*. _____ can be passed from person to person but _____ ones cannot. Diseases that last a long time are called _____. Other diseases, called _____, last only a short time.

❷ Give two examples of acute diseases.

❸ Critical Thinking Why is it best for you to stay home from school when you have a communicable disease?

❹ ⭐ **COMPARE AND CONTRAST** Draw and complete this graphic organizer to show how asthma and a cold are alike and different.

Topic: Asthma and a Cold
Alike   Different

❺ Write to Inform—Description

Amos has a fever, a sore throat, and a cough. How can Amos explain how he feels? In your answer, include whether his disease is communicable or noncommunicable and whether it is chronic or acute.

Caring

Help People Who Are Ill

Another type of health condition is a disability—a mental or physical problem that keeps the body from working as it should. People who have illnesses or disabilities want to be treated with care and understanding. Here are some tips to help you to be more caring:

- **Visit. People with some chronic noncommunicable illnesses may miss a lot of school. They might like to have you visit them at home.**

- **Get to know someone with a disability. Think about how an illness or disability would affect you and how you would want to be treated.**

- **Never tease. If you hear or see schoolmates making fun of a person with an illness or disability, ask them to stop, or tell an adult. Pages 268–276 can help you be a good role model.**

- **Help a person with a physical disability if you can. Be aware of the person's feelings. Like everyone else, people with disabilities like to do as much as they can on their own.**

Activity

Suppose a classmate uses a wheelchair. Brainstorm how you could adapt group activities to include this student. List ideas for involving a variety of individuals with differences in your activities.

Communicable Diseases

Causes of Disease

Pathogens (PATH•uh•juhnz) are organisms or viruses that cause communicable diseases. There are several kinds of pathogens. A **virus** (VY•ruhs) is the smallest kind. Viruses multiply inside the cells of living things. Viruses cause colds, flu, chicken pox, and many other diseases.

Bacteria (bak•TIR•ee•uh) are one-celled living things that also can cause disease. Most bacteria are harmless. In fact, your body needs many kinds of bacteria. But a few kinds of bacteria cause diseases, including pinkeye, ear infections, and strep throat.

◄ German scientist Robert Koch (1843–1910) proved that certain kinds of bacteria cause certain diseases. Before his work, people thought that "bad air" caused most diseases.

This lab technician is observing some pathogens through a microscope. Bacteria and many fungi are so small that this is the only way to see them. Viruses are even smaller. They can be seen only by using a very powerful electron microscope. ▶

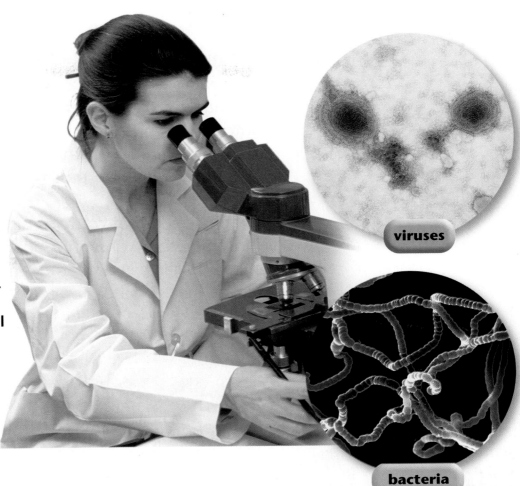

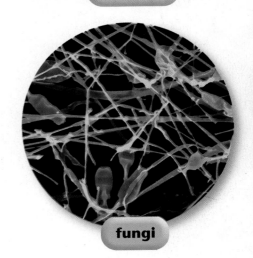

viruses

bacteria

fungi

Fungi (FUN•jy) are another kind of pathogen. Fungi are small, simple living things such as yeasts and molds. As with bacteria, not all fungi cause disease. The fungi that do cause disease often affect the skin. Two examples are athlete's foot and ringworm. Athlete's foot is a fungus infection of the skin between the toes. Ringworm is actually not a worm, but a fungus that causes itchy, red skin.

All pathogens multiply, or grow in large numbers. An infection (in•FEK•shuhn) is the growth of pathogens somewhere in the body. If your body gets an infection, you may become ill.

CAUSE AND EFFECT What can happen when pathogens enter a person's body?

How Pathogens Spread

Pathogens can spread in many different ways. For example, you use a pencil that someone who is ill has used. Pathogens from the pencil can get onto your hands. If you don't wash your hands, you could pass the pathogen to your mouth or eyes. You could also pass the pathogen to someone else.

Something that contains pathogens is *contaminated* (kuhn•TAM•uh•nayt•id). Water, air, and food can spread pathogens. If you drink contaminated water, for example, you will probably get sick.

▼ When someone coughs or sneezes, droplets with pathogens can be sprayed into the air. If you are nearby, you may breathe in those pathogens.

Pathogens multiply in food that is spoiled or is not properly prepared. When you eat spoiled or contaminated food, you may get food poisoning. Some forms of food poisoning can make you very ill or even kill you.

Some pathogens can spread from one food to another. Some are spread when people who handle foods don't wash their hands. Others multiply whenever food is left out of the refrigerator. See pages 84–86 for a reminder of ways that you can avoid food poisoning and food contamination.

MAIN IDEA AND DETAILS Name four ways that pathogens can be spread. Give an example for each.

▲ Stream water often looks clean, but it might not be safe to drink. Take drinking water with you when you go hiking.

▲ Animals such as insects and birds sometimes spread pathogens to people.

Lesson 2 Summary and Review

① Summarize with Vocabulary

Use vocabulary from this lesson to complete the statements.

There are several types of _____ that cause disease. They include _____, _____, and _____. If any of them multiply in your body, you can get a(n) _____.

② Name three illnesses caused by viruses and three caused by bacteria.

③ Critical Thinking If your best friend has a cold, what are two ways that the pathogens in your friend's body could be spread to you?

④ (Focus Skill) COMPARE AND CONTRAST Draw and complete this graphic organizer to show how bacteria and viruses are alike and different.

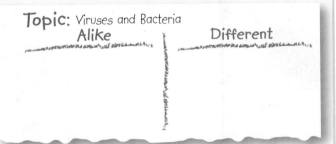

Topic: Viruses and Bacteria
Alike   Different

⑤ Write to Inform—How-To

Jamie wants to help his father prepare breakfast. Make a list of things Jamie can do to make sure he doesn't spread pathogens as he helps prepare breakfast.

Fighting Communicable Diseases

Lesson Focus

You can help your body fight disease.

Why Learn This?

You can use what you learn about preventing disease to promote health at home and at school.

Vocabulary

immune system
antibodies
immunity
vaccine

Your Body Fights Disease

You are ill. Your throat hurts. You're coughing, you have a fever, and your body aches. You have symptoms of flu. *Symptoms* (SIMP•tuhmz) are signs or physical feelings of a disease.

You don't get ill every day. You are usually healthy because your body defends itself against pathogens. Your body's defenses are described on the next page. If pathogens get past your first defenses, your immune system goes to work. The **immune** (ih•MYOON) **system** is the body system that fights disease. White blood cells are an important part of the immune system because they kill pathogens.

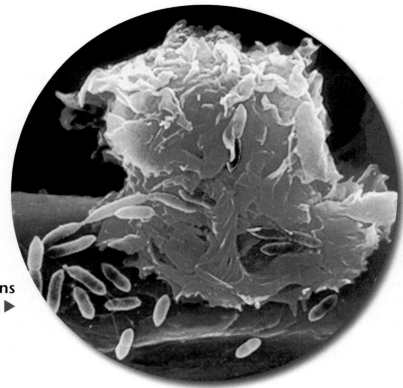

You have several kinds of white blood cells. Some surround pathogens and destroy them. ▶

Some white blood cells fight pathogens by making antibodies. **Antibodies** (AN·tih·bahd·eez) are chemicals that the body makes to fight disease.

An antibody attaches itself to a pathogen and tries to destroy it. If the pathogen is not destroyed, white blood cells then attack and destroy it.

Once your body has made antibodies for a pathogen, the antibodies stay in the body. Some stay for several months. Some stay your whole life. If that pathogen ever attacks again, your body usually has enough antibodies to keep you from getting ill. The body's ability to defend itself against certain kinds of pathogens is called **immunity** (ih·MYOON·uh·tee).

DRAW CONCLUSIONS If you have had a certain viral disease, can you get that disease again? Explain.

Did You Know?

A fever, or above-normal body temperature, is a symptom of many diseases. A fever shows that your body is fighting an infection. It is a normal response of the body to foreign invaders such as bacteria and viruses.

The Body's Defenses

Tears kill and wash away pathogens that might enter the body through your eyes.

Mucus (MYOO·kuhs) is a thick, sticky substance that traps and destroys pathogens.

Chemicals in saliva, the liquid in your mouth, kill many pathogens.

The skin's tough outer layers block many pathogens from entering your body. Sweat on skin may destroy some pathogens, too.

Earwax traps pathogens that might enter through your ears.

Cilia (SIL·ee·uh) are small hairs that line the body's air passages. Cilia help move pathogens out of the body.

Chemicals in the digestive juices in your stomach kill many pathogens.

Quick Activity

Avoiding Disease
Look at this picture. With a partner, come up with a list of two or three ways you see pathogens being spread. For each example you list, write ways to avoid or kill the pathogens. Present your work in a table.

▲ Why is this student's friend avoiding contact?

Myth and Fact

Myth: Soap is what kills bacteria when you wash your hands.

Fact: Rubbing your hands together loosens dead skin cells. Soap makes the pathogens on those cells stay suspended (floating) in the warm water, so that you can rinse them off your hands.

Help Your Body Avoid Disease

You can avoid pathogens by not touching things someone ill has touched. For example, pinkeye is a bacterial eye infection. If someone with pinkeye rubs his or her eyes, the bacteria get on the person's hands. The bacteria can get on objects he or she touches, too. If you touch the same objects and then touch your eyes, you could get pinkeye. Pathogens can also be spread through coughing and sneezing. Stay away from people who have a communicable disease, such as flu or a cold.

Hospitals and medical offices have rules to follow to avoid the spread of disease. Your school might ask you to stay home if you are ill. Following rules can help you avoid disease.

SEQUENCE You have flu. Your mother takes your temperature. Then she has something to eat without washing her hands. What might happen next?

Practice Healthful Habits

One of the best ways to avoid disease is to keep your hands clean. Wash your hands often. Always wash before eating, after using the bathroom, and after playing with pets. Use soap and warm water. Rub your hands together for at least 15 seconds. You should also avoid touching your eyes, nose, and mouth.

Remember, bacteria can enter your body if you cut your skin. Wash cuts with clean water. Follow the tips on pages 350–351. Another way to avoid disease is by obeying school rules that say not to share combs, drinks, or foods. Practicing healthful habits can help avoid the spread of disease.

SUMMARIZE How can you keep pathogens from spreading?

Personal Health Plan ▶

Real-Life Situation
Pathogens can spread from objects and surfaces that people touch every day.
Real-Life Plan
Make a list of three surfaces or objects in your classroom. Next to your list write down what you can do to protect yourself from the spread of pathogens. Refer to the additional information about hand washing on page 34.

▼ How are these students helping keep pathogens from spreading?

ACTIVITY

Building Good Character

Responsibility One of the ways you show that you have responsibility is by the way you cooperate with others. Name two ways that you can cooperate with parents and health-care providers in the treatment or management of disease.

Vaccines Can Protect You

Fernando is getting his flu vaccine shot. A **vaccine** is a substance made to prevent and control a disease. Fernando does not like getting shots, but he knows the shots will help keep him from getting ill. Fernando's parents make sure that he and his brother get their vaccines. Some states require students to have all their vaccines before they begin the school year. The schedule below shows when some of these vaccines should be given.

There are different kinds of vaccines to protect people from diseases. For example, a flu vaccine is made each year to protect against the kind of flu virus expected to strike that year.

Immunization Schedule

Vaccine	When Needed
Hepatitis B protects against hepatitis B virus.	birth–2 months, 1–4 months, 6–18 months
DTaP protects against diphtheria, tetanus, and pertussis bacteria.	2 months, 4 months, 6 months, 15–18 months, 4–6 years, 11–12 years (tetanus and diphtheria only), tetanus booster every 10 years
MMR protects against measles, mumps, and rubella viruses.	12–15 months, 4–6 years
Hib protects against *Haemophilus influenza* bacterium.	2 months, 4 months, 6 months, 12–15 months
IPV protects against polio virus.	2 months, 4 months, 6–18 months, 4–6 years
Pneumococcal conjugate protects against pneumococcal bacteria.	2 months, 4 months, 6 months, 12–15 months
Varicella protects against chicken pox virus.	12–18 months

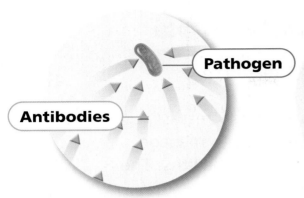

Antibodies

Pathogen

▲ Your body makes antibodies against the pathogens in the vaccine.

▲ Antibodies are ready to destroy this kind of pathogen.

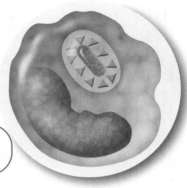

White Blood Cell

▲ White blood cells surround and destroy the pathogens.

Some different vaccines can be mixed and given together in a single shot. Some vaccines give you immunity to a disease for life. Others give you immunity for a limited time. Because of this, you need to get a booster shot before the time is up.

DRAW CONCLUSIONS How is getting a vaccine similar to getting a disease?

Lesson 3 Summary and Review

1 Summarize with Vocabulary

Use vocabulary from this lesson to complete the statements.

The _____ system in your body fights disease. White blood cells fight pathogens by making _____. The body's ability to defend itself against certain kinds of pathogens is called _____. You can get protection against some diseases by receiving a _____.

2 Name five of your body's first defenses against disease.

3 Critical Thinking Explain how seeking the services of the school nurse, a doctor, or others can be helpful to your health.

4 (Focus Skill) **COMPARE AND CONTRAST** Draw and complete this graphic organizer to show how flu and pinkeye are alike and different.

Topic: Flu and Pinkeye

Alike	Different

5 Write to Inform—Explanation

Explain what you would do if you started having symptoms of a communicable disease. Include adults you would ask for help to stop the spread of the disease.

Manage Stress
at the Doctor's Office

Everybody feels stress sometimes. Stress is mental or emotional strain. Learning to manage stress is an important part of staying healthy. The steps to **Manage Stress** can help you.

Jason needs a tetanus shot, so he must go to the doctor's office. Just thinking about the shot gives Jason a stomachache. How can he deal with the stress?

1 Know what stress feels like and what causes it.

2 Try to determine the cause of the stress.

Jason is feeling nervous. He gets stressed when he visits the doctor's office.

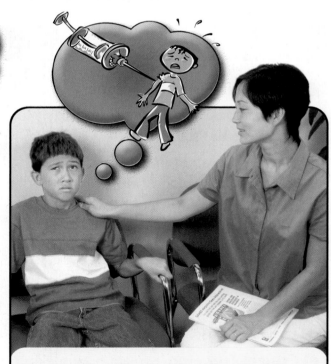

Jason doesn't like getting shots. He knows they hurt. He also knows thinking about getting a shot gives him stress.

③ Visualize yourself in a more pleasant situation.

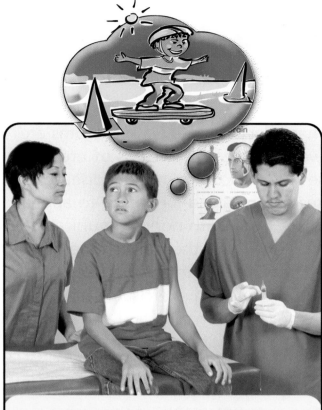

Jason decides to look away and to think of something that he enjoys. He imagines himself on his skateboard with his friend.

④ Think positively rather than negatively.

All done!

Wow! Not that bad.

Jason finds that thinking about something pleasant helps relieve his stress. He hardly feels the s'

 Problem Solving

Natalie's grandmother has a chronic illness. Natalie is so upset and worried that she can't sleep. She knows that this much stress can harm her own health, but she does not know what to do about it. Use the steps to **Manage Stress** to help Natalie. Suggest ways that she can demonstrate caring to her grandmother, which will help her handle the stress that she feels herself.

LESSON 4

Noncommunicable Diseases

Lesson Focus

Some diseases cannot be spread from person to person.

Why Learn This?

You can make choices that lower your risk of disease.

Vocabulary

cancer
allergy
asthma
diabetes
arthritis

Health & Technology

It's Electric Doctors can ~ a test called an ~trocardiogram, or EKG, ~d out if the heart is w~ properly. An EKG ca~ doctors that a pati~ heart disease befor~ isease gets bad.

Heart Disease

Ms. Cole has heart disease. Its symptoms are chest pain, weakness, and shortness of breath. Heart diseases are noncommunicable diseases. These diseases often take a long time to appear. Some people are born with noncommunicable diseases, while others get them over time.

Ms. Cole's heart disease may have been caused by her not getting enough exercise or from not eating right. Poor health habits and smoking can increase a person's risk for getting heart disease. Heart disease is the leading cause of death among adults in the United States.

DRAW CONCLUSIONS **Did Ms. Cole catch heart disease? Explain.**

◀ Ms. Cole is having a stress test. While she exercises on the treadmill, her heartbeat rate and blood pressure are being checked.

Cancer

Some people get cancer. **Cancer** occurs when body cells that are not normal grow out of control. Cancer cells often form lumps called tumors. Cancer can occur in nearly every part of the body, including the bones and blood. Cancer can also spread from one part of the body to another. Cancer is the second-leading cause of death in the United States.

Scientists know what causes some forms of cancer. Tobacco, for example, is one cause. There are many other kinds of cancers for which scientists still do not know the cause. The sooner a cancer in the body is found, the more likely it can be treated successfully.

MAIN IDEA AND DETAILS **What is cancer, and in what parts of the body can it occur?**

▲ You can get skin cancer if your skin is exposed to too much sunlight. Using sunscreen helps prevent this form of the disease. What other protection is the boy using?

Did You Kn

Skin cancer is ncer common typ han 1 in humans ound million c e who each y get sily, and hav y history of su have greater f getting this than other people.

◄ This cat's scratching could make someone's eyes water and cause sneezing.

◄ Allergies can cause asthma episodes. A person who is allergic to grass should stay away from mowing. The exhaust from the mower could also cause an episode.

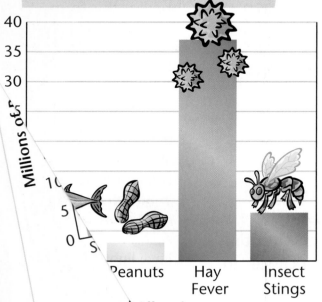

Numbers of People with Common Allergies in the United States

Millions of

40
35
30

10
5
0

Peanuts   Hay Fever   Insect Stings

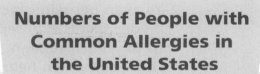

Allergies at Allergies
in the Unite... ...han 40 million people
common alle... ...hich is the most
...n the graph?

Allergies

An **allergy** (AL·er·jee) is a noncommunicable disease in which a person's body reacts badly to a certain thing. People can be allergic to animals, plants, medicines, and even foods. Some allergic reactions are so severe that they can cause death.

If you have allergies, you should avoid the things you are allergic to. Medicines can help make the symptoms go away and can even save your life if you have a severe reaction. Some people can get shots for their allergies. Over time, they no longer have allergic reactions.

MAIN IDEA AND DETAILS What symptoms might suggest that you have an allergy to cats?

Asthma

Keiko has asthma. **Asthma** (AZ•muh) is a noncommunicable disease of the respiratory system. Her asthma episodes can be scary. Her chest feels tight. She has trouble breathing, and she coughs or wheezes. Episodes are sometimes called *attacks.*

Asthma episodes are caused by allergies, cigarette smoke, and dust. Cold weather and exercise can also cause them. Keiko has more episodes than usual if she has a cold or other disease that affects the lungs.

Asthma cannot be cured, but some children stop having episodes as they get older. A doctor can find out what things cause the episodes and tell ways to avoid them. Doctors can also give medicines to help people manage the disease.

SUMMARIZE **What is asthma, and how can you get help for it?**

Myth and Fact

Myth: **People with asthma should never exercise.**

Fact: Exercise is important for good health. People with asthma usually can avoid episodes when they exercise by not exercising too long. They can also take medicine before exercising.

◀ Keiko gets directions from her doctor on the use of a fast-relief inhaler for proper management of her asthma.

Diabetes

Nancy has **diabetes** (dy•uh•BEET•eez), a disease that occurs if the body stops making insulin or stops using it properly. Insulin (IN•suh•lin) is a substance that helps body cells take up sugar from the blood. People who have diabetes feel weak and tired.

When sugar cannot enter body cells, it builds up in the blood. High blood sugar causes many health problems. If diabetes is not treated, blood vessels as well as the heart, kidneys, and eyes can be damaged.

Diabetes cannot be cured, but it can be treated. People with diabetes must follow a balanced diet, get regular exercise, and measure their blood sugar levels. Some take insulin or other medication.

DRAW CONCLUSIONS Why do people with diabetes feel weak and tired?

Nancy is learning how to measure her blood sugar level. If it is too high, she will get a shot of insulin. Nancy has to take insulin every day to control her blood sugar level. ▶

Arthritis

Will's grandmother has **arthritis** (ar•THRYT•is), a noncommunicable disease in which one or more of the body's joints become swollen and painful. Joints are places, such as wrists and knees, where your body bends. These joints can be red, swollen, stiff, and painful. Some mornings Will's grandmother is so stiff that it is hard for her to get out of bed.

There is no cure for arthritis, but doctors can give medicines to help the pain and swelling. A physical therapist taught Will's grandmother daily stretches that help keep full motion in her joints. She also takes walks and swims often.

CAUSE AND EFFECT Will's grandmother rotates her wrists in an exercise. How does this help her arthritis?

▲ Walking helps Will's grandmother stay limber and also helps her manage stress by taking her mind off her disease.

Lesson 4 Summary and Review

❶ Summarize with Vocabulary

Use vocabulary and other terms from this lesson to complete the statements.

_____ diseases are not caused by pathogens. These diseases include _____, which affects the joints, and _____, which affects the level of sugar in the blood. _____ develops when cells that are not normal grow out of control.

❷ Name some things that can cause an allergic reaction.

❸ Critical Thinking If you were planning a snack for yourself and a friend who has diabetes, what foods would you select?

❹ (Focus Skill) COMPARE AND CONTRAST Draw and complete this graphic organizer. List ways in which cancer and heart diseases are alike and different.

Topic: Cancer and Heart Diseases

Alike | Different

❺ Write to Inform—Description

Suppose that one of your friends has just found out that he or she has cancer. Describe one or two ways you could show your friend that you care.

Live a Healthful Lifestyle

Lesson Focus

A healthful lifestyle lowers your chances of getting ill.

Why Learn This?

Setting and meeting personal health goals and managing stress can help you feel good and stay well.

Vocabulary

resistance
abstinence

Ways to Stay Well

The choices you make about such things as what to eat and what activities to take part in all affect your health. A healthful lifestyle can help you stay well.

Eating healthful foods gives your body the energy that it needs to be active, fight diseases, and repair itself. Exercise helps prevent heart disease and some types of diabetes. It also helps your body fight off pathogens. Getting enough sleep helps your body grow and repair itself.

By making healthful lifestyle choices, you protect your body's resistance. **Resistance** (rih•ZIS•tuhnts) is your body's natural ability to fight off diseases on its own. The higher your resistance, the less often you will become ill, and the sooner you will get well when you do.

▲ What are these children doing to stay healthy and keep up their resistance?

180

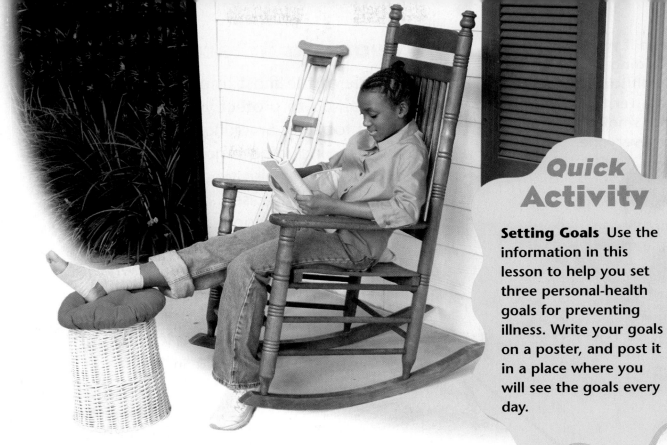

▲ When Bobbie is feeling a lot of stress, she relaxes with a good book.

Quick Activity

Setting Goals Use the information in this lesson to help you set three personal-health goals for preventing illness. Write your goals on a poster, and post it in a place where you will see the goals every day.

Managing stress is another important part of a healthful lifestyle. Everybody has stress from time to time. Sometimes stress comes from outside, for example, from school. Other times stress comes from you. Perhaps you tell yourself that you're not smart enough. Stress you put on yourself can be the hardest of all.

It's important to know the difference between normal stress and unhealthful stress. Feeling a little nervous before a big game might help you play better. But feeling stressed all the time is the kind of stress you need to get rid of. Too much stress can reduce your body's resistance to disease and can make you ill.

DRAW CONCLUSIONS **Why might a person who has problems at home get colds more often than one who doesn't?**

Consumer Activity

Accessing Valid Health Information A number of TV and magazine ads say that taking large amounts of vitamins will strengthen your resistance. Don't believe all the ads that you see. Talk with a parent or guardian or doctor before adding vitamins or minerals to your diet.

▼ Even if you don't smoke, avoiding tobacco smoke can be difficult. Jamal is making a poster to remind people that smoking is unhealthful for everyone.

Avoiding Tobacco

One of the most important things you can do to protect your health is to avoid tobacco. Smoking can cause many diseases, including cancer, heart disease, and asthma. It also weakens your resistance to disease.

People who choose not to use tobacco are practicing abstinence. **Abstinence** (AB•stuh•nuhnts) is avoiding a behavior that can harm the health. One reason it is important to abstain from tobacco is that it is addictive, or hard to give up. Practicing abstinence is a healthful lifestyle choice.

CAUSE AND EFFECT How does using tobacco affect a person's health?

Lesson 5 Summary and Review

❶ Summarize with Vocabulary

Use vocabulary and other terms from this lesson to complete the statements.

You can increase your _____ to disease by making wise lifestyle choices. Choosing _____ foods and getting enough _____ are very important. Practicing _____ from tobacco is also important.

❷ What things could you do to improve your body's resistance?

❸ Critical Thinking If you know someone your age who smokes, what can you say to persuade and help that person to quit?

❹ (Focus Skill) COMPARE AND CONTRAST Draw and complete this graphic organizer to show how the effects of stress and smoking are alike and different.

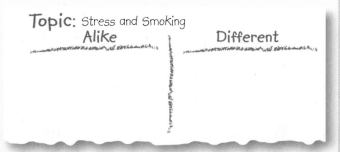

Topic: Stress and Smoking
Alike   Different

❺ Write to Express—Idea

Sylvia wants to help her family make healthful food choices. Help Sylvia by writing a paragraph that gives her family some suggestions and explains the importance of a healthful diet.

ACTIVITIES

Science

Home & Community

Research Bacteria Most bacteria are not pathogens. In fact, many bacteria in our bodies actually protect us from diseases. Research good bacteria. Find out how some of these bacteria help us. Use an encyclopedia or other library resource in your research. Present your findings in an oral report.

Communicating Talk with your family about what you've learned about good health habits and how they can keep pathogens from spreading. Write on note cards two or three of the health habits that you discuss. Post the note cards on the refrigerator or another place where family members will see them and be reminded to act healthfully.

Math

Calculate the Cost If one pack of cigarettes costs $4.00, how much would it cost to smoke one pack of cigarettes every day for one year? For two years? How much would it cost to smoke two packs of cigarettes every day for one year? For two years?

Career Link

Licensed Practical Nurse (LPN) Under the guidance of physicians or registered nurses, licensed practical nurses care for sick or injured people. Many LPNs work in nursing homes. Suppose that you are an LPN working in a nursing home. You provide care for a woman who has arthritis. The woman feels sad because she misses living in her own home. Write some tips to help your patient manage her disease and handle her stress.

Technology Project

Use a computer to make a slide presentation of about seven tips for creating a healthful lifestyle. Present your slide show to your classmates and family.

GO ONLINE **For more activities, visit The Learning Site.** www.harcourtschool.com/health

Reading Skill

COMPARE AND CONTRAST
Draw and then use this graphic organizer to answer questions 1 and 2.

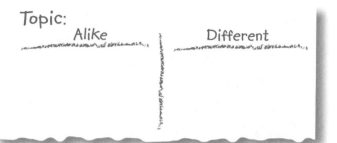

Topic:

Alike | Different

1 Write how communicable and noncommunicable diseases are alike.

2 Write how communicable and noncommunicable diseases are different.

Use Vocabulary

Use a term from this chapter to complete each sentence.

3 Communicable diseases are caused by _____. (p. 162)

4 The body system that fights disease is the _____ system. (p. 166)

5 Signs or physical feelings of disease are _____. (p. 166)

6 _____ is a noncommunicable disease caused by cells growing out of control. (p. 175)

7 Avoiding behavior that can harm your health is called _____. (p. 182)

8 Chemicals made by the body to help fight disease are called _____. (p. 167)

9 An illness is a(n) _____. (p. 158)

10 Substances made to prevent certain diseases are called _____. (p. 170)

11 _____ is a noncommunicable disease in which one or more of the body's joints become swollen and painful. (p. 179)

Check Understanding

Choose the letter of the correct answer.

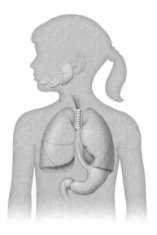

12 Small hairs that line the body's air passages are called _____. (p. 167)
  A saliva   **C** cilia
  B mucus   **D** fur

13 Your body's natural ability to fight off diseases on its own is called _____. (p. 180)
  F antibody   **H** defense
  G resistance   **J** immunity

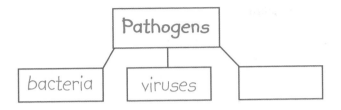

14 What pathogens are missing from the graphic organizer? (p. 163)

A fungi   **C** insulin

B vaccine   **D** mucus

15 If you are trying to prevent the spread of pathogens, which of these should you do? (p. 169)

F    **H**

G    **J**

Think Critically

16 Marianne has allergies. If Marianne sneezes on Ted, will he get allergies too? Explain your answer.

17 Several people in Matt's family have heart disease. Describe Matt's chances of getting heart disease. Tell how Matt can lower his chances.

Apply Skills

18 **LIFE SKILLS**

Manage Stress Suppose you are nervous about going onstage in your first play. Explain what you could do to feel more relaxed.

19 **BUILDING GOOD CHARACTER**

Caring After studying this chapter, you decide to help your friends and family take better care of their health. What are some ways that you can set a good example?

Write About Health

20 **Write to Inform—Explanation** Amy needs a booster shot, but she is scared. She has complained so much that her mom is about to give in and let Amy put off the booster. Write a note explaining why Amy needs to get her booster on time.

CHAPTER 8

Medicines, Drugs, and Your Health

ABOUT
ALCOHOL AND
OTHER DRUGS
A COLORING & ACTIVITIES BOOK

This coloring and activities
book belongs to

Reading Skill

SUMMARIZE A summary is a short statement that includes the main ideas and most important details in a passage. Use the Reading in Health Handbook on pages 340–341 and this graphic organizer to help you read the health facts in this chapter.

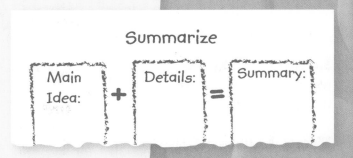

Health Graph

INTERPRET DATA Did you ever hear "Everyone is doing it"? Information about marijuana use among students ages 12 to 17 tells a different story. Do most teenagers use marijuana? What does this graph tell you?

Marijuana Use Among Students
Ages 12–17

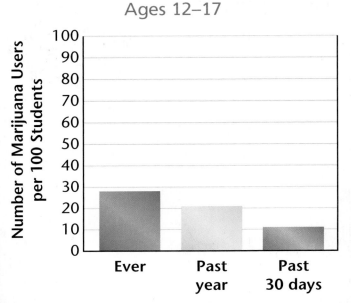

Daily Physical Activity

Keep your body healthy. Stay active and drug free.

 *Be Active!* Use the selection Track 8, **Jumping and Pumping**, to make your body feel better.

Medicines Affect the Body

Medicines Are Drugs

Has a parent or guardian ever given you a pill for a cold or put antibiotic cream on a cut? Then you have some idea of what a medicine is.

A **medicine** (MED•uh•suhn) is a drug used to prevent, treat, or cure a health problem. A **drug** is a substance other than food that changes the way the body works. All medicines are drugs, but not all drugs are medicines. Pain relievers and antibiotic creams are medicines. Drugs that are not medicines do not prevent, treat, or cure health problems. Instead, they can cause health problems and if misused can hurt you.

▼ Medicines come in many forms.

The medicine in some sprays is breathed in. An inhaler is used to take the medicine into the lungs.

Liquid medicines are swallowed. The medicine is carried through the blood.

Creams are placed directly on the area being treated.

Eardrops take medicine right to where it's needed.

Sucking on these cough drops releases medicine right where it's needed, to help you feel better.

Some pills are chewed, then swallowed. The medicine dissolves in the stomach and is carried through the blood.

▲ Medicines come in many forms. The way a medicine is used depends on its purpose.

When you are hurt or ill, your parents or other trusted adults decide if you need medicine. They decide how much and what kind of medicine to give you. They teach you to use medicines properly so that when you are old enough to take them yourself, they do not harm you.

Even when used properly, medicines may have side effects. **Side effects** are unwanted changes in the body caused by a medicine. Doctors and pharmacists can tell you about a medicine's side effects. Most are not harmful. If you feel worse after taking a medicine, always tell a trusted adult.

 SUMMARIZE Explain the similarities and the differences between medicines and drugs.

Myth and Fact

Myth: **Medicines are different from drugs.**
Fact: The word *drug* can refer to medicines—helpful drugs that cure or treat illness. Other times, the word *drug* refers to substances that do not help or prevent illness, but can harm the user.

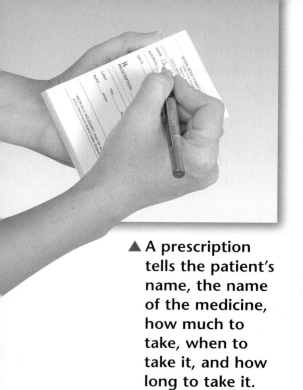

▲ A prescription tells the patient's name, the name of the medicine, how much to take, when to take it, and how long to take it.

Prescription Medicines

For some health problems, you need to see a doctor. After the doctor carefully decides what kind of medicine you need, he or she writes a prescription. A **prescription** (prih•SKRIP•shuhn) is a doctor's order for a medicine. When an adult takes the prescription to a pharmacy, a pharmacist (FAR•muh•sist) fills the order for the medicine and labels the container. Medicine that an adult can buy only with a doctor's order is called a **prescription medicine**. A prescription medicine is meant for just one person. Never take another person's prescription medicine. This can be dangerous to your health.

SEQUENCE **What are the steps for getting a prescription medicine?**

The label tells the name, address, and phone number of the pharmacy as well as the doctor's name.

Instructions tell how much of the medicine to take, how often to take it, and for how long.

Each prescription is meant only for the person named on the label.

The name and strength of the medicine are given.

Med Mart
145 Cutter Drive, Anytown, USA 54321

DR. MILLER
456 STATE DRIVE
ANYTOWN, USA 54321

Rx# 56489

JOHN SMITH
123 Main Street, Anytown, USA

USAGE DIRECTIONS:
ONE TEASPOONFUL (5mL) ORALLY
EVERY FOUR TO SIX HOURS AS
NEEDED FOR CONGESTION O
NOSE.

Allergy Syrup   4oz

◀ The pharmacist includes other important information on each medicine label.

◀ Labels on OTC medicines tell people what they can be properly used for. What are the uses for this medicine?

Over-the-Counter Medicines

For some health problems, you don't need to see a doctor. Your parents or guardians may give you a medicine from a drugstore or a grocery store. Medicines that can be bought without a prescription are called **over-the-counter medicines**, or OTC medicines. Many pain relievers, antibiotic creams, and cough medicines are OTC medicines.

The label on an OTC medicine tells what health problem the medicine treats and the dose. The **dose** is the amount of the medicine that you should take every time you use it.

OTC medicines can be harmful if taken incorrectly. Never take an OTC medicine on your own. Tell a parent or another trusted adult if you do not feel well.

CAUSE AND EFFECT When can OTC medicines be harmful?

Quick Activity

Read and Compare
Look at the prescription medicine label on page 190 and the OTC medicine label above. How are they alike and different?

Consumer Activity

Make a Buying Decision
At a drugstore or a grocery store, find three OTC cough medicines with the same active ingredients. Compare the costs of the medicines. Which is the best value?

Caring Chad is worried about his older sister. She is always taking medicine, even though she's not sick. Chad wants to talk with someone about his sister, but he is worried that she will get into trouble. What actions would best show that Chad cares about his sister?

Safe Use of Medicines

Everyone must learn the safe use of medicines. For example, medicines should not be used if the expiration date has passed. The **expiration date** (eks•puh•RAY•shuhn) tells you the last date it is safe to take the medicine. Always check a medicine's expiration date. The safety seal should also be checked. Medicine should not be bought if the seal is broken. Whenever you take medicine, follow the rules on the Medicine Safety Checklist.

▼ Always have a parent or another trusted adult give you medicine. Never take *any* medicine on your own.

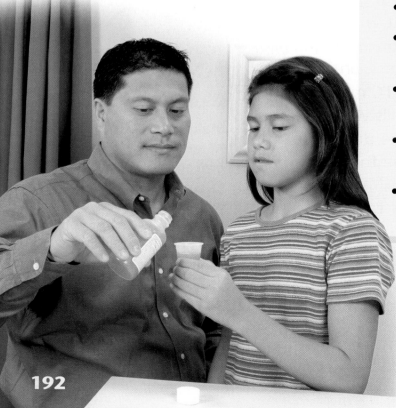

Medicine Safety Checklist

- Take medicines only from a parent or another trusted adult—never on your own.

- Follow directions on the medicine label.

- Do NOT use a medicine after its expiration date.

- Do NOT take another person's medicine.

- Do NOT buy an OTC medicine with a broken or missing safety seal.

- Do NOT crush or break capsules or pills without a doctor's permission.

- Store medicines in a locked cabinet, out of the reach of small children.

- If a medicine makes you ill or has side effects, tell an adult.

Throw away medicine that is too old to use. Age can make medicines change. They might not work or might cause harmful effects.

Child-resistant safety caps are used on many medicines. ▶

◀ Always follow the directions on the label. This includes taking the right dose at the right time.

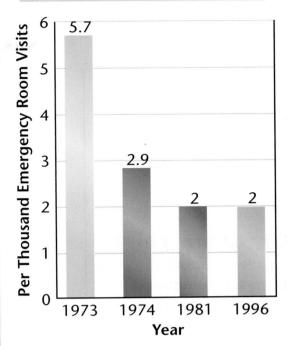

Children Under 5 Poisoned by Medicines

Per Thousand Emergency Room Visits

- 1973: 5.7
- 1974: 2.9
- 1981: 2
- 1996: 2

Year

In 1972 a law about the use of safety caps on medicines was passed. How has this helped keep small children safe and healthy?

Focus Skill SUMMARIZE How can you use medicines safely?

Lesson 1 Summary and Review

❶ Summarize with Vocabulary

Use vocabulary from this lesson to complete the statements.

_____ change the way the body works. Those used to treat or cure illnesses are called _____. _____ can be bought without a doctor's order, but _____ can not.

❷ Critical Thinking Distinguish between helpful and harmful medicines and drugs.

❸ OTC medicine labels describe the health problem the medicine treats. Prescription medicine labels do not. Why not?

❹ Focus Skill SUMMARIZE Draw and complete this graphic organizer to describe the information found on a prescription medicine label.

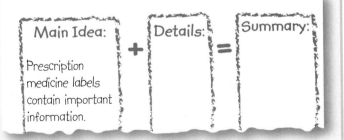

Main Idea:

Prescription medicine labels contain important information.

+ Details:

= Summary:

❺ Write to Inform—How-To

Write a pamphlet designed to teach your family how to use medicines safely.

Substances That Can Be Harmful

Lesson Focus

Common household products and OTC medicines can be harmful if they are misused.

Why Learn This?

If you learn about the dangers of common substances, you are less likely to be harmed by them.

Vocabulary

addiction
caffeine
inhalants

Harmful Effects and Misuse

You probably have heard about the dangers of drugs. Did you know that common substances around your home can also be dangerous?

OTC medicines can clear your stuffy nose. They can take away pain, soothe a sore throat, or stop an itch. But OTC medicines can harm you if you misuse them.

Some people misuse medicines. In most cases they simply don't read the labels or follow the directions. Medicines can be harmful to your body if you take more than the right dose. They can be harmful if you take them more often than you should or for the wrong reasons.

▲ Don't misuse medicines. Always follow the dose directions.

Directions

Adults and children 12 years and over: Take 2 caplets at bedtime.

Should not be used by children under 12 years of age.

▼ OTC medicines can impair a user's driving ability and may cause car crashes.

Misuse of some medicines can cause car crashes. For example, some medicines make people feel sleepy. This affects the way they drive.

The misuse of medicines and drugs can lead to addiction. An **addiction** (uh•DIK•shuhn) is a craving that makes a person use a drug even when he or she knows it is harmful. People who are addicted to a drug feel sick if they don't use it. It's very hard for them to stop using the drug. No one can predict who is likely to develop an addiction.

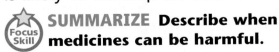 **SUMMARIZE** Describe when medicines can be harmful.

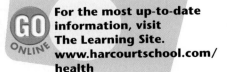

Personal Health Plan ▶

Real-Life Situation
Suppose you are about to choose a drink from a soda machine. You know that drinks with little or no caffeine are more healthful than ones with a lot of caffeine.

Real-Life Plan
Write how you might avoid choosing a drink with caffeine.

Caffeine

Caffeine (ka•FEEN) is a drug found in coffee, tea, chocolate, and some soft drinks. Like all drugs, caffeine changes the way you feel, think, and act. It speeds up the heart and makes most people feel more awake.

Small amounts of caffeine will not harm most people. However, too much caffeine can be harmful. Caffeine can make your heart beat too fast. It can make you nervous and keep you from sleeping. People can become addicted to caffeine. To avoid these effects, choose water, milk, or other caffeine-free drinks.

DRAW CONCLUSIONS How can reading a beverage label help you make a healthful drink decision?

Compare these drinks. Which has the most caffeine? The least? ▼

Some kinds of water contain vitamins, caffeine, and even sugar.

This sports drink has more than 50 mg of caffeine.

Iced tea has about 30 mg of caffeine per cup.

A cup of coffee has about 75 mg of caffeine.

Colas aren't the only soft drinks with caffeine. Other soft drinks with caffeine are root beer and some brands of orange soda.

Inhalants

Some chemicals when mixed can produce harmful fumes. Many household products give off dangerous fumes. When these fumes are used as a drug, they are called **inhalants** (in•HAY•luhnts). The fumes from these products are poisonous and should not be breathed.

Inhalants can cause clumsiness, headache, nausea, confusion, and memory loss. They can damage the brain and other organs. They can even cause death. Some people die the very first time they breathe the poisons. Others become addicted to inhalants.

CAUSE AND EFFECT What should you do if you have to use a product that gives off fumes?

▼ When used where there is plenty of fresh air, these products are safe. When inhaled directly, the fumes are poisonous.

DANGER
EXTREMELY FLAMMABLE
VAPORS CAN EXPLODE
HARMFUL OR FATAL IF SWALLOWED
IF SWALLOWED, DO NOT INDUCE VOMITING.
CALL PHYSICIAN IMMEDIATELY
KEEP OUT OF REACH OF CHILDREN
AVOID PROLONGED BREATHING OF VAPORS
DO NOT SIPHON BY MOUTH
DO NOT STORE IN VEHICLE OR LIVING SPACE
STORE AND USE IN WELL VENTILATED AREA
VAPORS CAN BE IGNITED BY A SPARK OR FLAME
SOURCE MANY FEET AWAY

nor puncture or incinerate. **Keep out of reach of children.** Use in adequate ventilation. Use only as directed. Intentional misuse by deliberately concentrating and inhaling the contents can be harmful or fatal.

sources. Do n... accumulate and concentrate such as basements, bathrooms or small enclosed areas. USE ONLY WITH ADEQUATE VENTILATION TO PREVENT BUILDUP OF VAPORS. Whenever possible, use outdoors in an open air area. If using indoors open all windows and doors and maintain a cross ventilation of moving fresh air across the work area. If strong odor is noticed or you experience slight dizziness, headache, nausea or eye-watering - STOP - ventilation is inadequate. Leave area immediately. If the work area is not well ventilated you MUST use a properly fitted and maintained NIOSH approved respirator for organic solvent vapors. A dust mask does not provide protection against vapors. DANGER! HARMFUL OR FATAL IF SWALLOWED. D...

Lesson 2 Summary and Review

❶ Summarize with Vocabulary

Use the vocabulary from this lesson to complete the statements.

An _____ is a craving a person has to use a drug. The drug _____ is found in coffee, tea, and some soft drinks. Common household products that give off fumes can also cause addiction if they are used as drugs called _____.

❷ How can reading the label before using a household product protect you from harm?

❸ Critical Thinking Why is it important to know how caffeine affects your body?

❹ (Focus Skill) SUMMARIZE Draw and complete this graphic organizer to describe how common substances can be harmful.

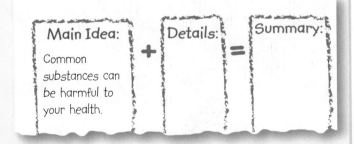

Main Idea: Common substances can be harmful to your health. + Details: = Summary:

❺ Write to Express—Business Letter

Draft a letter asking the maker of your favorite soft drink how much caffeine the product has.

LIFE SKILLS

Refuse
OTC Medicines

People sometimes think OTC medicines are safer than prescription medicines. That's why they might try OTC medicines they don't need. Using the steps for **Refusing** can help you refuse medicines you don't need.

Lucy and Sofia are studying together. Lucy says her brother gave her some caffeine pills. He said they would help her stay awake. She offers one to Sofia.

1 Say *no* firmly, and state your reasons for saying so.

"No, thanks," Sofia says. "I'm not allowed to take medicine unless my parents give it to me."

2 Remember a consequence, and keep saying *no*.

"Try one. It helps me stay awake so I can study," Lucy says. Sofia says, "But it might make you sick."

3 Suggest something else to do.

"Besides, you don't need pills to stay awake," Sofia says. "Why don't you just go to bed earlier?"

4 Repeat *no* and walk away.

"Just one won't hurt," Lucy offers. "No. I don't need pills to stay awake. I'll see you later," Sofia says as she walks away.

 # Problem Solving

Richard finds a package of OTC pills on his big brother's desk. When his friend Cory comes over, Richard shows the pills to him. He suggests that they each take a pill and see what happens.

Explain the importance of refusal skills. How can Cory use the steps for **Refusing** to refuse the pill? Explain how his decision can demonstrate caring for his health.

Marijuana and Cocaine

Marijuana

Some drugs are so harmful that they are illegal (ih•LEE•guhl). An **illegal drug** is a drug that is not a medicine and that is against the law to sell, buy, have, or use. A drug abuser is someone who uses illegal drugs. Drug abusers harm their health and break the law. They often spend time in jail.

Marijuana (mair•uh•WAHN•uh) is an illegal drug made from the hemp plant. It is sometimes called grass or pot. Marijuana users usually smoke it.

▼ It is illegal to grow marijuana in the United States. Illegally grown marijuana is destroyed, and the people who grow it are arrested.

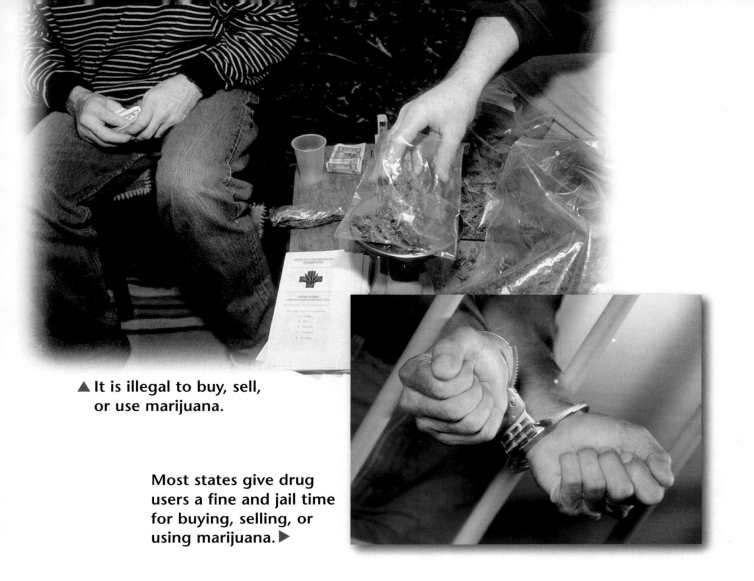

▲ It is illegal to buy, sell, or use marijuana.

Most states give drug users a fine and jail time for buying, selling, or using marijuana. ▶

Marijuana harms users' health. It has more than 400 substances in it. Marijuana use can lead to dependence on the drug. **Drug dependence** is the need to take a drug just to feel normal.

Smoking marijuana causes breathing and heart problems and makes it hard for the body to fight infections. It can also cause cancer.

 SUMMARIZE How does marijuana use affect the body?

Did You Know?

At one time, drug experts did not think that marijuana use was dangerous. The latest evidence shows that marijuana *is* harmful.

ACTIVITY

Life Skills

Manage Stress

Some drug users say they use drugs to relieve stress. However, there are safe, healthful ways to manage stress. Name some things you can do to manage stress and stay drug-free.

Cocaine

Cocaine (koh•KAYN) is a powerful drug made from the leaves of the coca plant. Cocaine affects the way a user feels. But the feelings last for only a short time.

Crack is a solid form of cocaine. It causes the same effects as cocaine, only faster. Crack is probably one of the most addictive illegal drugs.

Dependence on cocaine can happen after using the drug just once. The drug abuser often needs more and more of the drug to get the same effect. This can lead to serious illness or death.

Cocaine and crack are illegal drugs. Some cocaine and crack users commit crimes to get money to buy drugs. People who sell or use cocaine often get arrested and spend time in jail.

DRAW CONCLUSIONS Why might users of crack and cocaine lose friends and family?

▼ Cocaine is responsible for almost a third of all drug-related emergency room visits.

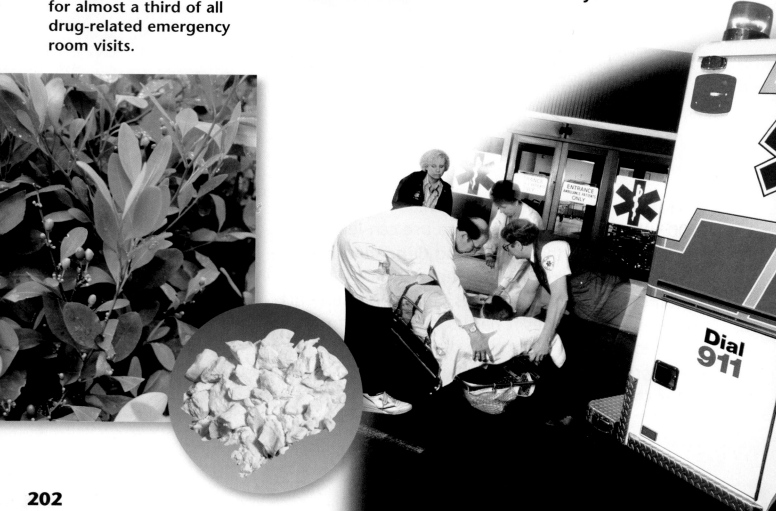

Effects of Marijuana and Cocaine

Marijuana

- trouble learning
- trouble remembering
- confusion
- nervousness
- trouble judging time and distance
- heart works harder
- lung damage
- cancer

Cocaine

- confusion and anger
- nervousness, sadness, and sleeplessness
- seizures
- heart works harder
- chest pain
- higher blood pressure
- heart failure
- heart attack
- trouble breathing
- lung damage
- cancer

COMPARE AND CONTRAST
What effects are the same for marijuana use and cocaine use? What effects are different?

Quick Activity

Identify Body Systems Make a table showing which body system these drugs affect and each organ affected. You can refer to pages 12–14 and 20–23 if you need help.

203

Effects of Drug Use on Others

You know that drug use is harmful to the drug user. Did you know that it also hurts others? Family members suffer when they live with the effects of drug use. Even the community is affected. Drug users often end up in car crashes that injure others.

Law enforcement and drug treatment cost a great deal of money. There are many hospital, legal, and jail expenses due to drug abuse. Because tax dollars help pay for these expenses, everyone is hurt by drug use.

DRAW CONCLUSIONS
How does drug abuse affect people who do not use drugs?

Lesson 3 Summary and Review

① Summarize with Vocabulary

Use vocabulary and other terms from this lesson to complete the statements.

Marijuana and cocaine are _____. A person who abuses these drugs is called a _____. Drugs harm not only the person who uses them, but also his or her family and the _____.

② Critical Thinking Why does marijuana use make it hard to do well in school?

③ What is cocaine, and what are some of its effects on the body?

④ **SUMMARIZE** Draw and complete this graphic organizer to show how marijuana use affects the body.

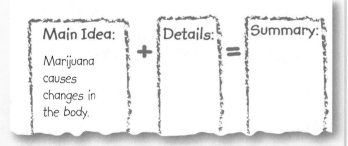

Main Idea: Marijuana causes changes in the body. + Details: = Summary:

⑤ Write to Inform—How-To
Imagine that you want to teach a younger child how to say *no* to marijuana and cocaine use. Write a how-to pamphlet that describes the effects of the drugs and teaches refusal skills.

Responsibility

...g Self-Control

...e people know that their actions affect others.
...control. They choose actions that will not harm
...emselves. Here are some ways to practice self-

- ...od judgment in what you do. Make good
  ...ions.
- ...NOT choose actions that harm yourself or
  ...ners.
- ...o NOT do anything that is against your family's
  rules or against the law.
- **Remember that your actions have short-term and long-term effects.**
- **Think of your long-term goals. Do NOT do things that will harm your future.**
- **Be responsible for your own actions. Do NOT give in to peer pressure. See page 207 for more about peer pressure.**

Activity

Take turns practicing self-control with a friend.
Suppose that you have been offered drugs.
How would you use self-control
to say *no*? What questions
would you ask yourself
before deciding what
to do? What things
would you think about
before saying *no*?

LESSON 4

Refusing

Refusing Is a Healthful

Refusing drugs is one of the most
decisions you can make. It helps you b   ion
self-respect, the feeling you have about
when you like yourself and are proud of w
do. Saying *no* to drugs helps you keep your
safe from harm and keep your mind clear. It
means you obey the law and want to stay out o
trouble. It allows you to do the things that are
important to you and to go after your goals.

Lesson Focus

Knowing the facts about drugs makes it easier to say *no* to them.

Why Learn This?

When you refuse drugs, you have a better chance to stay healthy.

Vocabulary

self-respect
peer pressure

Quick Activity

Demonstrate Ways to Refuse Drugs Use the reasons shown here to help you and a partner role-play refusing drugs. Take turns offering one another drugs and saying *no*. List your reasons for saying *no*.

▼ **Respect Yourself:** "I don't need drugs to feel good about myself."

▲ **Feel Healthy:** "I don't want to hurt my body."

There are many reasons to refuse drugs. Remember what you learned about drugs. When you know the risks of using drugs, saying *no* to drugs is easy.

Only you can decide what is right for you. When you make a decision to refuse drugs, stick to it. Do not give in to peer pressure. **Peer pressure** is the strong influence people your own age can have on you. It can create a desire to follow the crowd and do what others are doing. Others may tell you that using drugs is cool. Is putting your health at risk a cool thing to do? Peer pressure is *negative* if someone wants you to do something you know is wrong. Most people do not use drugs. Ask yourself: Do you want to harm your body?

SUMMARIZE Explain why you should resist peer pressure to use drugs.

Personal Health Plan ▶

Real-Life Situation
Saying *no* to drugs helps you stay healthy. It shows that you respect yourself and others. Saying *no* lets you pay attention to the important things in your life.

Real-Life Plan
Write how you might say *no* to drugs. How does saying *no* help you stay healthy?

◀ **Pursue Your Interests:** "I don't want anything that will hurt my future."

Do Well in School: "I want to be proud of my schoolwork and reach my goals." ▶

Ways to Say *No* to Drugs

If you are ever tempted to try drugs, think about what might happen. If you use drugs, you will have to deal with the harm they do to your body. You will have to deal with the problems you could cause your family and your friends. If you are caught, you will also have to deal with the law.

It is *your* responsibility to keep yourself healthy and safe. Other people can give you reasons to avoid drugs, but you are the only one who can decide to say *no* to drugs. You are the only one who can stick to that decision.

Ways to say *No*:

- I don't want to hurt my body.
- I don't want to get into trouble.
- I don't want to disappoint my family.
- It's against the law.
- It's against my family rules.
- My friends don't use drugs.
- I have better things to do.
- If you are trying to get me to use drugs, then you are not my friend.

◀ This girl has thought about how she will say *no* to drugs. How will you say *no*? It helps to have a plan. Then you can say *no* with confidence.

What will you say if someone tries to get you to use drugs? Having a plan can help you say *no* with confidence. One way to avoid being tempted is to have friends who don't abuse drugs. Another way is to go to places where drugs are not used. Getting involved with activities you enjoy will help you find friends who don't use drugs.

Organizations in your community may offer activities for people your age. Check out a community center, your school, or a religious center for fun things to do. You might join a sports team, a club, or a musical group.

If you have a problem, don't turn to drugs. Instead, talk with a parent or another trusted adult about your problem.

▼ If you have a problem, talk with your parents or other trusted adults.

★ Focus Skill SUMMARIZE Identify ways to cope with or seek assistance when confronted with situations involving drugs.

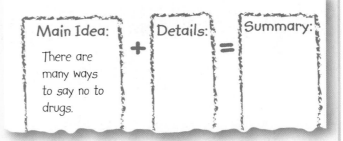

Lesson 4 Summary and Review

❶ Summarize with Vocabulary

Use vocabulary and other terms from this lesson to complete the statements.

If you know the ways that drugs can harm you, it is easier to resist _____. Planning ways to say *no* can make it easier to _____. Refusing drugs will help you like yourself and feel proud of your actions and will help build _____.

❷ Critical Thinking Why is it important to talk to a trusted adult to get help with your problems?

❸ What are three healthful alternatives to drug use?

❹ ★ Focus Skill SUMMARIZE Draw and complete this graphic organizer to show ways to refuse drugs.

Main Idea:		Details:		Summary:
There are many ways to say no to drugs.	+		=	

❺ Write to Express— Solution to a Problem

Write about how you would respond if you are ever offered drugs.

2

How Drug Abusers Can Get Help

Lesson Focus

It's important to know the warning signs of a drug problem and where to go for help.

Why Learn This?

You can use what you learn to get help for yourself, family members, or friends who might need it.

Know the Warning Signs

People who abuse drugs need help. If you know the warning signs of drug abuse, you may be able to get help for someone you know who might be using drugs. Once a person admits that he or she has a drug problem, that person can get help.

Changes in mood and behavior are clues that a person might be using drugs. Drug abusers might be nervous or tired. They might get angry easily. Some users may avoid friends and stop doing things they used to enjoy. Others might not seem to care about how they look. Or their grades may drop, and they may not do well in other activities.

Focus Skill **SUMMARIZE Why should you know the warning signs of drug abuse?**

◀ Does a friend suddenly seem moody or sad? Has he or she stopped doing things with you? Your friend might have a drug problem and need help.

Tell a trusted adult. ▶

When Does Someone Need Help?

Yes answers to one or more of these questions might mean you need to find help for yourself or someone else.

- Do you have friends who use drugs?
- Have your friends tried to get you to use drugs?
- Have you ever used drugs just for fun?
- Have you ever taken OTC medicines just to improve your mood?
- Do you have friends who sell drugs?

Take Action

You might think that someone else's drug problem is not your business. You might think that you will hurt the user if you tell others about the problem. But taking illegal drugs is harmful. Trying to help the user is the caring thing to do.

If you, a friend, or a family member needs help, talk with your parents or other trusted adults. They will know how to get help. If a parent or guardian needs help, speak to another adult you trust.

There are organizations that can help with recovery, the process a user goes through to stop taking drugs. You can find the names of these organizations in a school or community library.

▼ There are people in your family, school, and community to talk with about drug problems.

▲ Your parents

PEOPLE WHO CAN HELP

▲ Your doctor

▲ Your teacher, school nurse, or counselor

DRAW CONCLUSIONS Why is it important to talk with a trusted adult about a drug problem?

▲ Another trusted adult

Lesson 5 Summary and Review

1 Summarize with Vocabulary

Use terms from this lesson to complete the statements.

Mood swings and poor grades may be _____ of drug use. Many organizations can help drug users with _____, the process of stopping drug use.

2 Critical Thinking What should you do if you think a friend has a drug problem?

3 List three warning signs of drug use.

4 (Focus Skill) **SUMMARIZE** Draw and complete this graphic organizer to show how you can take action to help someone who wants to stop using drugs.

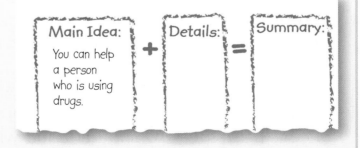

Main Idea: You can help a person who is using drugs. **+** Details: **=** Summary:

5 Write to Inform—How-To

Write how to tell if someone you know has a possible drug problem.

212

ACTIVITIES

Science

Caffeine-Containing Plants Do some research on plants that contain caffeine, such as coffee beans, tea leaves, and cola nuts. Find out how these plants are used in food and beverage products and where they come from.

Physical Education

Find Your Heart Rate Find your heart rate by holding your first two fingers at the base of your jaw line or at the inside of your wrist. Then count heartbeats for fifteen seconds, and multiply that number by four to find the heart rate. Report on how using large amounts of caffeine might affect a person's heart rate.

Technology Project

Think of the ways drug use affects each member of a family. Use a computer to make a slide presentation showing the effects of one person's drug use on each family member. Present your slide show to your family or classmates. If a computer is not available, you can draw a flowchart on paper or make overhead transparencies.

GO ONLINE For more activities, visit The Learning Site.
www.harcourtschool.com/health

Home & Community

Communicating Discuss with family members the information and safety rules you have learned about taking medicines. Make a medicine safety checklist like the one shown on page 192 to post near places where medicines are stored.

Career Link

Drug Rehabilitation Counselor Drug rehabilitation counselors help people who have problems with drug addictions. They help users identify the behaviors and problems that cause their addictions. They have counseling sessions for individual users, their families, or groups. The counselors work closely with doctors to help an addict overcome his or her addiction. Describe how you might try to help someone if you were a drug rehabilitation counselor.

Reading Skill

SUMMARIZE

Copy this graphic organizer, and then use it to answer questions 1 and 2.

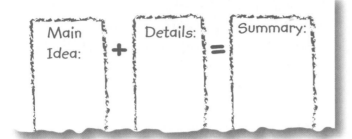

1 How can medicines be used safely?
2 How does marijuana affect the body?

 Use Vocabulary

Match each term in Column B with its meaning in Column A.

Column A	Column B
3 Influence from others	A side effects
	B drug abuser
4 Changes caused by a medicine	C peer pressure
	D medicine
5 Drug used to prevent or treat a health problem	E dose
	F recovery
6 Amount of medicine taken	
7 Stopping the use of drugs	
8 Someone who uses illegal drugs	

 Check Understanding

9 The feeling you have about yourself when you like yourself is called _____. (p. 206)
 A addiction   **C** self-respect
 B peer pressure   **D** dependence

10 Refusing drugs allows you to _____. (pp. 206–207)
 F do poorly in school
 G hurt your family relationships
 H lose self-respect
 J work toward your goals

11 How did the use of safety caps affect the number of children poisoned by medicines? (p. 193)
 A It caused the number to drop.
 B It did not change the number.
 C It caused more children to be hurt.
 D None of these.

12 Using marijuana can cause _____. (pp. 200–201, 203, 204)
 F health problems   **H** legal problems
 G family problems   **J** all of the above

13 Medicines that can be bought without a doctor's order are called _____. (p. 191)
 A cough medicines
 B over-the-counter medicines
 C prescription medicines
 D antibiotics

14 Which of the following belongs in the blank? (p. 190)

Go to doctor		Go to pharmacy

   F Try OTC medicine
   G Get prescription
   H Go to doctor
   J Go to pharmacy

15 Which does **NOT** describe an effect of cocaine on the body? (p. 203)
   A It makes it hard to learn.
   B It makes the heart work harder than it should.
   C It causes lung damage.
   D It makes it hard to breathe.

Think Critically

16 Study the OTC medicine label shown. What does it tell you about the safety of this medicine for someone your age?

> **Directions**
> Adults and children 12 years and over: Take 2 caplets at bedtime.
>
> Should not be used by children under 12 years of age.

17 Why is it important to know the warning signs of drug abuse?

Apply Skills

18 **BUILDING GOOD CHARACTER**
Responsibility One of your friends has started hanging around with people who use drugs. He has stopped doing activities he used to enjoy. His clothes look messy, too. You think he might be using drugs, but you don't want to get him into trouble. What is the best way to show responsibility in what you know about your friend's situation?

19 **LIFE SKILLS**
Refuse Suppose you have just returned from a long hike. Your legs are tired, and your feet hurt. Your friend offers you some medicine to make you feel better. What do you do? Explain how you will respond to your friend.

Write About Health

20 **Write to Inform—Description** Imagine that you are participating in a school health fair. Create a pamphlet that describes how medicines can be harmful as well as helpful.

215

Harmful Effects of Tobacco and Alcohol

Reading Skill

Focus Skill

IDENTIFY CAUSE AND EFFECT
Effect is what happens. Cause is the reason, or why, it happens. Use the Reading in Health Handbook on pages 334–335 and this graphic organizer to help you read the health facts in this chapter.

Identify Cause and Effect

Cause: → Effect:

Health Graph

INTERPRET DATA In the 1920s, it was against the law to drink alcohol in the United States. At that time, Americans drank less alcohol than at any other time in history. How did the amount of alcohol drunk by American adults change from 1934 to 1980?

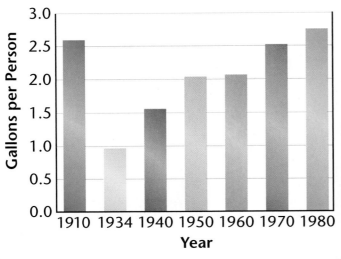

Yearly Amount of Alcohol Drunk by American Adults

Daily Physical Activity

You can stay healthy and free from the effects of tobacco and alcohol. Be physically active.

 **Be Active!**
Use the selection Track 9, **Hop To It**, to practice some healthful activity choices.

How Tobacco Harms Body Systems

Tobacco

The brown material inside a cigarette is called tobacco. It comes from dried leaves of the tobacco plant. When people smoke cigarettes, they breathe tobacco smoke into their lungs. It can harm the lungs and other parts of the body.

Another kind of tobacco—chewing tobacco—comes in small bags. People who use chewing tobacco put small wads of it into their mouths. Snuff is another tobacco product. People suck on pinches of it that they put in their mouths.

▼ The use of tobacco products is dangerous. In many places, it is against the law for people under 18 years old to use tobacco products.

Harmful Chemicals in Cigarette Smoke

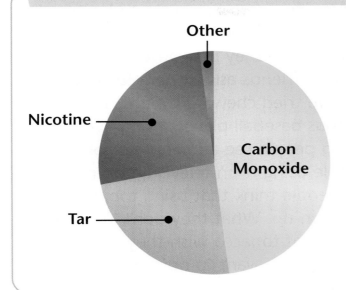

Other

Nicotine

Carbon Monoxide

Tar

Quick Activity

Interpret Graphs
Look at the circle graph on this page. What chemical is found the most in cigarette smoke? How do the other chemicals compare to this chemical?

▲ Most chemicals in cigarette smoke are harmful. Just a little nicotine can kill a person.

All forms of tobacco contain nicotine. **Nicotine** is a very addictive chemical that speeds up the nervous system. People addicted to nicotine have a constant need, or craving, for this chemical. They find it hard to stop using nicotine.

Another dangerous chemical in tobacco smoke is tar. **Tar** is a dark, sticky material that coats the lungs and air passages of smokers. Tar buildup makes it hard for a smoker to breathe.

Tobacco smoke also contains many other harmful chemicals. In fact, tobacco smoke contains more than 4,000 chemicals. About 50 of those chemicals are known to cause cancer.

(Focus Skill) **CAUSE AND EFFECT** Why is smoking tobacco unhealthful?

▲ Diseased lung tissue

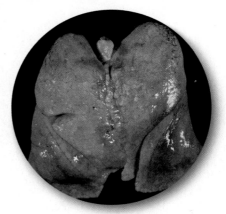

▲ Healthy lung tissue

219

The Trap of Tobacco

Most adults who use tobacco started when they were young. They may have tried tobacco because they were curious. Or they may have started smoking because friends asked them to try it. Others may have tried chewing tobacco because they saw famous baseball players using it.

Many young people see adults using tobacco. They see people using it on television or in movies. Some young people think that using tobacco is a way to act grown-up. What they don't know is that most adult users of tobacco wish they had never started using it! They want to quit, but they have a hard time doing so.

▲ Tobacco use may seem like fun, but it causes more problems than it's worth! Smoking can make you lose your friends and your health.

▲ Smoking is not cool. It makes your breath and clothes smell bad and your teeth turn yellow.

Many people cough the first time they smoke. They might get dizzy or have an upset stomach. These are warning signs that cigarette smoke is harmful. People's bodies are telling them not to smoke.

Some first-time users will stop smoking, but many will smoke again and again. Soon, the body gets used to the smoke. In a short time, quitting becomes hard for the smoker. The person begins to crave the nicotine in cigarettes. The smoker may get nervous or depressed when he or she doesn't smoke. He or she has become addicted to nicotine.

SEQUENCE Explain how the social aspects of smoking can lead to an addiction to tobacco.

Harmful Effects of Tobacco

Smoking can change a person's health. Over time, a smoker is much more likely than a nonsmoker to develop cancer and other diseases.

Cancers caused by tobacco use are lung cancer and mouth cancer. Lung cancer grows in a smoker's lungs. It blocks the lungs' air passages and can cause death. Mouth cancer happens most often in people who use chewing tobacco and snuff. To treat it, doctors often must cut away part of the face, lips, or tongue to remove the cancer. Some cancers can't be treated and can lead to death.

Carbon monoxide can cause brain damage. This can lead to memory loss and difficulty learning new information.

Nicotine shrinks blood vessels. This makes the heart work harder. This condition can lead to high blood pressure, heart disease, and stroke.

Tar coats the lungs and air passages. This leads to coughs and diseases of the lungs and air passages.

◄ Your health and fitness can be ruined if you use tobacco or alcohol products.

Tobacco users are more likely to develop heart disease and high blood pressure than nonsmokers. That's because the gases in cigarette smoke take the place of oxygen in the blood. The heart has to work much more to get the oxygen the body needs.

Environmental tobacco smoke (ETS) is smoke in the air. It can cause the same diseases in nonsmokers as in smokers. ETS comes from burning cigarettes, pipes, or cigars and from smoke that is breathed out by smokers.

Children who live with smokers are likely to get infections and develop asthma more often than children who live in smoke-free homes.

DRAW CONCLUSIONS Describe the short-term and long-term effects of tobacco use.

▲ ETS is not only a bother—it can also make you ill.

Lesson 1 Summary and Review

❶ Summarize with Vocabulary

Use vocabulary and other terms from this lesson to complete the statements.

When somebody smokes _____, he or she breathes in dangerous chemicals such as the sticky, black substance called _____. Also, smokers become addicted to _____. These chemicals are released into the air as _____.

❷ Critical Thinking What are two short-term and two long-term social effects of tobacco use?

❸ List three harmful chemicals in tobacco.

❹ (Focus Skill) CAUSE AND EFFECT Draw and complete this graphic organizer to show how choosing to use tobacco products affects the body.

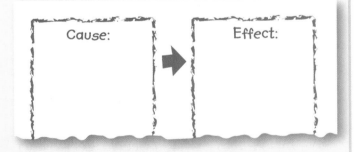

Cause: Effect:

❺ Write to Inform—Explanation

Interview an adult who started smoking cigarettes as a child. Ask if he or she regrets the decision now.

How Alcohol Harms Body Systems

Lesson Focus

Alcohol is an addictive drug that can harm the body and affect behavior.

Why Learn This?

Knowing the dangers of alcohol can help you refuse to use it.

Vocabulary

alcohol
intoxicated
alcoholism

Alcohol

Alcohol is a drug found in beer, wine, and liquor. The use of alcohol is legal only for adults 21 years of age and older. When a person drinks alcohol, it enters the blood. The amount of alcohol in a person's blood is called the *blood alcohol level (BAL)*. The more a person drinks, the higher his or her BAL will become.

Alcohol changes the way people feel, act, and think. It also changes the way the body works. After drinking alcohol, a person may find it is hard to walk or to speak clearly. The size and age of a person affect the way his or her body reacts to alcohol. A small person will have a higher BAL than someone larger who drinks the same amount.

These effects are based on a 150-pound adult. People who weigh less may have these effects with fewer drinks. ▶

How Alcohol Affects the Body

Number of Beers	BAL	Effect on a Person's Body
1 beer	0.015	reduced concentration, reflexes slowed
2 beers	0.04	short-term memory loss
4 beers	0.1	seven times more likely to have a car crash if driving
12 beers	0.3	vomiting/unconsciousness

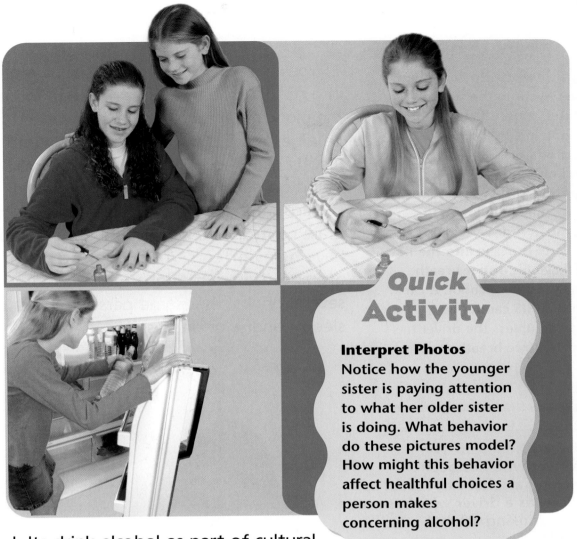

Quick Activity

Interpret Photos
Notice how the younger sister is paying attention to what her older sister is doing. What behavior do these pictures model? How might this behavior affect healthful choices a person makes concerning alcohol?

Some adults drink alcohol as part of cultural events, or celebrations. For example, some people drink champagne at weddings. Others drink a small amount of wine as part of religious ceremonies.

Some adults drink to relax or because they feel lonely, nervous, or depressed. These people may become addicted and need alcohol more often.

Some young people see adults or their peers using alcohol, so they want to try it. They are curious about its effects. They think drinking alcohol will make them seem grown-up. Many young people think that drinking alcohol is a fun activity. Others may try alcohol because their friends pressure them to try it. They want to feel like they are part of a group.

DRAW CONCLUSIONS **List three reasons a young person may want to try alcohol.**

Ways Alcohol Harms the Body

You've learned that food is slowly digested into nutrients that are small enough to enter the bloodstream. Alcohol does not need to be digested. Instead, it goes directly into the bloodstream from the stomach and small intestine. Blood quickly carries alcohol to the brain.

Alcohol slows down the brain. Because the brain controls the body's functions, alcohol can have many effects. After just one drink, an average-size adult might feel relaxed. After several drinks, that same person might feel ill, sleepy, angry, or depressed.

Effects of Alcohol

- difficulty walking
- memory loss
- blurred vision
- slurred speech
- decreased ability to think clearly
- dizziness

Slowed Reaction Time
A driver who has been drinking alcohol can't react as quickly as a driver who has not been drinking alcohol.

Lack of Coordination
Steering, braking, and speeding up all depend on coordinating different muscles. Alcohol makes it hard to control muscles.

Dizziness
Alcohol can make a person feel dizzy. This can affect vision, which is important to driving.

Difficulty Thinking
Alcohol makes it hard for a person to think clearly. A driver who has been drinking alcohol is not able to make clear, quick decisions about traffic and road conditions.

Long-term use of alcohol can damage the brain. Drinking too much alcohol can cause heart disease. Heavy drinking can damage other organs too, especially the liver. The liver cleans the blood of poisons. Alcohol affects the liver's ability to work. That may lead to cirrhosis. Cirrhosis is a liver disease that results from drinking too much alcohol. Cirrhosis can cause death.

Many people who drink do not eat well. Alcohol makes it hard for the body to absorb nutrients from food. The health of someone who drinks a lot may suffer because the body doesn't get all the nutrients it needs.

 CAUSE AND EFFECT **List two short-term and two long-term effects of alcohol use.**

Personal Health Plan ▶

Real-Life Situation
Suppose a friend invites you to a party where you know alcohol will be served.
Real-Life Plan
Make your own plans. Invite your friend to come to your activity instead. Write down some suggestions for some fun things that you could do.

Health behaviors affect body systems. For example, choosing to drink alcohol can harm your nervous, cardiovascular, and digestive systems. ▶

Nervous System
Heavy drinking damages parts of the brain linked with memory, vision, and coordination.

Cardiovascular System
Alcohol makes the heart beat faster and raises blood pressure. Heavy drinking can permanently raise blood pressure.

Digestive System
Heavy drinking can lead to sores in the stomach, called ulcers. Alcohol can also damage the pancreas, causing severe pain and vomiting.

Alcohol Can Affect Behavior

A problem drinker is often drunk, or intoxicated (in•TAHK•suh•kay•tuhd). Being **intoxicated** means being strongly affected by too much alcohol. Problem drinkers don't behave as they would if they were not drinking. They have trouble thinking clearly and making good decisions. They may get into serious situations that hurt themselves and others.

Problem drinkers often miss work. They do poorly when they are at work. They may have trouble keeping a job. Young drinkers can't concentrate well and often miss school. As they lose interest in their classes, their grades fall.

▼ Problem drinkers often say things that make others angry. Because of this, they lose friends.

228

Problem drinkers are often addicted to alcohol. They cannot stop drinking without help. They have a disease called **alcoholism**. A person who has this disease is called an alcoholic.

The families of alcoholics often suffer. Family members feel pain and frustration at not being able to live without worry. A family member who is an alcoholic cannot be depended upon to help in everyday chores or responsibilities. Alcoholics can't think about the needs of others—not even family members. Alcohol makes some people say hurtful things and become violent. They may hurt others or be arrested by the police. Their behavior can change from day to day.

 CAUSE AND EFFECT What are some social and legal consequences of alcoholism?

WINE

▲ Alcoholism affects every part of an alcoholic's life.

Lesson 2 Summary and Review

❶ Summarize with Vocabulary

Use vocabulary and other terms from this lesson to complete the statements.

When people drink too much _____, they become drunk, or _____. Long-term use of alcohol can lead to _____. Many _____ develop the liver disease _____.

❷ List three mental effects of drinking alcohol.

❸ Critical Thinking How is the blood alcohol level related to body weight?

❹ **CAUSE AND EFFECT** Draw and complete this graphic organizer to show how choosing to drink alcohol affects body systems.

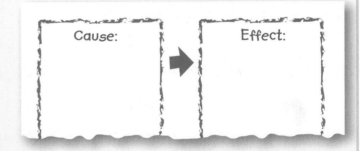

Cause: →   Effect:

❺ Write to Inform—Explanation

Write a paragraph explaining why NOT drinking alcohol is a responsible behavior. Explain how this choice can affect one's health.

Saying *No* to Alcohol and Tobacco

Be Prepared to Say *No*

Many adults choose not to use tobacco or alcohol. You, too, have a choice. Someday, someone may offer you alcohol or tobacco. What will you say?

Earlier in this chapter, you learned about the harmful effects of these products. For many people, knowing about the harmful effects of alcohol and tobacco is enough for them to choose to say *no*. But there are other important reasons for saying *no*.

◀ Practice different ways to say *no* so that you will know what to do if someone offers you alcohol or tobacco.

Ways to Say *No*

- Politely say *no* and walk away.

- Say that you have something else to do.

- Explain that you won't use these products because of their health risks.

- Explain that it is against the law for young people to use these products.

- Change the subject.

It is against the law for young people to use alcohol and tobacco. If you are caught using these products, you could be fined or arrested. Your family will be upset. If you break the rules of your family and use these products, you may lose your family's trust.

Some people refuse to use alcohol and tobacco because tobacco makes them feel ill and alcohol makes them feel nervous, sad, or out of control. Others refuse to let alcohol and tobacco rule their lives. People who want to live a healthful lifestyle know that alcohol and tobacco use should be avoided. They have more fun and feel better without using these drugs.

 CAUSE AND EFFECT Explain why it is responsible behavior for you to say *no* if someone offers you alcohol or tobacco.

▼ Knowing why other people don't use alcohol and tobacco can help you prepare to say *no*.

Alcohol and Tobacco Use

If You Say *Yes*—

You may develop lung, heart, or liver disease. Your breath, clothing, and hair will smell. You are more likely to be in a car crash or a fire. You may have problems at home or at school. You may become depressed or angry. You may be arrested.

If You Say *No*—

Your organs are more likely to be healthy. You are more likely to be alert and in control. Your body is more likely to be healthy, and you will have more energy. You will have a better chance to do your best.

Dealing with Peer Pressure

In Chapter 8 you learned that peer pressure can sometimes affect you. Sometimes friends get you to do healthful things, such as playing sports or studying. Sometimes friends may try to get you to use alcohol and tobacco. The best way to say *no* to alcohol and tobacco is to avoid peer pressure to use them.

There are plenty of activities you can do to have fun without using alcohol or tobacco. ▶

No   **Yes**

Young people often find it hard not to give in to peer pressure. You can avoid peer pressure by staying away from people who use alcohol and tobacco. Don't go to places where alcohol is being served to young people. Make friends with people who share your decision not to use these drugs. Finally, if the pressure becomes too much, always seek help from a parent or another trusted adult, such as a teacher, who will help you resist this kind of peer pressure.

MAIN IDEA AND DETAILS List other things you can do instead of using alcohol or tobacco.

Make friends with other alcohol-free and tobacco-free students! ▼

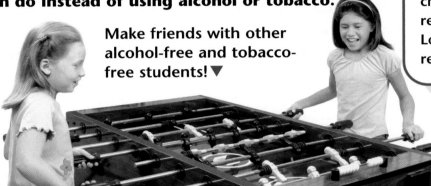

Lesson 3 Summary and Review

❶ Summarize with Vocabulary

Use terms from this lesson to complete the statements.

Some people choose to use tobacco or alcohol because of _____, which can be resisted by learning how to say _____ to these drugs.

❷ Critical Thinking What are some of the reasons people choose to use alcohol or tobacco?

❸ Identify ways to cope with or seek assistance when confronted with situations involving alcohol and tobacco.

❹ (Focus Skill) CAUSE AND EFFECT Draw and complete this graphic organizer to show how knowing how to refuse alcohol and tobacco can affect a person's mental and physical health.

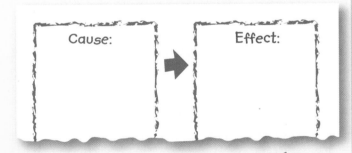

Cause: → Effect:

❺ Write to Inform—Description

Write a paragraph describing how adult family members and school staff can be role models for healthy behaviors such as not using tobacco and alcohol.

REFUSE
To Use Alcohol and Tobacco

Someone may someday offer you alcohol or tobacco. Using the steps to **Refuse to Use Alcohol and Tobacco** can help you say *no* and can help you make a healthful choice.

Rodney's friend Kevin is thinking about trying to smoke tobacco. Some students have asked Kevin to join them while they smoke some cigarettes. Kevin wants Rodney to come with him. How can Rodney refuse?

1 **Say *no* and tell why not.**

"Some of the guys are going to try some cigarettes after school. Want to come?" asks Kevin.
"*No.* Smoking is against the law, and it's bad for you," Rodney says.

2 **Suggest something else to do.**

"Come on. Everybody does it. It's the cool thing to do," Kevin says.
"Not me. Let's go play some soccer instead," says Rodney.

3 Reverse the peer pressure.

4 Repeat *no* and walk away. Leave the door open for the other person to join you.

"You don't need to use tobacco. Besides, real cool people don't waste their money on tobacco," Rodney says.

"Smoking isn't for me. I'm going to play soccer. You can come too," says Rodney.
"Wait for me," says Kevin. "I'd rather play soccer too."

Problem Solving

Celia and Mattie walk home together after school every day. One day, they see a friend from class with some older students. Their friend calls them over, saying, "Celia, Mattie, do you want to try a cigarette?" Use the steps to **Refuse to Use Alcohol and Tobacco** to describe how Celia and Mattie might respond and reverse the peer pressure. Explain how Celia and Mattie's behavior might demonstrate caring for their friend's health.

Tobacco and Alcohol Users Can Get Help

Lesson Focus

There are warning signs that a person needs help in quitting the use of tobacco and alcohol.

Why Learn This?

Knowing about the sources of help for users of tobacco and alcohol may allow you to help yourself and others.

Consumer Activity

Accessing Valid Health Information Make a list of community resources for people who are addicted to tobacco. Who do you think are the best people to ask about products that help tobacco users overcome their addiction?

Joanie sees her sister smoking with friends. She thinks her sister might have a problem. ▶

Help for Users of Tobacco or Alcohol

Tobacco users who get nervous when they don't smoke or chew tobacco probably need help. People who hide tobacco use feel uneasy about what they are doing. So do those who lie about smoking or chewing tobacco. These signs show that the person needs help to quit using tobacco.

As with alcohol use, if you are worried about someone using tobacco, talk with a trusted adult. The adult can find help. There are many health organizations that can help people who are addicted to tobacco.

▼ Talk to your parents if you're worried about someone's tobacco or alcohol use.

Some organizations are the American Lung Association and the American Cancer Society. There are some products that can help tobacco users overcome their addiction. Nicotine gums and patches can help people reduce their need for nicotine. The best prevention is to never start using tobacco.

Have you ever been afraid to ask someone for help? Alcoholics need help. It's hard for them to stop drinking. They may be afraid to ask for help.

If you are worried about someone who uses alcohol, there are warning signs of alcoholism that you should know. The signs, listed here, can help you decide if an alcohol user needs help. You may also notice that the user has trouble doing things most people do normally. For example, young users may not do schoolwork or home chores. Adult users may forget to pay their bills. All alcoholics need help.

> **SUMMARIZE** **List three people you can turn to if you know someone with a tobacco problem.**

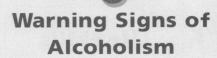

Warning Signs of Alcoholism

1. Often seems tired
2. Has an unhealthful diet
3. Often misses school or work
4. Has trouble controlling moods
5. Gets angry when he or she drinks
6. May not wash hair or clothing
7. Smells like alcohol

Life Skills
Communicate

Curt's mother is an alcoholic. Sometimes when his mother is drinking, she yells at Curt and he feels hurt. Name some trusted adults Curt could talk to. What could Curt say to these adults? Use the steps for **Communicating** shown on pages 46–47.

More Help for Alcohol Users

Where can you go for help if you're worried about someone's alcohol use? Talk to an adult you trust, such as a parent, another relative, or a family friend. You could also talk to a teacher, counselor, school nurse, family doctor, or religious leader. Telling someone else about the problem might help you feel better.

Don't worry that telling someone will hurt the person with the alcohol problem. The adult you talk to may be able to find help for the alcoholic. There are many programs to help alcoholics and their families. Alcoholics Anonymous (AA) and Al-Anon are just two.

DRAW CONCLUSIONS Why is it important for an alcoholic to get help?

Lesson 4 Summary and Review

❶ Summarize with Vocabulary

Use terms from this lesson to complete the statements.

Tobacco users can get support from organizations such as _____ and _____. _____ and their family members can go to organizations such as _____ or _____ for help with their alcohol problems.

❷ What are three signs that a person is an alcoholic?

❸ Critical Thinking Why should alcoholics and tobacco users try to stop their addictions?

❹ **CAUSE AND EFFECT** Draw and complete this graphic organizer to show two possible effects of talking with a trusted adult about a brother's alcohol problem.

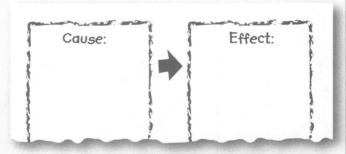

Cause:

Effect:

❺ Write to Inform—Explanation

Write about why it may be difficult for a user of tobacco or alcohol to quit. Write how a user can find help to recover from his or her addiction.

Trustworthiness

Building Good Character

Report Dangerous Events

Trustworthiness involves being honest, telling the truth, and keeping promises so that people know they can count on you. You are trustworthy when you report dangerous events. Reporting dangerous events makes your home, community, and school safer. You should report dangerous events, such as when you

- **see young people drinking alcohol**
- **see young people using tobacco**
- **see people fighting**
- **smell smoke or gas**
- **see somebody who is hurt or unconscious**
- **see a stranger around your home or on school grounds**

You can report these events to
- **a parent**
- **another adult relative**
- **a teacher**
- **your school counselor**
- **your school principal**
- **a police officer**
- **another trusted adult**

Activity

With a friend, role-play how to report a dangerous event. Be sure to tell the person playing the trusted adult what you saw, where it was, and how long ago you saw it.

Tobacco, Alcohol, and the Media

Lesson Focus
Advertisers and the media do not always present alcohol and tobacco in a truthful manner.

Why Learn This?
Understanding the purpose of ads can help you make good decisions about not using tobacco and alcohol.

The Job of Advertising

Companies that make tobacco and alcohol products use advertisements, or ads, to send messages. They want you to think that people who use their products have lots of fun. The people in the ads are young and attractive. They wear stylish clothes and drive high-priced cars. Advertisers want young people to think that using alcohol and tobacco is exciting, fun, and healthful.

Cigarette companies are not allowed to advertise on television. But you still might see the names of their products in other places—in magazines or displayed at sporting and cultural events.

▼ The job of advertising is to sell products, not to show the truth.

BEACH BEER
For a fun time on the beach!

Beer makers use TV commercials to advertise their products during sporting events and other popular programs. They hope you will think that drinking beer is fun and exciting.

Alcohol products are sometimes advertised on billboards, in magazines, and on the radio. It's important to know that what is shown in tobacco and alcohol ads is not true. Alcohol and tobacco can't make you happy, popular, or successful. The truth is, alcohol and tobacco use may ruin your health, cause you to lose friends, and keep you from doing well at school or work.

COMPARE AND CONTRAST How do alcohol and tobacco ads compare with the facts about these drugs?

Consumer Activity

Analyze Advertising and Media Messages
Take notes about TV or magazine ads for alcohol or tobacco. How do the ads make tobacco and alcohol use seem exciting? Use the Tips for Analyzing Ads and Media Messages, found on pages 48–50, to help.

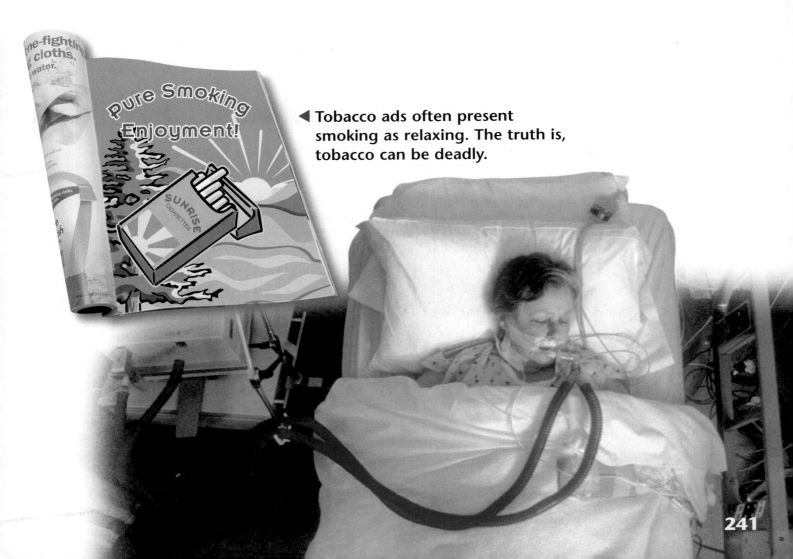

◄ Tobacco ads often present smoking as relaxing. The truth is, tobacco can be deadly.

Resist False Media Messages

Look at ads for alcohol or tobacco on billboards, in magazines, or on television. Think about what really happens to people who use alcohol or tobacco. People who use these drugs have a greater risk for disease and injury. They really don't have much fun either. Knowing these facts can help you resist the false messages in ads about alcohol and tobacco.

DRAW CONCLUSIONS Why is it important that you know the facts about alcohol and tobacco when you see ads?

▲ Information is available that tells the truth about alcohol and tobacco use.

Quick Activity

Make a Poster Many organizations publish ads or brochures that tell the truth about alcohol and tobacco. Make an anti-alcohol or anti-tobacco poster that one of these organizations could use.

Lesson 5 Summary and Review

❶ Summarize with Vocabulary

Use terms from this lesson to complete the statements.

Tobacco and alcohol companies use _____ to sell their products. These companies want you to _____ their products. You need to know the _____ about alcohol and tobacco product ads.

❷ How do ads show alcohol and tobacco?

❸ Critical Thinking Why should you resist false media messages about the use of alcohol and tobacco?

❹ (Focus Skill) CAUSE AND EFFECT Draw and complete this graphic organizer to show the possible effects of believing alcohol and tobacco ads.

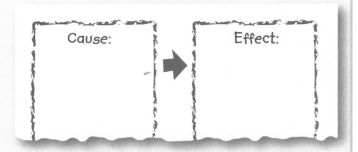

Cause: → Effect:

❺ Write to Inform—Description

Write a paragraph describing how media messages can influence a person's health-related buying choices.

ACTIVITIES

Science

Make a Body Atlas Decorate a bulletin board with a full-size picture of the human body, showing organs that are affected by alcohol and tobacco. Color the organs that are affected by tobacco one color. Use another color to show the organs affected by alcohol.

Social Studies

Historic Beverages When settlers first came to North America, people drank beverages other than water. Find out what they drank. Did any of these beverages have alcohol in them? How were they made? Write a magazine article that reports your findings.

Technology Project

Use the Internet to research an organization such as Mothers Against Drunk Driving (MADD), SADD, AA, Al-Anon, or Alateen. Write a report about the resources the organization has to help someone overcome an alcohol problem. If you do not have access to a computer, find a book about one of these organizations.

GO ONLINE **For more activities, visit The Learning Site.** www.harcourtschool.com/health

Home & Community

Promote Health Talk to your classmates about ways to say *no* to tobacco and alcohol use. Make posters that show your ideas. Hang the posters in your school library, where other students can see them. Then take your poster home and share what you have learned with your family.

Career Link

Social Worker Social workers help people with many kinds of problems. Imagine that you are a social worker. An alcoholic father and his family have come to you for help. Write a list of things that you think the family should do to overcome their problems. Be sure to include in your list some organizations that help alcoholics and their families.

Reading Skill

CAUSE AND EFFECT

Draw and then use this graphic organizer to answer questions 1 and 2.

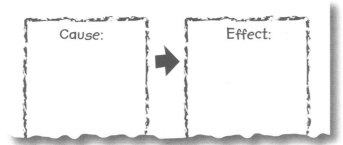

Cause: → Effect:

1 Write two effects that alcohol and tobacco have on the nervous system.

2 Write two effects that alcohol and tobacco have on the cardiovascular system.

 Use Vocabulary

Match each term in Column B with its meaning in Column A.

Column A	Column B
3 Strongly affected by alcohol	**A** alcohol
4 Smoke in the air from burning tobacco	**B** alcoholism
	C environmental tobacco smoke
5 Addiction to alcohol	**D** intoxicated
6 A dark, sticky material in tobacco	**E** nicotine
	F tar
7 A drug found in beer, wine, and liquor	
8 An addictive substance in tobacco	

 Check Understanding

9 Which of the following has about 50 cancer-causing chemicals? (p. 219)

A

C

B

D

10 Which is one way to avoid harmful peer pressure? (pp. 232–233)

F Make friends who don't do drugs.

G Go to parties where alcohol is available.

H Don't practice refusal skills.

J Choose friends who use tobacco.

11 Which group could help somebody quit smoking? (p. 237)

A Alcoholics Anonymous

B American Lung Association

C Al-Anon

D none of these

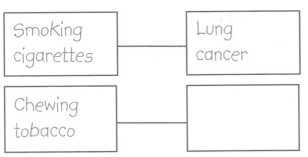

Smoking cigarettes — Lung cancer

Chewing tobacco —

12 Which disease would best complete this graphic organizer? (p. 222)

F cirrhosis   **H** mouth cancer
G heart disease   **J** alcoholism

13 Gases in cigarette smoke take the place of _____ in the blood. (p. 223)

A nicotine   **C** nitrogen
B carbon monoxide   **D** oxygen

14 Which of the following is **NOT** a sign of alcoholism? (p. 237)

F clothes not clean
G seems tired
H has more energy
J often gets angry

15 People start using tobacco or alcohol for all of the following reasons **EXCEPT**_____. (pp. 220, 225)

A to improve health
B peer pressure
C to feel grown-up
D curiosity

Think Critically

16 Since smoking is dangerous, why do so many adults continue to do it?

> SURGEON GENERAL'S WARNING: Smoking Causes Lung Cancer, Heart Disease, Emphysema, And May Complicate Pregnancy

17 Study the warning label shown above. Similar warnings appear on alcohol bottles and cans. How would this warning help people refuse to use the product?

Apply Skills

18 **BUILDING GOOD CHARACTER**
Trustworthiness You are walking to class one day when you see some students sharing a beer outside the school. What should you do?

19 **LIFE SKILLS**
Refuse Some older students start talking to you after school one day. You're really excited to have their attention. Then one of them offers you a cigarette. What should you do?

Write About Health

20 Write to Inform—Description
Describe how using alcohol or tobacco makes life less fun.

Your Needs and Feelings

IDENTIFY MAIN IDEA AND DETAILS
The main idea is the most important thought in a passage. Details tell about the main idea and help you understand it. Use the Reading in Health Handbook on pages 336–337 and this graphic organizer to help you read and understand the information in this chapter.

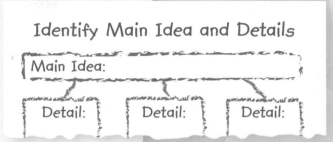

Identify Main Idea and Details

Main Idea:

Detail: | Detail: | Detail:

Health Graph

INTERPRET DATA A magazine for young people asked readers what bothered them the most. This graph shows how they replied. What bothered these young people even more than a test?

What Bothers You?

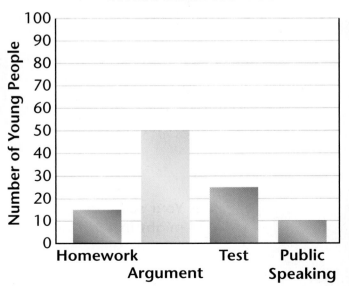

Daily Physical Activity

You can feel better about yourself. Be physically active, and exercise.

 Be Active!
Use the selection Track 10, **Super Stress Buster**, to relax you and give your mood a boost.

Learning About Yourself

Lesson Focus

Learning about yourself helps you appreciate who you are.

Why Learn This?

Knowing who you are helps you make healthful decisions and get along well with others.

Vocabulary

self-concept
self-confidence

Getting to Know You

In Chapter 1, you learned *traits* are the physical characteristics or other qualities that make you special. People are also described by their traits. For example, one person might be friendly. Someone else might be shy.

Knowing your traits gives you a picture of yourself. The picture you have of yourself most of the time is your **self-concept**. If your self-concept is positive, you have self-respect. *Self-respect* means that you value yourself and your ideas.

A positive self-concept leads to *self-confidence* and *self-esteem.* **Self-confidence** means that you are sure of yourself. You can handle most problems. When you have self-esteem, you respect yourself and are happy with yourself.

When you have self-respect, you always try your best.▼

▲ Your family helps you have respect for yourself and your abilities.

▲ Your self-concept might include having athletic skills.

▲ Self-confidence gives you the courage to challenge yourself.

In addition to physical traits, you also have mental, emotional, and social traits.

Your mental and emotional traits affect the way you think, learn, and act. These traits might include a good memory or a sense of humor. One of your traits might be a *talent*, or natural ability. You may play the violin or draw well.

Your social traits affect the way you act with others. Maybe you are a leader. Maybe you prefer to work on your own. You might be a good listener. Perhaps friends turn to you for help.

Your many traits make you who you are. Knowing your traits helps you learn about yourself.

 MAIN IDEA AND DETAILS Explain how personal characteristics contribute to your self-confidence and self-esteem.

Did You Know?

Every year, about one million people from 150 countries compete in the Special Olympics. The athletes all take this oath: "Let me win. But if I cannot win, let me be brave in the attempt."

249

Building Good Character

Respect You have a science report due this Friday and you want to get a good grade. List things you can do to reach this goal. How will your work show you respect yourself?

What Makes You Special

Your self-concept is partly shaped by your *environment*, all the people and things around you. For example, if your family is musical, you might have inherited a musical talent, too. If you are the oldest child in your family, you might have more responsibility.

You cannot change most of your physical traits. You can, however, change some of your other traits. If your family is not musical, you can still learn to play an instrument. Maybe you have a temper. You can find ways to control that behavior. If speaking to a group makes you nervous, you can change that, too. If you change your traits and behaviors, you can change your self-concept.

DRAW CONCLUSIONS Think of a trait someone might want to change. How could changing that trait change his or her self-concept?

You have talents and skills you can develop. ▼

Valuing Yourself

Your self-concept is also shaped by your attitude. *Attitude* is how you look at things. You respect yourself and your skills if you have a positive attitude. If you have a negative attitude, you expect to do poorly.

If you expect to do poorly, you probably will. If you expect to do well, you probably will. The more successes you have, the more confidence you gain. Your attitude then becomes more positive.

Learn more about yourself. What is your self-concept? What are your abilities? After you know yourself, you can decide which traits to value and which ones to change.

COMPARE AND CONTRAST **How are *self-concept* and *self-respect* different?**

Lesson 1 Summary and Review

1 Summarize with Vocabulary

Use vocabulary and other terms from this lesson to complete the statements.

Your _____ is how you picture yourself. When you value your own ideas, you show _____. When you are sure of yourself, you have _____. Everyone has qualities, or _____, that make them special. Your self-concept is shaped by your _____.

2 What traits do most family members share?

3 Critical Thinking How can you demonstrate personal characteristics that contribute to self-confidence and self-esteem?

4 (Focus Skill) MAIN IDEA AND DETAILS Draw and complete this graphic organizer to show two more things that are part of self-concept.

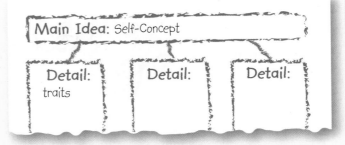

Main Idea: Self-Concept

Detail: traits   Detail: Detail:

5 Write to Inform—Description

Choose a character in a story you have read. Describe some physical, mental, emotional, and social traits of this character.

We All Have Needs

Your Basic Needs

People all have physical, mental, emotional, and social needs. These are called **basic needs**.

To stay healthy, you need food, water, clean air, and a place to live. These are your physical needs. When you were a baby, your family met all of your physical needs. Now that you are older, you can meet some of these needs. For example, you get your own snacks or drinks. When you are grown-up, you will meet all of your physical needs.

You also have wants. *Wants* are things you would like to have. You *need* to eat food, but you may *want* to eat a hamburger. You may not need a hamburger. You just want one!

Everyone has physical needs. People can help each other meet mental and emotional needs. ▶

Mental needs include thinking, learning, and using your mind. For example, you need to know math so you can count, use money, and measure. You learned to read so you can read words and enjoy a story. To use your mind, you might read new books or learn how to play a new game.

Emotional needs include love, security, and a feeling of belonging. Everyone needs to feel accepted. You need to be able to talk with others about your feelings and personal thoughts. You need to trust others and feel that they trust you.

Your family probably meets most of your emotional needs. Friends and other people also help meet your emotional needs.

SUMMARIZE **What is a physical need?**

Quick Activity

Interpret an Illustration List the physical needs this picture shows being met. Then write a paragraph describing any emotional and mental needs that the picture shows are being met.

253

Consumer Activity

Analyze Ads and Media Messages If you watch television this week, pay attention to any messages about social needs. Do people seem to always be with other people? Is anyone ever happy alone? What influence do you think these shows or ads have on your social needs?

Social Needs and Setting Goals

Social needs include getting attention. They also include being part of a group. They can also include time to be alone.

Almost everyone likes to get attention. You also appreciate being able to express yourself. When you were a baby, you got attention mostly by crying. Now you can talk to people and express your needs. You can raise your hand in school if you have a question. Politely asking for someone's attention is another healthy way of getting attention.

People have different social needs. For example, you might need **privacy** (PRY•vuh•see), or time by yourself. You might be the only one in your family who wants a quiet place to read.

People might have different social needs at different times.▼

As you get older, you will be responsible for meeting more of your own needs and wants. Learning to set goals will help with this. A **goal** is something you are willing to work for. The tips here show how to set and meet a goal.

Be clear about your goals. For example, if your goal is to get to school on time every day, work on things to help you reach the goal. What takes up your time each morning? Look at ways to save time. As you work toward your goal, check your progress. Are you getting closer to meeting your goal? Do you need to do something different?

Meeting your needs will be up to you someday. If you know how to set and meet goals, you'll be ready!

SEQUENCE What should you do after you set a goal?

How to Set and Meet Goals

- Set a goal.

- Plan the steps to meet your goal. Will you need help? How long will it take?

- Work toward your goal.

- Evaluate your progress, and make any necessary changes.

Lesson 2 Summary and Review

1 Summarize with Vocabulary

Use vocabulary and other terms from this lesson to complete the statements.

To stay healthy, you must meet your _____. Things you would like to have are called _____. Having someone to trust is an _____ need. Many people like to have time alone, so they need _____. To meet a need or a want, you can set a _____.

2 Name a mental need. How do people meet this need?

3 Critical Thinking Describe three healthy ways that you can get attention.

4 (Focus Skill) MAIN IDEA AND DETAILS Draw and complete this graphic organizer to show three important details about a goal.

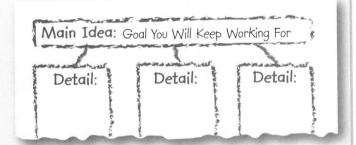

Main Idea: Goal You Will Keep Working For

Detail: Detail: Detail:

5 Write to Inform—Narration

Tell about a goal you worked to meet. For example, your goal might have been to get on a team, make a new friend, earn money, or learn a new skill.

We All Have Feelings

Your Feelings

You have the same feelings as everyone else, but you may not share the same feelings at the same time. For example, you might feel happy about a school field trip, but a friend might be anxious about it. Understanding what you feel and why you feel it is an important part of growing up. Learning about feelings can help you get along with others.

Feelings are not good or bad, but feelings that are uncomfortable can be a warning signal. When you feel angry or afraid, something is not always right. If you feel that you are being abused, or bothered physically, emotionally, or in a way that violates your privacy, talk to a parent or trusted adult.

Quick Activity

Interpret Photographs Study these pictures. Then write what you think each person is feeling and why.

You might try to hide uncomfortable feelings, but your body often gives you away. *Body language* is movements, such as frowning or slouching, that can express your real feelings.

One uncomfortable feeling is *stress*. You can feel stress when you have too much to do. Stress can show in tense shoulders. Your face can look pained from a headache or a stomachache.

Grief is another uncomfortable feeling. Grief is a great sadness. For example, you might feel grief after the loss of a pet or of a family member.

If you feel grief, tell someone. Helping others is another way to deal with grief. Exercise and writing are also good ways to cope with grief.

COMPARE AND CONTRAST Which do you think tells more about someone's feelings—words or body language? Why?

Myth and Fact

Myth: Any stress is bad for your health.
Fact: People need a certain amount of stress, called *eustress*, to do their best. However, too much stress, called *distress*, is not healthful.

▼ People's feelings show in their words and on their faces. Even young children can figure out other people's feelings through body language.

257

Controlling Your Feelings

Did You Know?

Self-control can also mean you choose what actions you will take in situations. Self-control involves making choices about what you will do or will not do. You do not have self-control if you let your friends make decisions for you.

Part of growing up is learning how to express your feelings responsibly. When you express feelings calmly, you have **self-control**. Like any skill, self-control takes practice.

For example, imagine that someone keeps teasing you at school. You begin to feel angry. Your face gets red, and your stomach hurts. Your hands curl into fists, and you feel like hitting. Finally you shout, "Stop that!" You might even call the teaser names.

You are out of control, and it's not a comfortable feeling. You can, however, learn how to manage your anger and stay in control. Then you can *choose* how to respond to your anger.

▼ Before you can manage anger, you must first calm down.

The steps shown can help you manage angry feelings and stay in control. You might use an "I" message to express your feelings. An "I" message tells someone how you feel without placing blame on him or her. You might say, "I feel very angry and I wish this would stop." You might also try acting as though the teasing doesn't bother you. Laughing or making light of it may cause the teaser to lose interest.

Another way to become responsible for yourself is to learn how to deal with uncomfortable feelings. When you are in control, you choose how you will express your feelings.

SEQUENCE What should you do before you express feelings of anger?

Steps for Anger Management

1. Stop what you are doing or saying.

2. Calm down by counting to ten or by taking long, slow breaths.

3. Think about what is happening.

4. Take action—either walk away or express your feelings calmly in "I" messages.

Lesson 3 Summary and Review

1 Summarize with Vocabulary

Use the vocabulary and other terms from this lesson to complete the statements.

People express their feelings with words and _____. Someone who has too much to do might feel _____. When a pet dies, you might feel _____. When you express feelings calmly, you have _____.

2 Critical Thinking Why is it important to know what you are feeling?

3 Identify types of physical or emotional abuse and ways that you could seek help from a parent or another trusted adult.

4 **MAIN IDEA AND DETAILS** Draw and complete this graphic organizer by providing two more details to explain the main idea.

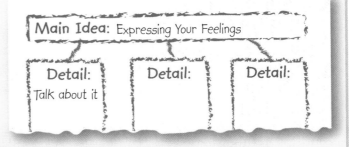

Main Idea: Expressing Your Feelings

Detail: Talk about it

Detail:

Detail:

5 Write to Express—Idea

Choose a song you like, and write about how it makes you feel. Include why you think the song makes you feel that way.

The Challenge of Friendship

Lesson Focus
Knowing how to solve conflicts and keep friends is a valuable skill.

Why Learn This?
The ideas in this lesson will help you be a true friend.

Vocabulary
conflict
conflict resolution
negotiate
compromise

▼ Friends can help you have self-respect.

The Value of Friends

Friends meet your social need to belong to a group. Friends, along with your family, encourage and support you.

You probably have several friends. Friendships often begin between people who share an interest or a goal. You might have friends in different places. For example, you might see some friends only at school. Others may be where you live.

You can express different parts of yourself through different friends. For example, your friends in art class may know you as a painter. Friends you skate with may know you as an athlete.

You and your friends may share the same feelings as well as the same goals and interests.

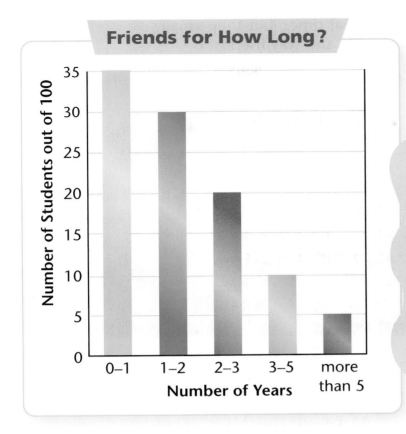

Friends for How Long?

Number of Students out of 100

35
30
25
20
15
10
5
0

0–1   1–2   2–3   3–5   more than 5

Number of Years

Quick Activity

Interpret a Graph
How long had the largest group of students known their friends? What else can you tell about friendships by studying the bar graph?

Some friendships last a lifetime. Some last only a day or two. Young people often make new friends as their interests change.

If a friend starts spending time with someone else, don't be sad. This is normal. You will probably find a new friend soon, too.

To find a friend quickly, join a club or group. Then you may find a friend who likes the same things you do. Maybe your school has a club you would like to join. You could find a friend there who likes to do things you do. Or you could join a sports team.

Making and keeping friends takes practice. Still, having friends is worth the effort. Just remember that to have a friend, you must be a friend.

CAUSE AND EFFECT Describe **some appropriate ways that you have used to make new friends.**

▼ **Friendships often start with sharing.**

Friends have conflicts at times, but they usually can resolve them fairly and stay friends.▼

ACTIVITY

Life Skills

Communicate

You have difficulty communicating with a friend who is deaf. Analyze your strengths and weaknesses. Then explain how improving your communication skills can demonstrate consideration for your friend.

Solving Conflicts with Friends

Do you and any of your friends ever get angry at one another? It is normal for friends to have conflicts at times. You cannot avoid them. A **conflict** is a disagreement that happens when people have different needs or wishes. You can learn how to resolve conflicts and remain friends by using conflict resolution. **Conflict resolution** (rez•uh•LOO•shuhn) is the solving of problems you and your friends may have. Learning to resolve conflicts can also help you when you are an adult. Following rules like those below can also help.

- Don't talk behind each other's backs.

- Tell the truth.

- Avoid hurtful comments and put-downs.

- Solve disagreements peacefully.

- Set up a time to talk about problems.

- Listen to each other carefully.

When you and your friends have problems, you can **negotiate** (nih•GOH•shee•ayt). That is, you can work together to resolve the conflict. You might decide on a compromise (KAHM•pruh•myz). A **compromise** is a kind of solution in which each side gives up some of what it wants.

Suppose you want to sit in the cafeteria with a new student at school. Your best friend wants just the two of you to sit together, as usual. You and your friend could negotiate and find a compromise. You might sit with the new student one day and with your best friend the next day. Maybe your best friend will join you and the new student. Many conflicts have a workable solution.

DRAW CONCLUSIONS How does finding a compromise help resolve conflicts?

Ways to Handle Disagreements

- Ignore small problems.
- Laugh at the problem together.
- Say you're sorry and forgive each other.
- If the problem is serious, you should both walk away. Maybe you can resolve the conflict later or ask an adult for help.

Quick **Activity**

Interpret Photographs What do you think these two friends are arguing about? How might they resolve this conflict?

Getting Help for Harassment

You and your friends can settle most of your conflicts. But at times when you both get angry it is good to seek the help of a parent or another trusted adult. Talking to an adult might help you think of a solution. Maybe an adult can help you both talk things out.

A situation that may require you to seek the help of a parent or trusted adult is harassment. *Harassment* is when someone teases or bothers you repeatedly in a hurtful way. An older person can offer help and suggestions on how to deal with harassment.

Your parents have had problems with friends, too. They may be able to help you with your problem. ▶

264

Someone who wants you to do things that make you uncomfortable is not a true friend. If he or she asks you to go against your values, talk with a parent or another trusted adult. It may be time to make new friends—friends who share your values.

There's nothing wrong with friends having different opinions. True friends respect each other. They can agree to disagree about things.

 MAIN IDEA AND DETAILS **What is harassment and how can you get help?**

A school counselor can help you sort out your feelings about a friendship.▶

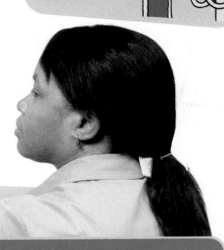

Lesson 4 Summary and Review

1 Summarize with Vocabulary

Use the vocabulary from this lesson to complete these statements.

A _____ is a disagreement between people. People can try to resolve conflicts through _____. When you work together to solve a problem, you _____. Sometimes you reach a _____, in which each side gives up some of what it wants.

2 Why is it normal for friends to have conflicts?

3 Critical Thinking Why is it important to stand up for your values, even if you lose a friend?

4 **MAIN IDEA AND DETAILS** Draw and complete this graphic organizer. In the boxes, name three places where you could find a friend.

Main Idea: Friends are everywhere

Detail: | Detail: | Detail:

5 Write to Inform—How-To

Describe the qualities of a good friend.

Resolve Conflicts
At School

Every day you face conflicts. It's easy to become angry, but you can use the steps for **Resolving Conflicts** to settle conflicts peacefully.

Joe wants to use the classroom computer, but Ashley is using it. They are both working on reports that must be finished in class before lunch.

1 **Use "I" messages to tell how you feel.**

2 **Listen to each other. Consider the other person's point of view.**

Joe says, "Ashley, I'm worried. I have to get my report done. I need to use the computer now."

Ashley says, "I have to finish my report, too. I was here first. You can use the computer later."

3 Ask for a mediator. A mediator is someone who listens to both sides of a problem and helps find a fair solution.

4 Find a way for both sides to win.

Joe says, "That won't help. Let's ask Ms. Williams what to do." Ashley agrees. They ask their teacher to act as mediator.

Ms. Williams suggests a schedule. Ashley will use the computer for an hour, and then Joe will use it. Both of them are happy with that.

Problem Solving

Joe and Ashley resolved their conflict even though Ashley is deaf. Ashley reads Joe's lips. Joe understands Ashley's signing.

Suppose you were working on a project with a student who is deaf. In what ways could you communicate with the student? Describe how this would demonstrate consideration for the student.

Working with Others

Lesson Focus
Part of growing up is learning how to work respectfully with others.

Why Learn This?
Respecting differences helps you get along with others.

Vocabulary
compassion
role model

Understanding Others

Imagine going to a school where no one makes fun of you. No one teases you for getting glasses or a new haircut. New students are welcomed. Someone with a *disability* (dis•uh•BIL•uh•tee), a physical or mental impairment, is included in groups and activities.

How can you help make a school like that? You can help by keeping an open mind. You can show respect and compassion for others. When you have **compassion** (kuhm•PASH•uhn), you understand the needs and feelings of others. You help someone who is having a bad day because you know how that can feel.

DRAW CONCLUSIONS How can showing compassion help friends feel good about themselves?

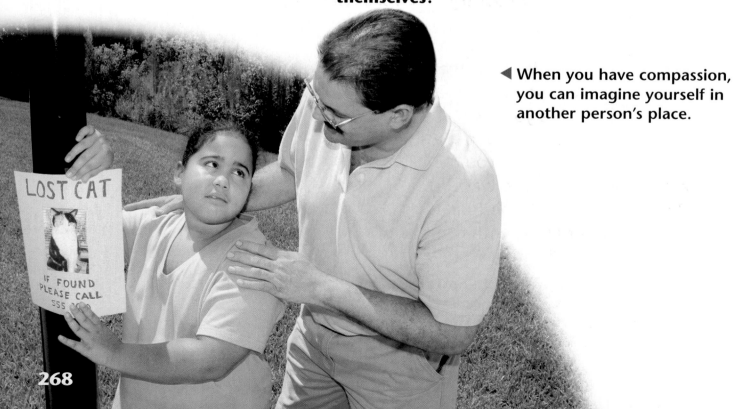

◀ When you have compassion, you can imagine yourself in another person's place.

268

▲ We can see some of our differences. However, many differences do not show on the outside.

Dealing with Differences

You might feel nervous when you first meet someone who is different from you. Perhaps he or she is from another country or speaks with an accent. Maybe the person has a problem speaking or has trouble saying some words. If you listen closely, you may understand the words. You can ask questions to see if you understand. For example, you might ask, "Are you looking for the cafeteria?"

Besides these examples, people may be different in other ways. The more you get to know others, the more you will notice ways you are all the same.

You do not have to be friends with everyone. Still, you can get along with others and respect their right to be different from you.

Did You Know?

By the year 2050, almost half the people living in the United States will be Hispanic, African American, Asian, or from the Pacific Islands.

CAUSE AND EFFECT How might someone with a speech defect or someone who does not speak English feel if you took the time to speak with him or her?

269

Making a Difference

You can make a difference in your home, at school, and in your community. You might not make the news. But you and the people you help will know what you do.

You can make a difference at home. If you have younger brothers or sisters, you know that they might cry or scream to demand things. You can teach them to get attention in other ways. You can practice listening and find ways to be helpful. When you respect your family's rules, you show that you are responsible and caring.

You can make a difference at school, too. You can show compassion and respect for other students and for teachers. Try seeing things from their points of view.

Quick Activity

Interpret Photographs Look at these pictures of ways students make a difference. Then write three ways that you can make a difference in your community.

270

At school, you can make sure that everyone is included in activities. You can welcome new students and discourage hurtful teasing. You can help keep the classrooms and other areas clean. By doing these things and encouraging others to do the same, you show respect for your school, the people in it, and yourself.

You can also make a difference in your community. Visit people in care centers, or volunteer to help in youth programs. You can make a difference all by yourself. You already have the skills you need!

 MAIN IDEA AND DETAILS Explain the three important points made on these two pages.

Personal Health Plan ▶

Real-Life Situation
Suppose you want to be more of a help at home.
Real-Life Plan
Write a plan that you can follow to help you meet this goal.

Setting an Example

When you make a difference, you serve as a role model. A **role model** is someone who sets a good example. When you set a good example, you encourage others to do the same, and they can make a difference, too. Another way you can make a difference is by not being a member of a clique. A *clique* (KLEEK) is a group that excludes other people.

Some adults also serve as role models. By observing how they behave, you can learn to be honest, to follow rules and laws, and to respect others. Some adults are role models because they make healthful choices about food, exercise, and safety. You can encourage others by being a positive role model. How many people did you encourage today?

SUMMARIZE Why should young people set good examples?

Lesson 5 Summary and Review

❶ **Summarize with Vocabulary**

Use vocabulary and other terms from the lesson to complete these statements.

When we try to understand others' needs and feelings, we show ____. Some students face challenges because they have a physical or mental ____. When we try to make a difference, we serve as a ____.

❷ "The more you learn, the less you fear." How does this statement relate to respecting differences?

❸ **Critical Thinking** Explain why you would not be a good role model if you were a member of a clique.

❹ (Focus Skill) **MAIN IDEA AND DETAILS** Draw and complete this graphic organizer by adding three ways to show compassion.

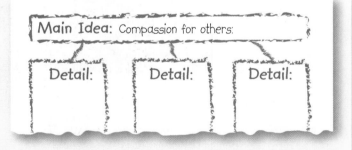

Main Idea: Compassion for others:

Detail: Detail: Detail:

❺ **Write to Express—Business Letter**

How could your community be more compassionate to people, such as the elderly or the disabled? Explain your idea in a letter to the editor of your local newspaper.

272

Caring

Being a Good Friend

How can you be a good friend? The most important thing to remember is to treat others as you want them to treat you. Here are some things you can do.

- **Communicate clearly, share your feelings, and encourage your friend to share his or hers. This is important when you have a disagreement. Explain your point of view, and then listen to your friend's viewpoint.**

- **Show compassion, if your friend is having a bad day. Use your best listening skills. Sometimes you can show support just by being there.**

- **Show respect. Your friend has a right to disagree, just as you have a right to your own opinion.**

- **Take responsibility for your words and actions. If you have accidentally hurt your friend's feelings, apologize. Be ready to forgive if your friend has hurt you.**

- **Be open-minded. Are you passing up a really good friend because he or she is different from you in some way?**

Activity

Keep a friendship journal. Every night for two weeks, write down the ways you showed friendship that day. Did you invite a new student to eat with you at lunch? Did you find a way for a friend who has a disability to be a part of your basketball game? You can be caring at home, too. After two weeks, review your journal. Describe how your observations helped contribute to self-confidence and self-esteem.

Dealing with Peer Pressure

Lesson Focus

Knowing how to recognize the two kinds of peer pressure can help you know how to respond to peer pressure.

Why Learn This?

When you resist negative peer pressure, you help build a strong self-concept. You also encourage your friends to do the same.

Kinds of Peer Pressure

In Chapter 8, you learned that *peer pressure* is the strong influence someone your own age can have on you. Remember that peer pressure is *negative* if someone wants you to do something you know is wrong. For example, someone wants you to let him or her look at your paper during a test.

Peer pressure can be *positive*, too. For example, some friends may want you to help collect food for a food drive. Positive peer pressure doesn't ask you to do something wrong. It helps you build a strong self-concept. A strong self-concept can help you resist negative peer pressure.

▼ Did you ever invite friends to join you in a fun, healthful game or sport? If you did, you used positive peer pressure.

How do you deal with peer pressure? First, determine if it is positive or negative pressure. You might ask yourself these questions:

- Does this activity go against my values?
- Would my parents approve?
- What might happen if I do this?
- How will I feel about myself afterward?
- Is this something I want to do?

After you answer these questions, you will know if you should say "Let's do it!" or "No way!"

COMPARE AND CONTRAST **What is the difference between positive and negative peer pressure?**

Health & Technology

Pocket Keyboard Staying in touch with friends is getting easier. Soon you may be able to fold up a full-size keyboard for your cell phone and put it in your pocket. Wires can now be woven into cloth. The cloth can then be made into a keyboard.

"We'll have fun!"

"Just try it!"

"Let's play!"

▲ When a friend asks you to do something, think before you respond. Someone who wants you to do something harmful is not really your friend.

Saying *No*

How can you say *no* to negative peer pressure? Sometimes friends just need you to set an example. Suggest a more healthful activity. They may go along with your idea.

You might tell why you won't do the harmful activity. For example, "It's not safe to swim without a lifeguard." You could make a joke. Say, "I can't believe you want to do that!" If they still want to do something harmful, walk away.

Do not give in to negative peer pressure. Your friends will admire your courage. Use positive peer pressure. True friends will respect you for it!

SEQUENCE You have refused several times to go along with something harmful. Now what should you do?

▼ You can use peer pressure to encourage your friends to do their best.

Lesson 6 Summary and Review

❶ Summarize with Vocabulary

Use the terms from this lesson to complete these statements.

_____ is getting someone your age to do something. _____ peer pressure is encouraging a friend to study. You should say _____ to _____ peer pressure.

❷ Why might people think all peer pressure is bad?

❸ Critical Thinking Why might it be hard to resist negative peer pressure?

❹ (Focus Skill) MAIN IDEA AND DETAILS Draw and complete this graphic organizer to show examples of positive peer pressure. Do not use examples from the lesson.

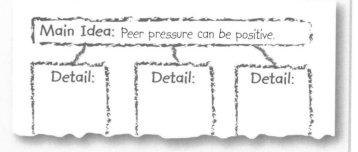

Main Idea: Peer pressure can be positive.

Detail: Detail: Detail:

❺ Write to Inform—How-To

Explain how you might use peer pressure to ask a friend to do something positive.

ACTIVITIES

Science

Plants Have Needs Like you, plants have needs. Do some research to find out about some of the needs of plants. Then do an experiment to see for yourself. Select three plants of the same type and size. Put each plant in a different environment in your home. Observe and compare their growth after a month.

Physical Education

Reducing Stress Pick a partner and find out about exercises that can help reduce stress. Consider talking to a physical education teacher for ideas. Then share what you have learned with the rest of the class. One partner could explain what the other is demonstrating. Then you could switch roles.

Technology Project

Make an outline of the main ideas and the important details of this chapter. Use a computer to make slides of the outline, if possible. Or make colorful posters of your outline.

GO ONLINE **For more activities**, visit **The Learning Site.** www.harcourtschool.com/health

Home & Community

Communicating Share what you have learned about resolving conflicts. Make a poster to show at least four ways to resolve conflicts with friends. Display your poster in a hallway outside your classroom, in the media center, or at home for your family.

Career Link

School Counselor Suppose you are the counselor in your school. A teacher has sent Benjamin to you. Other students are upset because Benjamin keeps teasing them. Benjamin does not understand why the other students are making such a big deal out of it. Explain how you would help settle this conflict.

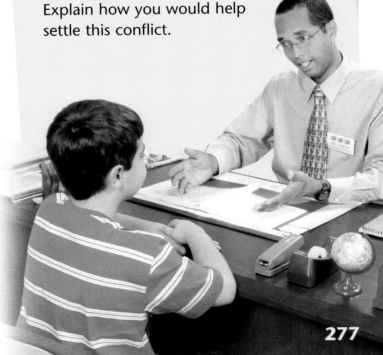

Chapter Review and Test Preparation

 Reading Skill

MAIN IDEA AND DETAILS

Draw and then use this graphic organizer to answer questions 1 and 2.

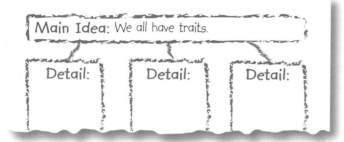

1 Write a different trait in each box.

2 Label each trait as *physical*, *mental*, *emotional*, or *social*.

 Use Vocabulary

Match each term in Column B with its meaning in Column A.

Column A	Column B
3 Feeling sure of yourself	**A** compromise
4 Ability to express feelings calmly	**B** self-control
5 Time by yourself	**C** role model
6 Someone who sets a good example	**D** self-confidence
7 A solution in which each side gives up some of what it wants	**E** disability
8 A physical or mental impairment	**F** privacy

 Check Understanding

Choose the letter of the correct answer.

9 What must you meet in order to stay healthy? (p. 252)

   A goals

   B basic needs

   C wants

   D role models

10 Being shy is a _____. (p. 248)

   F need

   G want

   H trait

   J goal

11 What is the older boy showing? (p. 268)

   A self-confidence

   B peer pressure

   C conflict resolution

   D compassion

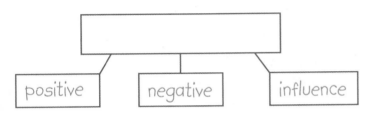

```
┌─────────────────────┐
│                     │
└──┬───────┬───────┬──┘
   │       │       │
┌──┴──┐ ┌──┴───┐ ┌─┴────────┐
│positive│ │negative│ │influence│
└─────┘ └──────┘ └──────────┘
```

12 Which term goes in the top box?
(p. 274)

F peer pressure

G conflict resolution

H basic needs

J compromise

13 Which of these is **NOT** a step in conflict resolution? (pp. 266–267)

A Explain how you feel.

B Laugh at the other person.

C Listen to the other person.

D Find a way for both sides to win.

14 Your brother has just grabbed the last cookie, and you tell him it was yours. You are having a _____. (p. 262)

F compromise   **H** conflict

G compassion   **J** conflict resolution

15 A classmate says that he will write the group's report if you present it to the class. He is trying to _____ with you. (p. 263)

A negotiate   **C** respect

B conflict   **D** joke

Think Critically

16 Describe a time when a person might lose self-control. How could that person stay in control?

17 Describe something a friend might encourage you to do. How can you decide if this peer pressure is positive or negative?

Apply Skills

18 **BUILDING GOOD CHARACTER**
Caring A classmate is teasing another student about his new shoes. How can you show this boy that you are a friend?

19 **LIFE SKILLS**
Resolve Conflicts Suppose that you and your friend want to play a sport together after school, but you each like a different sport. How could you resolve this conflict peacefully?

Write About Health

20 **Write to Inform—Explanation** Explain why young people need to learn how to use self-control when expressing their feelings.

279

11 Families Together

SUMMARIZE A summary is a short statement that includes the main ideas and most important details in a passage. Use the Reading in Health Handbook on pages 340–341 and this graphic organizer to help you remember the main points as you read this chapter.

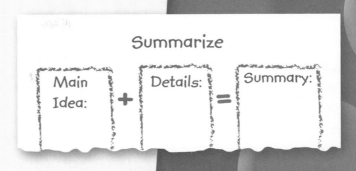

Summarize

| Main Idea: | + | Details: | = | Summary: |

Health Graph

INTERPRET DATA Today many American adults are living in families with their own children, with children who are not related, without children, or with other relatives. Of 100 American families surveyed, how many were traditional married couples with their own children?

U.S. Families and Households

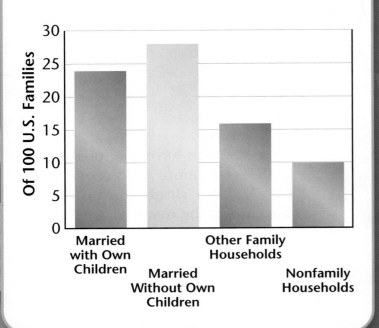

Daily Physical Activity

Find ways that you and your family can stay active for healthful living.

 **Be Active!**
Use the selection Track 11, **Funky Flex**, to practice exercises you can share with your family.

Families Meet Their Needs

Lesson Focus

Families are different from one another. It is in families that most people's basic needs are met.

Why Learn This?

Family life runs more smoothly when all family members find ways to respect and appreciate one another.

Vocabulary

traditions
nuclear family
single-parent family
blended family
extended family

Types of Families

Families can differ in many ways. Almost all families help meet the needs of their members. You get food, clothes, a place to sleep, and other things from your family. Family members take care of you and make sure you are safe. When you are afraid or sad, family members protect and help you. Most parents try hard to make a safe and loving home for their children.

Some families have **traditions** (trah·DIHSH·unz), or customs family members follow. Traditions are part of the way a family celebrates holidays and special occasions.

Some families have a mother, a father, and one or more children. This type of family is called a **nuclear family**.

Some families have only one parent with one or more children. Children may live in a **single-parent family** because of the death of a parent or because their parents are divorced.

Grandparents pass down traditions to their children and grandchildren. Traditions help keep family members close together.

A nuclear family includes two parents and their children. But some children do not grow up with both of their natural parents. Some children may grow up with only one parent, in a single-parent family.

Sometimes two single parents marry and form a blended family. Their children become part of the new family. The new parent is a stepparent, and the children become stepsisters or stepbrothers.

Other children live in extended families. These families may include other close relatives, such as grandparents, aunts, uncles, or cousins.

★ **SUMMARIZE** **What are the types of families?**
Focus Skill

Did You Know?

Extended families may become more common as Americans live longer. Population projections for the year 2010 estimate that there will be about 131,000 Americans over the age of 100!

Quick Activity

Think About Families Look at the pictures on these pages. Make a table listing the ways these families are alike and different.

An **extended family** often has many members. Besides parents and children, there may be grandparents, cousins, uncles, and aunts.

When two single parents get married, they create a **blended family**. Each parent's child or children are now part of the blended family.

283

When your parents are busy, a grandparent may be able to help you. ▶

ACTIVITY

Building Good Character

Caring Emil's mother has had a baby and just returned home from the hospital. Write a paragraph describing ways Emil can help out and show that he cares.

The Roles of Family Members

All family members are important, including you. Each family member has a different role. A parent's main role is to support and take care of the children in the family. Your main role is to learn to be a responsible family member.

Family members' roles may change over time. When you were a baby, your family had to do everything for you. Now you are older and can do things to help the family. If there is a new baby in the family, you become an older brother or sister. You may then have to do chores or jobs to help out.

▼ A new baby does not replace other children.

▼ Parents love you just as much as they always have.

Members of a family also respect each other. When you respect family members, you value them for who they are. They value you, too.

Think about your family. What is special about each person in it? What roles does each person have? Do you help by taking out the trash? Does your older sister or brother help take care of a new baby?

Everyone's role in a family changes over time. Everyone gets older. Everyone has new things to do. Through it all, you and your family members can love, respect, and support one another in all you experience together.

COMPARE AND CONTRAST What is your role in your family? How will it change as you get older? Make a chart to compare your role now with your role when you were younger.

Health & Technology

Keeping in Touch It is sometimes difficult to keep a family together during outings. One way some families have found to keep in touch and to communicate is through the use of inexpensive shortwave radios. These pocket-size radios run on batteries and can act as a pager and as a walkie-talkie. Some of these devices have a range of up to 5 miles.

▼ Having fun together is one role everyone in a family can enjoy.

285

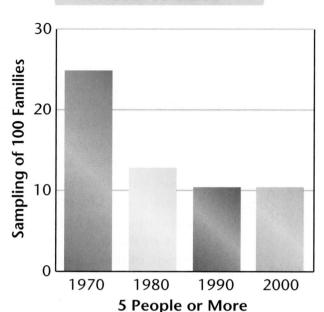

Size of Households 1970 to 2000

Sampling of 100 Families

30
20
10
0

1970　1980　1990　2000

5 People or More

In what year was the number of families with five or more people the greatest?

Benefits of Extended Families

When you live in an extended family, you have grandparents or other adult relatives you can talk to. When you need encouragement and help with problems, they can help. Relatives can teach you things and tell you stories.

You may live with cousins who are close to your age. They can help with chores and be there to play with and share feelings with. Living in an extended family can be interesting and fun. Extended families can give you a lot of support.

CAUSE AND EFFECT Make a list of reasons the roles of family members change. Write what the changes are.

Lesson 1 Summary and Review

❶ Summarize with Vocabulary

Use vocabulary from the lesson to complete the statements.

A _____ has a mother, father, and children. Some people live in an _____ with grandparents, aunts, or uncles. Others live with only one parent in a _____. Children who have stepparents live in a _____. No matter what kind of family you live in, you likely have _____ you follow, especially when you celebrate holidays.

❷ Critical Thinking What do nearly all families have in common?

❸ What roles do different family members have in a family?

❹ SUMMARIZE Draw and complete this graphic organizer to show the roles a child has in a family over time.

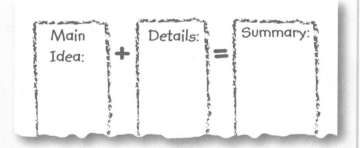

Main Idea: + Details: = Summary:

❺ Write to Inform—Description

Think about how you will change over the years. What will you be like when you are older—in middle school, high school, and then college? Write how you think your role in your family will change at each new time in your life.

286

Fairness

Not Taking Advantage of Others

Family members help one another in different ways. Children often help prepare meals, set the table, or wash the dishes after dinner.

When all family members are fair and help out cheerfully, everyone gets along. If family members try to avoid doing their share, arguments may start. A family member who doesn't help out is taking advantage of others in the family. He or she is not showing respect for other family members.

Sharing family responsibilities is fair to everyone. Here's how you can do your part.

- **Do your family chores cheerfully, knowing you are helping the people who care about you.**

- **Do your chores when they should be done, without having to be asked or reminded.**

- **If you see something that needs to be done, offer to do it. Don't hope someone else will do it instead.**

- **Don't avoid your chores by watching TV, playing video games, or going to a friend's house.**

- **If your brothers or sisters don't do their chores, don't fight with them. Explain to them that helping out shows respect for family members. Explain that avoiding or refusing to do their share takes advantage of others. Someone else will then have to do more than his or her share.**

Activity

Practice fairness by role-playing the following situation with your family. Your older brother is watching a show on TV instead of preparing dinner, which he is supposed to do. Your mom is due home soon. You know she'll be upset. What do you say to your brother? What can you do to help?

Families Communicate

Ways Families Communicate

When family members communicate, or talk with one another, they feel closer to one another.

Family members support one another. Try talking to your parents, brothers, and sisters about your feelings. Tell them about the good things that happen to you in school or with friends. Tell about things that make you sad or worried. Often, a family member can help you solve a problem.

For example, talk with your parents about your report card. Maybe you did not do as well as you had hoped in one subject. Your parents can work with you to help you do better.

▼ Whether you have good news or bad news, share it with your parents. Your parents are there to help you.

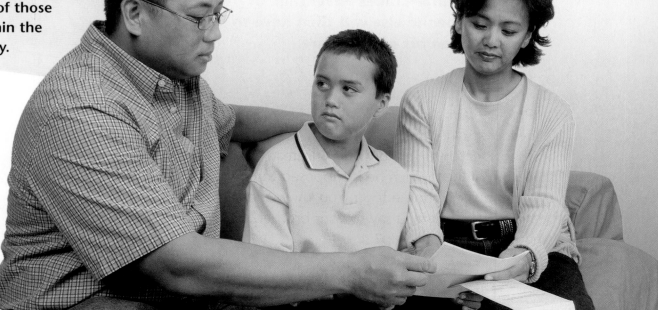

When you share your problems and feelings with your parents, you are communicating with them. You are showing them that you love and trust them.

Show family members you appreciate them. Thanking a family member helps you make him or her feel appreciated.

Sometimes family members are very busy and have little time together. You can share your feelings or your news by writing notes or letters.

Actions are also a form of communication. Doing a favor for a family member shows that you care. The way you act toward others affects the way they act toward you. When you are nice to family members, you encourage them to be nice to you. That helps the whole family.

MAIN IDEA AND DETAILS **Why is communication important in families? List some ways family members communicate.**

Quick Activity

Write a Letter Write a letter to someone in your family. In your letter, describe something special that has happened in school.

Family Relationships

In Chapter 8 you learned that *peer pressure* is the strong influence someone your own age can have on you. Peer pressure can sometimes be negative and hard to resist. One way to deal with peer pressure is to ask for advice from a parent, a grandparent, or another adult. He or she may have good advice about how you can resist peer pressure.

Sometimes what your friends want you to do may not be what your family thinks is right. As a family member, you need to consider your family's wishes and rules.

If you have a problem or are unsure about something, talk with your parents. They care about you and can give you good advice you can trust.

Your family cares about you. When you are torn between your family's expectations and your friends' wishes, talk to your parents about your feelings. ▶

What should you do when a family member does something that makes you angry? Take a deep breath. Try to relax and stay calm. Learning to control your anger can be very difficult, and it takes time.

Try talking or writing a note to the person. Communicating your feelings may help prevent an argument. Tell your family member how you feel. This shows that you trust him or her and want to get along.

If you keep cool and communicate honestly with family members, you'll settle conflicts more easily. Afterward, do a special favor for a member of your family to show that you care.

SEQUENCE What steps would you take to resolve the conflict when a family member has made you angry? Give the steps in order.

Ways Families Communicate

- Express your feelings to family members.
- Show you care.
- Do something special.
- Write letters or notes.
- Plan activities together.

Lesson 2 Summary and Review

1 Summarize with Vocabulary

Use terms from this lesson to complete the statements.

You should resist _____ when it may lead you to do something you don't want to do. There are many ways to _____, including talking, writing notes, and doing things together.

2 Critical Thinking How can you show family members that you appreciate them?

3 What are three ways you can communicate your feelings to members of your family?

4 **SUMMARIZE** Draw and complete this graphic organizer to show ways being a good listener helps you improve communication among the members of your family.

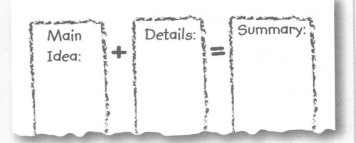

| Main Idea: | + | Details: | = | Summary: |

5 Write to Inform—How-To

Write a paragraph to a younger sister or brother. Tell her or him what to do to practice controlling anger, both with friends and with family members.

291

COMMUNICATE
With Your Family

Family members need to respect one another. Working on communication skills will help you get along with your family. Using the steps for **Communicating** will help you improve your skills.

Katrina and her new friend call each other every evening. Katrina's family has put a ten-minute limit on phone conversations. Katrina doesn't think this new rule is fair. What should she do?

1 Understand your audience.

Katrina knows that she needs to talk to the whole family about the phone rules. She asks her dad to plan a family meeting.

2 Give a clear message.

Katrina tells her family that she and her new friend don't have enough time to talk at school. She explains that ten minutes isn't long enough to say everything she wants to say.

Listen carefully, and answer any questions.

"If the phone is always busy, we might miss important calls," Katrina's mom explains.
"I need to use the phone to plan my activities, too," says her brother.

4 **Gather feedback.**

Katrina realizes that everyone else feels the rule is fair, so she agrees to the ten-minute limit. Then the family thinks of other ways Katrina can spend more time with her friend.

 # Problem Solving

Matt shares a room with his brother Dan. Sometimes Dan goes to play with friends and leaves the room in a mess. Matt finds it hard to do his homework when the room is a mess. He is really upset.

Use the steps for **Communicating** to help Matt solve his problem. What would you suggest Matt do to help Dan be more responsible?

How You Learn from Your Family

Family members care about you and teach you values (VAL•yooz). **Values** are strong beliefs about how people should behave and live.

Families pass down values from earlier generations (jen•er•AY•shunz), family members who came before. These include parents, grandparents, and great-grandparents.

Family members may teach you to be honest, kind, generous, and helpful. They may teach you to do things that help keep you safe and healthy. These values are shared by people everywhere.

CARING

A caring person understands other people and offers to help them whenever possible.

TRUSTWORTHINESS

FAIRNESS

When you are trustworthy, people know that you are honest and truthful.

When you treat people fairly, you show that you value them and that you know right from wrong.

RESPECT

Helping people is one way of showing respect.

CITIZENSHIP

Being a good citizen means respecting your country.

RESPONSIBILITY

Everyone in a family should take some responsibility for helping out with family chores.

Learning and practicing these values help you get along with other people. Parents and grandparents don't always use words to teach values. Sometimes they teach by example. This means that you learn values from seeing how they behave.

If your grandparents are always honest and fair, you will probably grow up to be that way. If your mother is always kind to others, you will learn the value of kindness. If your father works hard to do a job well, you could learn to take pride in doing your best.

Parents teach children to be responsible family members. Your family can teach you many important and helpful values.

MAIN IDEA AND DETAILS **What does it mean to teach by example? Describe some values that you can learn this way.**

ACTIVITY

Life Skills
Resolve Conflict

Suppose you and your family are planning to spend a day together. You disagree on what to do. What steps can you take to help your family choose an activity that satisfies everyone? For help, see the steps to Resolve Conflicts on pages 146–147.

Families can work together to help others in the community.▼

▲ Helping with projects is a way families cooperate and have fun.

Personal Health Plan ▶

Real-Life Situation
Suppose you have to study for a test, practice for a school team game, and write a school report—all in two days.

Real-Life Plan
Write a step-by-step plan that describes how you would handle all this. Use the steps for Managing Stress on pages 10–11.

How Families Work Together

You and your family will spend many years together. It's important for everyone in the family to cooperate with each other. When you **cooperate** (koh•AHP•er•ayt) with others, you work with them and help them. For example, if you do your chores, you are cooperating with your family. You are also showing them that they can depend on you.

Families cooperate in many ways. You may work together on projects to make your home look better. Together, you may help others in your community. Even having fun together is a way of cooperating. Everyone has a good time when all family members try to get along.

When you all cooperate, doing what needs to be done can be fun.▼

▲ Playing together is another way a family can spend time together.

Quick Activity

Plan Family Fun Make a list of activities you and your family could do together. Include activities that you think each person in your family could do and would enjoy.

When you cooperate, you show family members you respect them. For example, when you ask your brother if you may borrow his bike, you are showing him respect.

Families that cooperate have less conflict and stress. So family members are happier and healthier. When a conflict arises, family members can talk it over and solve the problem more easily.

If you have a problem, share your feelings with your parents. They have lots of life experience and can help with your problem.

SUMMARIZE What are three ways family members can cooperate?

Why Rules Are Important

People sometimes groan when they hear the word *rules*. But rules are important in a family. Like values, they help people learn what's important and how to behave. They can also help keep people safe from harm or injury.

If everyone follows the rules, family members get along well together. Family life can be a more enjoyable experience.

DRAW CONCLUSIONS **Why is family life happier when everyone follows the rules?**

Lesson 3 Summary and Review

❶ Summarize with Vocabulary

Use vocabulary and other terms from this lesson to complete the statements.

Parents often teach _____, such as respect, by example. They pass on values from people in earlier _____. Being able to _____ with others helps you work well with people.

❷ Why might rules about healthful behavior at home lead a child to have good health habits throughout life?

❸ Critical Thinking Why is there less conflict in a family in which everyone cooperates and works together?

❹ (Focus Skill) SUMMARIZE Draw and complete this graphic organizer to show three values that parents or other adults teach children.

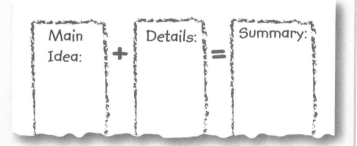

Main Idea: + Details: = Summary:

❺ Write to Inform—Explanation

Children learn many values from their parents. Choose one value you think is especially important. Write an essay explaining why you think this value is important. Use examples in your writing.

ACTIVITIES

 **Art**

Your Gift On your own, make a poster showing what you give to members of your family. It might be a love of shooting basketballs, patience, a sense of humor, or a talent in art. Think also of some of the ways that you are a help to other members of your family.

 Language Arts

Family Traditions Look in the library for books about family traditions. Find out about how some of these traditions were started. Then write about one of the traditions, and share with the class what you learned.

 Technology Project

Make an outline that lists important points about families from this chapter. Use a computer, if one is available, to make a presentation that includes your outline and pictures that show these important points. If you don't have a computer, make a colorful poster of your outline, with pictures.

 For more activities, visit **The Learning Site.** **www.harcourtschool.com/health**

 Home & Community

Communicating Make a bulletin board out of cork or cardboard to help family members communicate with one another. Decorate the bulletin board, and write a title above it, such as "Family Notes." Leave notepaper, a pencil, and tacks or tape near the bulletin board so family members can write and post messages to one another. With your parents' permission, attach the bulletin board to a wall in the kitchen or somewhere everyone can see and use it.

Career Link

Family Counselor At one time or another, every family has problems or conflicts. Sometimes families need someone to help them solve their problems. A family counselor is a professional who understands families and the problems they face. Suppose you are a family counselor. Write a paragraph explaining how you would advise family members on how to handle and resolve conflicts.

Reading Skill

SUMMARIZE

Draw and then use this graphic organizer to answer questions 1 and 2.

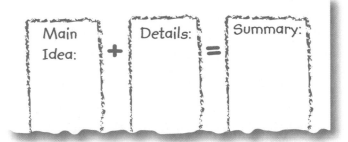

| Main Idea: | + | Details: | = | Summary: |

1 Write the main idea and details of how family members communicate.

2 Write values that make communicating with family members easy and useful.

Use Vocabulary

Match each term in Column B with its meaning in Column A.

Column A	Column B
3 Strong beliefs about how people should behave	**A** traditions
4 The influence of friends to get you to do things you don't want to do	**B** peer pressure
	C cooperate
5 A family that forms when two single parents marry	**D** extended family
6 Family customs	**E** values
7 To work with others	**F** blended family
8 A family of parents, children, and grandparents or other relatives	

 ## Check Understanding

Choose the letter of the correct answer.

9 Which of the pictures below shows family members communicating well? (p. 289)

A   **C**

B    **D**

10 The things that family members do are known as their _____. (p. 284)

  F needs   **H** homes
  G traditions   **J** roles

11 As you grow older, how does your role in your family change? (p. 284)

  A You no longer have to obey adults.
  B You can boss around the younger children.
  C You can stay up later at night.
  D You have more responsibilities.

12 Which of the following is a rule that parents make to maintain their children's good health? (p. 298)

  F Always say thank you.
  G Brush your teeth after meals.
  H Be a good listener.
  J Remember family stories.

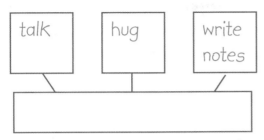

13 Which of the following words belongs in the empty box in the graphic organizer above? (pp. 288–289)
A communicate
B chores
C responsible
D proud

14 Two parents and their children are an example of _____. (pp. 282–283)
F an extended family
G a nuclear family
H a single-parent family
J a blended family

Think Critically

15 Getting enough sleep is important for good health. Young children must go to bed earlier than older children. What can you conclude about the need for healthful sleep at different ages?

16 How does cooperation help family members avoid conflict? Use one example in your answer.

17 If your mother had another baby, how would that change your role in your family? Give an example.

Apply Skills

18 **BUILDING GOOD CHARACTER**
Fairness You have just eaten a snack and put your dirty dishes in the sink. It's a family rule that everyone wash his or her dishes and not leave them in the sink. You have to study for an important test at school tomorrow, so you don't want to spend time washing the dishes you used. Anyway, your mother will probably wash them when she gets home from work. Should you wash your dishes, or should you leave them so you can study? Explain your decision.

19 **LIFE SKILLS**
Communicate Without asking your permission, your older sister took your CD player to a party. You are so angry, you don't know what to do. What is the best way to handle this situation? Whom should you tell about your feelings, and how should you describe the situation?

Write About Health

20 **Write to Inform—Explanation** Your parents said you could not go to a party on Friday night, even though they let your older brother go to weekend parties. You are very upset. Write a letter to a parent, explaining how you feel and asking if you can talk together about the situation.

CHAPTER 12

Living in a Healthful Community

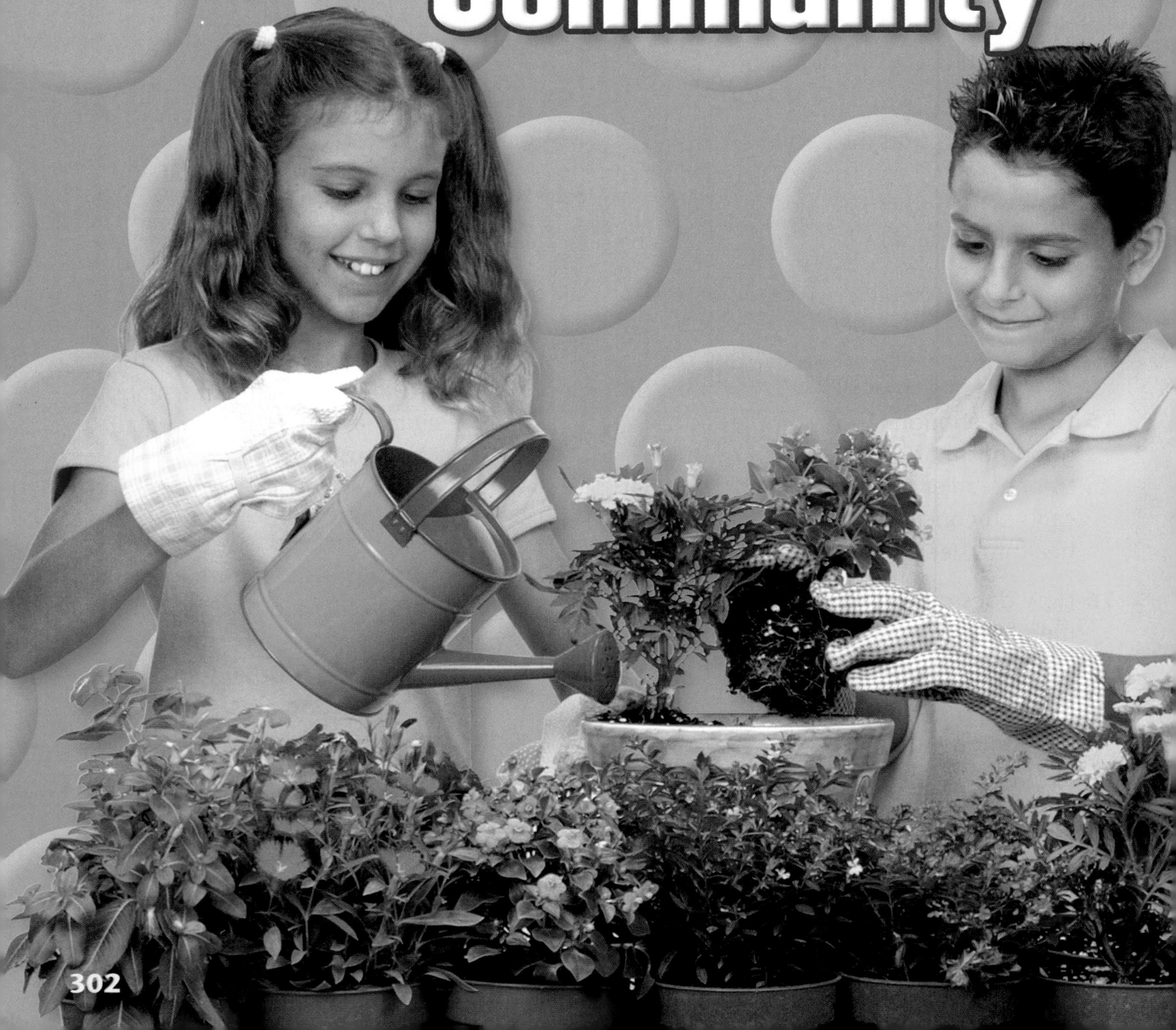

DRAW CONCLUSIONS Sometimes authors don't supply all the information. You have to use information from the passage plus what you already know to draw a conclusion. Use the Reading in Health Handbook on pages 332–333 and this graphic organizer to help you read the health facts in this chapter.

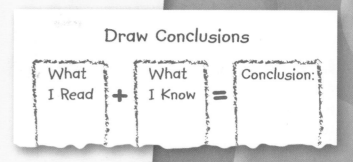

Draw Conclusions

| What I Read | + | What I Know | = | Conclusion: |

Health Graph

INTERPRET DATA Much lumber from trees is used in the United States. The circle graph shows softwood lumber use for a recent year. What were the top three uses for softwood lumber? What used the most softwood lumber in that year?

U.S. Softwood Lumber Consumption

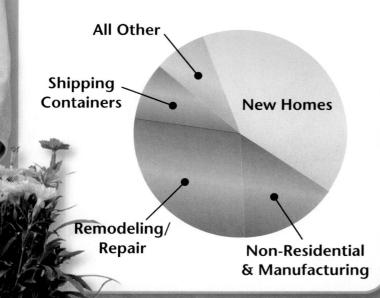

All Other

Shipping Containers

New Homes

Remodeling/ Repair

Non-Residential & Manufacturing

Daily Physical Activity

Live a healthful lifestyle. Exercise and be active in your community.

Be Active!
Use the selection Track 12, **Broadway Bound**, to share some exercise time with your classroom community.

Enjoying a Healthful Environment

Lesson Focus

A clean environment is important to your health.

Why Learn This?

You can use what you learn to enjoy your community in healthful ways.

Vocabulary

environment

A Healthful Environment

Your **environment** (en•vy•ruhn•muhnt) is made up of all the living and nonliving things that surround you. It includes plants, animals, air, water, soil, and even roads and buildings. A clean, healthful environment is important to your health. If your environment is dirty, you could become ill.

To stay healthy, people need to breathe clean air. Dirty air contains particles as well as harmful chemicals that can damage the lungs. Many people get asthma and other respiratory diseases from breathing dirty air.

Clean water is also extremely important for your health. People who drink water that has harmful chemicals or bacteria in it can become very ill and can even die.

Clean land, too, is important in many ways. We need it to grow healthful foods to feed ourselves and to feed animals. Plants that are grown on dirty land can become sick, unhealthful, or even poisonous. It is also important to keep land clean because most of our drinking water flows over the land or through the soil.

 DRAW CONCLUSIONS **What might happen to a person who lives in a dirty environment over a long period of time?**

In what ways does a park make a city a nicer place to live in? ▼

Healthful Community Activities

A healthful environment is important not just for your body. It is also important for your mental health. One way people enjoy a healthful environment is through outdoor *recreation* (rek•ree•AY•shuhn). Recreation is what you do to have fun or relax.

Cities and rural communities offer many forms of recreation. Many schools have playgrounds, softball fields, and basketball or tennis courts. A river, a lake, or a pond can be used for water sports such as swimming and fishing. Many people also enjoy other outdoor activities, such as gardening.

There are many good forms of recreation. ▶

Recreation areas can be added to a community. For example, railroad tracks no longer in use can be changed into trails for hiking and biking. Workers remove the old railroad tracks and change the land into a trail.

There are different kinds of rail-trails. In Boston, the Minuteman Trail takes people along a route that soldiers followed during the Revolutionary War. In Wisconsin, the Sugar Trail leads hikers through small towns and farms.

Some other kinds of trails are nature trails and exercise and fitness trails. Some trails go over water on boardwalks, while on still others, users need a canoe or boat.

SUMMARIZE What are some ways that communities can provide a healthful environment?

Lesson 1 Summary and Review

1 Summarize with Vocabulary

Use vocabulary and other terms from this lesson to complete the statements.

A healthful _____ is important to communities. Water, land, and air need to be _____ for people to have a healthful environment. In a healthful environment, many people enjoy outdoor _____, such as sports and gardening.

2 Explain what makes up an environment.

3 Critical Thinking Describe two of the recreation areas in your community. What makes these areas healthful?

4 **DRAW CONCLUSIONS** Draw and complete this graphic organizer to show the factors that create a healthful environment.

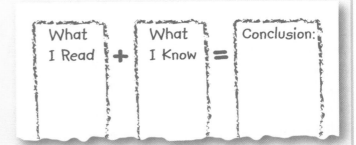

| What I Read | + | What I Know | = | Conclusion: |

5 Write to Inform—Description

Describe the kind of environment you need in order to enjoy your favorite form of outdoor recreation.

Protecting Your Community

Lesson Focus

Many people with different jobs work to keep your community clean and safe.

Why Learn This?

You can use what you learn to identify people who help take care of your community's health.

Vocabulary

graffiti

Keeping Your Community Clean

A community must be clean to protect the health of the people who live there. It takes many people to keep a community clean. For example, groundskeepers keep outside areas like parks clean and neat. They rake leaves and clean up trash and graffiti. **Graffiti** (gruh•FEET•ee) is writing or drawing made without permission on a public surface, such as a wall or a building.

Custodians and cleaners help keep inside areas clean by emptying trash cans, sweeping, and mopping floors. In hospitals, cleaners keep rooms, equipment, and supplies free from germs.

SUMMARIZE How are the jobs of custodians and cleaners important to the health of a community?

Quick Activity

Community Helpers
Think of a community worker you have seen. List ways this person helps keep the community and your environment safe.

◀ Garbage collector

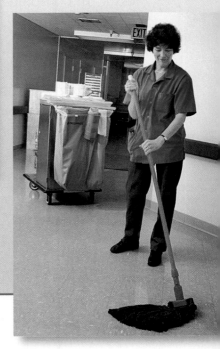

Custodian ▶

Keeping Your Community Safe

To be completely healthful, a community must be safe as well as clean. Many people work hard to keep your community safe. Police officers, for example, direct traffic, keep order, arrest criminals, and give first aid to accident victims.

Firefighters also help keep the community safe. They put out fires, rescue people, and perform first aid. They help prevent fires by giving people advice on how to keep their homes, schools, and workplaces safe.

Personal Health Plan

Real-Life Situation
Suppose you were in an unsafe situation.
Real-Life Plan
Make a list, with addresses and phone numbers, of people you can contact if you come across an unsafe situation in your community.

◀ The safety of a community depends on workers who respond to emergencies and help citizens stay safe.

▲ Firefighters

Mounted police officers ▶

Life Skills

Communicate

Imagine that you have an emergency and must call for help. Make a list of the information you will need to tell the dispatcher.

Emergency medical technicians (EMTs) are workers trained to handle serious injuries or sudden illnesses. EMTs give first aid at the scene of an accident and take care of patients on the way to a hospital.

If you call the police or fire station for help with an emergency, you are likely to talk to a *dispatcher*. Dispatchers tell safety workers like EMTs the information they need to find you.

DRAW CONCLUSIONS How does a dispatcher help save lives?

◀ Dispatchers work together with police officers, firefighters, and EMTs to help citizens in an emergency.

Lesson 2 Summary and Review

❶ **Summarize with Vocabulary**

Use vocabulary and other terms from this lesson to complete the statements.

Writing or drawing on buildings is called _____. A _____ takes calls and directs police officers, _____, and _____ to provide help in emergencies.

❷ Name five types of workers who help keep a community clean or safe.

❸ **Critical Thinking** Why is it important to community health to practice cleanliness when preparing food in a school lunchroom?

❹ **DRAW CONCLUSIONS** Draw and complete this graphic organizer to show the benefits of a safe and clean community.

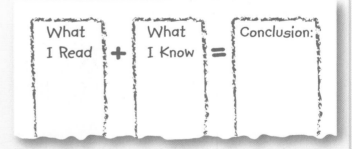

| What I Read | + | What I Know | = | Conclusion: |

❺ **Write to Inform—Description**

Describe what life might be like in a community that didn't have EMTs to help in emergencies. How would it be different from a community that does have EMTs?

Citizenship

Being a Good Neighbor

People in a community live and work together. They depend on one another to provide a clean and safe environment for everyone to enjoy. You can help, too! Here are some things you can do.

- **Volunteer to help out in your community. Organize a bake sale, and donate the proceeds to a local charity.**

- **Report unsafe or suspicious activity you see to your parents, teachers, or a police officer.**

- **Become involved. With adult supervision, work with some friends to clean up a local park or playground. Enjoy the clean and safe environment with a picnic afterward.**

- **Get to know your neighbors. Help a neighbor do yard work, take care of a pet, or clean the garage.**

- **Collect donations for a local shelter or Red Cross office.**

- **Become a *mentor*. A mentor is a positive role model to someone younger. As a mentor, or peer helper, you could help someone learn to read, for example.**

Activity

With your family, make a list of some useful things that could be done in your community. Choose one that you can do together. Plan how to do the task. When you have finished the task, write about how the experience helped make you a better neighbor.

311

Our Natural Resources

Natural Resources

Everything that we use comes from the environment. Energy, building materials, clothing, food, and medicines are all made from natural resources. **Natural resources** (REE•sawr•suhz) are materials from nature that people use to meet their needs. Our natural resources include rocks, minerals, plants, animals, air, sunlight, water, and soil. Oil, metal, cotton, clay, and wind are also natural resources.

We must have some of these resources, such as air and water. Without them, we could not live. We could live without some other resources, such as coal and gas, but our lives would be very different.

The pictures on these pages show eight kinds of natural resources. Which of these resources are nonrenewable? Which are renewable? ▼

▲ Trees

▲ Air

▲ Animals

Renewable resources are resources that can be replaced naturally. Trees, for example, are a renewable resource. When a tree is cut down, a new tree can be planted to grow in its place. Some renewable resources, such as water and wind, will never run out.

Other resources, however, take a very long time to replace or cannot be replaced at all. These are called nonrenewable resources . Oil is one of the most important nonrenewable resources. We use oil for energy. Oil is called a *fossil fuel* because it's made of the remains of tiny animals. Oil is found underground, and it takes millions of years to form. When we use oil, it's gone for good.

COMPARE AND CONTRAST How are renewable and nonrenewable resources alike and different?

▲ Minerals

▲ Water

▲ Coal, oil, and gas

▼ Soil and crops

How People Use Resources

Many resources went into building your home and the things in it. Paper and wood come from trees. Metal comes from minerals in rocks. Glass is made from sand. Concrete, cement, and plaster are all made from rocks. Plastics are made from oil.

Some clothes are made from plant fibers such as cotton or from animal products such as wool. Other materials, like plastic, are made from oil. Your food comes from plants and animals, whose energy originally came from soil, water, and sunlight. The medicines and all the chemicals in your house come from plants, animals, rocks, or minerals.

◀ Coal

▲ Coal is another fossil fuel resource that is nonrenewable. It is burned by energy plants to produce electricity.

▼ Energy plant

ACTIVITY

Life Skills
Communicate

Suppose that your little sister says nothing in her room was ever part of the environment. Choose at least two natural resources, and explain to her how those resources were used to make things in her room.

Natural resources are used to run your home. Electricity is made by burning coal or oil or by using sunlight, flowing water, wind, or heat from within the earth. The electricity runs through wires made of metals that come from rocks.

Your oven runs either on electricity or on gas, which comes from under ground. To heat your home, you might use oil, gas, wood, or electricity. Some homes are heated with corn-burning stoves.

 DRAW CONCLUSIONS In what way is water an important natural resource?

▲ Electricity travels through power lines. It can be used to run electrical appliances such as lights.

Lesson 3 Summary and Review

❶ Summarize with Vocabulary

Use vocabulary and other terms from this lesson to complete the statements.

Materials from nature that people use are called _____. Plants are examples of _____ resources, which can be replaced. Coal and oil, which are _____ resources, are examples of _____ fuels.

❷ Name five natural resources. Give an example of how people use each resource.

❸ Critical Thinking In what ways is water a renewable resource? In what ways is it nonrenewable?

❹ DRAW CONCLUSIONS Draw and complete this graphic organizer to show why people need to save natural resources.

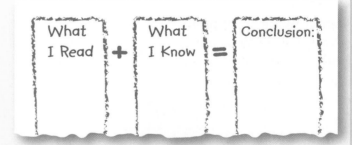

| What I Read | + | What I Know | = | Conclusion: |

❺ Write to Express—Business Letter

Write a letter to your local power company to request information about your power supply. Ask what natural resources are used to produce electricity and where those resources come from.

Preventing Pollution

Preventing Air Pollution

People need clean air to stay healthy. But in many places, especially near cities and factories, the air is polluted. **Pollution** (puh•LOO•shuhn) is harmful material in the air, water, or land. Air pollution includes dust and smoke particles and gases such as ozone and carbon monoxide.

Air pollution can cause eye and skin irritation and breathing problems such as asthma. Air pollution can even contribute to serious diseases like heart disease and cancer. People who breathe polluted air get diseases such as colds and flu more often.

▼ Smog is a form of air pollution. Laws to reduce smog have made some cities more healthful places to live.

Myth and Fact

Myth: **Air pollution affects only living things.**

Fact: Chemicals in polluted air can eat away at many kinds of building materials. Buildings and sculptures made from limestone or marble are especially likely to suffer damage from air pollution.

A lot of air pollution comes from factories and energy plants. Many energy plants burn fossil fuels such as coal. The smoke and gas that are released pollute the air. Burning **solid waste** such as garbage and litter also releases harmful gases and particles into the air. One way industries reduce this kind of pollution is by installing "scrubbers" in smokestacks. Scrubbers take out many of the pollutants before they get into the air.

Cars and trucks are some of the worst polluters. Over the years, manufacturers have made cars and trucks that pollute less. However, it's still important to use cars only when necessary. You can reduce air pollution by walking, biking, and using public transportation.

Focus Skill **DRAW CONCLUSIONS** How could using an electrical appliance in one place add to air pollution somewhere else?

This gas/electric hybrid car uses less gas, so it does not pollute as much as most cars. ▶

Health & Technology

Biofilters Some industries are trying a new way to reduce air pollution. Biofilters are being used to filter polluted air by using microorganisms. These organisms feed on the pollutants, removing them from the air. Biofiltration can be used by small businesses such as paint shops and garages as well as by large factories.

Preventing Water Pollution

Polluted water is bad for living things. There are many sources of water pollution. Some factories dump chemicals into water. In some places, untreated sewage flows into the ocean. Sometimes, people dump trash in rivers, and boats spill fuel.

Many water pollutants begin on land. For example, many farms use chemicals to kill insects and fertilize the soil. Rainwater flows over the soil, picking up the chemicals and fertilizers. They become pollutants when they flow into streams, rivers, lakes, and oceans.

▼ Fertilizers, pesticides, and industrial wastes are some of the sources of water pollution.

DANGER
SEWAGE CONTAMINATED
BEACH AND WATER

AVOID SHELLFISH HARVESTING, SWIMMING,
BEACH COMBING, OR OTHER CONTACT ACTIVITIES

▲ The Cuyahoga River in Cleveland, Ohio, was once so polluted with trash and oil that it caught on fire. The fire made many people realize how important it was to clean up the nation's rivers. Today the Cuyahoga River is much cleaner.

Water pollution can be very dangerous. Water that is polluted with human waste carries pathogens that can make people very ill or even kill them. Swimming in water that is polluted with chemicals can hurt your skin. Drinking polluted water, or eating fish that have lived in it, can cause serious diseases of the liver, kidneys, and brain.

We can protect our water supply. The Environmental Protection Agency (EPA) controls water pollution. The United States government's Clean Water Act protects water supplies. You can help by not throwing trash into water.

CAUSE AND EFFECT **What might be the effects of pouring untreated sewage into a lake?**

Quick Activity

Identify Water Pollutants Identify the kinds of water pollution shown on these pages. Choose one source of water pollution, and write about ways it can be controlled.

319

ACTIVITY

Building Good Character

Responsibility Keona has just finished drinking a bottle of water. There is no place to dispose of the plastic bottle because she is hiking in the woods. Name at least two ways Keona can show responsible behavior.

Preventing Land Pollution

Land pollution can harm your health and the environment. Littering is one kind of land pollution. Litter that is left in uncovered dumps can harm your health. Flies, mosquitoes, and rats that carry diseases often breed in dumps.

In many places, dumps are being replaced by sanitary landfills. In a *landfill*, trash is placed in a large pit that has a waterproof liner of plastic or clay. The trash is then covered with layers of soil. If the landfill is made properly, the waste won't harm the environment.

Poisonous chemicals and pollutants, like oil from cars, can be a problem. When it rains, chemicals on the road wash onto the land. They make the soil poisonous, which can kill plants and animals. These chemicals also get into the water supply.

◀ Salt makes an icy road safer to drive on. Since salt can harm plants and animals, many communities now use sand on icy roads.

▼ Litter that is not put in the proper place can cause disease.

People can reduce land pollution by not dumping trash or garbage. Take empty paint cans, batteries, and cleaning supply containers to collection centers in your community that accept poisonous waste.

Recycling materials instead of throwing them away can also reduce land pollution. For example, metal cans can be used to make new cans. Plastic containers can be reused. Another thing you can do is use a fabric bag to carry things home from the store instead of getting a plastic or paper bag from the store.

MAIN IDEA AND DETAILS **List three ways to reduce or prevent land pollution.**

▼ Many states have Adopt-a-Highway programs. Businesses or groups adopt a section of a highway and then work to keep it free of litter.

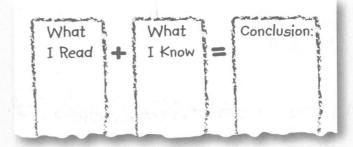

ADOPT A HWY LITTER CONTROL NEXT 2 MILES
S. W. SCHOOL OF ELECTRONICS

Lesson 4 Summary and Review

① **Summarize with Vocabulary**

Use vocabulary and other terms from this lesson to complete the statements.

People need to protect air, land, and water from _____. Burning _____ pollutes the air. One way factories remove some pollutants from smoke is by using _____. To reduce land pollution, dumps are being replaced by _____.

② Name one law that has helped reduce water pollution.

③ **Critical Thinking** What might happen if no one took responsibility for air pollution?

④ (Focus Skill) **DRAW CONCLUSIONS** Draw and complete this graphic organizer to show why people need to prevent pollution.

What I Read	+	What I Know	=	Conclusion:

⑤ **Write to Inform—Explanation**

Think of some rules that your school has, such as don't litter, keep the cafeteria clean, and so on. Write a paragraph explaining why these and other rules are important to your health and your classmates' health.

Set Goals
To Save Resources

Think about the amount of resources you use every day. What are some ways your family can save some of these resources? Using the steps for **Setting Goals** can help you plan to save resources.

Jane knows that water is an important resource. She notices some ways water is wasted in her home. She talks about this with her parents. What should Jane do next?

1 **Choose a goal.**

Jane and her parents decide that their goal will be to reduce the amount of water wasted in their home.

2 **List steps to meet the goal. Determine whether you will need any help.**

Jane discusses her goal and asks everyone to suggest ways to help reduce waste and save water.

3 Check your progress as you work toward the goal.

Jane and her mom check the water bill each month to see how much water the family is using. Jane records how much water is being saved.

4 Reflect on and evaluate your progress toward the goal.

Jane and her family discuss how many gallons of water they are saving. After a few months, her family finds that saving water is easy.

Problem Solving

Raoul hears on the news that the air in his city is becoming more polluted. Raoul knows that car exhaust causes air pollution. He notices that his family members drive the car a lot. They even drive to a store that is only two blocks away.

How might Raoul and his parents use the steps for **Setting Goals** to help them reduce air pollution? How does their effort demonstrate good citizenship?

Ways to Practice Conservation

Lesson Focus

Conserving resources such as water, air, and land is important to people's health.

Why Learn This?

You can use what you learn to practice conservation.

Vocabulary

conservation

Conservation Is Important

Clean air, water, and land are all part of a healthful environment. If not conserved, these resources and others will not last very long. **Conservation** (kahn•ser•VAY•shuhn) is the careful use of resources. Conservation makes resources last longer.

Conservation can help both renewable and nonrenewable resources last longer. For example, as long as people don't cut down trees faster than new ones grow, we should have forest resources. We can also conserve by using less of our resources such as fossil fuels and minerals. Recycling or reusing materials also reduces how much of our resources we use up.

Myth and Fact

Myth: Recycling aluminum cans saves only aluminum.

Fact: Recycling aluminum saves energy, too. The energy saved by recycling one aluminum can could run a television for three hours.

▼ Areas that protect animals and plants help conserve our natural resources.

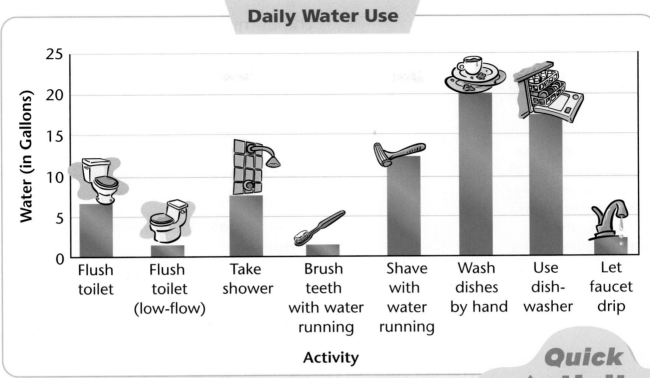

Daily Water Use

Water (in Gallons) vs. Activity

- Flush toilet
- Flush toilet (low-flow)
- Take shower
- Brush teeth with water running
- Shave with water running
- Wash dishes by hand
- Use dish-washer
- Let faucet drip

We can conserve water in many ways. For example, turn off the faucet when brushing your teeth. Take showers instead of baths. A five-minute shower uses about one-half as much water as an average bath. If you live in a dry area, plant your garden with plants that need little water.

People can also conserve water by installing low-flow toilets and low-flow showerheads. One type of low-flow showerhead adds air to the water. It can cut the amount of water used by one-half. Low-flow aerators can also be installed on faucets in your home. They mix air with water. The air helps the flow of water feel strong even though it has been reduced.

COMPARE AND CONTRAST How are tree conservation and coal conservation alike and different?

Quick **Activity**

Analyze Information Use the bar graph to estimate how much water a family of four uses each day for the activities listed. List ways this water use could be reduced.

▲ New energy-efficient light bulbs can save energy.

Other Ways to Conserve

The burning of fossil fuels produces most of the electricity used in the United States. Here are some ways your family can save fossil fuels.

- Replace regular (incandescent) light bulbs with fluorescent bulbs.
- Turn off lights when you leave a room for more than an hour.
- Put on sweaters instead of turning up the heat.
- Hang clothes to dry instead of using the dryer.
- Install ceiling fans to use instead of air conditioners.

SUMMARIZE **What are two ways people can change their use of electricity to conserve resources?**

Lesson 5 Summary and Review

1 Summarize with Vocabulary

Use vocabulary and other terms from this lesson to complete the statements.

_____ makes both renewable and nonrenewable resources last longer. When people _____ natural resources, they help the environment stay clean and they conserve resources.

2 Give two examples of renewable resources.

3 Critical Thinking Explain how conserving fossil fuels can also help conserve clean air, water, and land.

4 (Focus Skill) DRAW CONCLUSIONS Draw and complete this graphic organizer to show why people need to conserve resources.

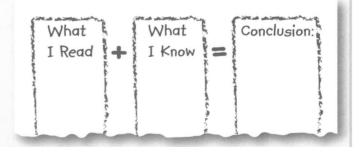

What I Read + What I Know = Conclusion:

5 Write to Entertain—Short Story

Write a story about how a family works together to conserve a natural resource, such as water. Use words like *save*, *reduce*, *conserve*, and *resources*.

ACTIVITIES

Science

Use It Again Recall that some resources can be replaced, while supplies of others are limited. Make lists of things you use at school and at home that are made from each of these two kinds of resources. Hint: Plastic products are made from oil, a fossil fuel. Make a plan for reusing some of them to conserve resources.

Home & Community

Pollution Prevention Work as a team to make a pollution prevention chart with three columns labeled *Air, Land, Water.* Discuss how you can prevent each of these kinds of pollution. Write the ideas on the chart, and then display it.

Physical Education

Physical Activities Find out what kinds of recreational activities are available in your community. Use the information to make a pamphlet to illustrate and map out where these activities take place. Invite others in your class to use the pamphlet to get ideas for recreational activities.

Career Link

Conservationist A conservationist is a person who works to conserve natural resources, such as forests. Conservationists often work with government agencies and private groups to help pass laws to protect resources and to educate the public about conserving resources. Most conservationists have a college degree in science. Choose a natural resource that interests you. Research the role of conservationists in conserving that resource. How might things be different if there were no conservationists?

Technology Project

Use Internet resources to find the story about Greenville, and read it. Using your community's name, write a similar real or imaginary story of a successful pollution cleanup.

GO ONLINE For more activities, visit **The Learning Site.** **www.harcourtschool.com/health**

Reading Skill

DRAW CONCLUSIONS

Draw and then use this graphic organizer to answer questions 1 and 2.

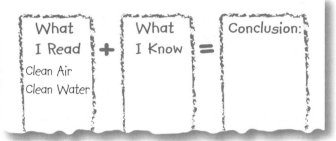

What I Read
Clean Air
Clean Water

+

What I Know

=

Conclusion:

1 In the second box write another thing people need.
2 Draw a conclusion and write it in the third box.

Use Vocabulary

Match each term in Column B with its meaning in Column A.

Column A	Column B
3 People who call EMTs	A emergency medical technicians
4 Handle serious injuries or sudden illnesses	B conservation
5 Living and nonliving things that surround you	C environment
	D dispatchers
6 Natural materials people use	E resources
7 Careful resource use	

Check Understanding

Choose the letter of the correct answer.

8 Graffiti is a type of _____. (p.308)
 A fossil fuel   C music
 B resource   D pollution

9 Which is **NOT** solid waste? (p. 317)
 F garbage   H trash
 G litter   J oil

10 In an unhealthful environment, the air, water, and land are _____. (pp. 316, 318, 320)
 A renewable   C nonrenewable
 B polluted   D conserved

11 Which is **NOT** a cause of air pollution? (p. 317)

F    H

G    J

12 A scrubber is used to remove pollutants from _____. (p. 317)
 A land   C water
 B smokestacks   D landfills

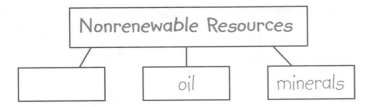

Nonrenewable Resources

oil   minerals

13 What nonrenewable fossil fuel is missing from the graphic organizer? (p. 314)

  F sun   **H** wind

  G coal   **J** rain

14 Recreation areas can be added to a community by _____. (p. 307)

  A illegal dumping

  B spreading organic fertilizer on fields

  C picking up litter in the community

  D turning old railroad tracks into trails

15 Dispatchers tell _____ where an emergency is and what kind of emergency it is. (p. 310)

  F hospital nurses

  G pollution technicians

  H EMTs

  J conservationists

Think Critically

16 Lisa and her friends had a picnic in the park. Lisa stayed to clean up, but her friends walked away. What could Lisa have said to her friends about why it's important to clean up their trash?

17 How is clean land related to clean water?

Apply Skills

18 **BUILDING GOOD CHARACTER**
Citizenship Mark lives across the street from Mrs. Lopez. She is retired and lives alone. She fell and broke her arm. What can Mark do to be a good neighbor to Mrs. Lopez?

19 **LIFE SKILLS**
Set Goals Mr. Carver notices that his electric bill is getting higher each month. He wants to lower his usage. What can Mr. Carver do to conserve electricity?

Write About Health

20 **Write to Inform—Description**
Describe what an ideal, healthful community would include.

Compare and Contrast

Learning how to compare and contrast information can help you understand what you read. You can use a graphic organizer like this one to compare and contrast.

Topic: List the two topics you are investigating.

Alike	Different
List ways the things are alike.	List ways the things are different.

Tips for Comparing and Contrasting

- To compare, ask—*How are people, places, objects, ideas, or events alike?*
- To contrast, ask—*How are people, places, objects, ideas, or events different?*
- When you compare, look for signal words and phrases such as *similar*, *both*, *the same as*, *too*, and *also*.
- When you contrast, look for signal words and phrases such as *unlike*, *different*, *however*, *yet*, and *but*.

Here is an example.

Compare ⟶

Abby and Halley both have an after-school snack every day. However, their choices are quite different. Abby has a piece of fruit and a glass of milk. Halley has potato chips and soda instead. Abby likes to eat right. Halley thinks eating right is not important. ⟵ Contrast

Here is what you could record in the graphic organizer.

Topic: Abby's and Halley's Snack Habits

Alike	Different
Both eat a snack every day.	Abby /fruit and milk
	Halley/potato chips and soda
	Abby/eating right is important
	Halley/eating right is not important

More About Compare and Contrast

Identifying how things are alike and how they are different can help readers understand ideas, events, people, and places. Use the graphic organizer from page 330 to sort the information given in the chart below.

Halley	likes to run	does not like apples	loves to eat hot dogs	enjoys soccer
Abby	loves to eat apples	enjoys soccer	likes to run	never eats hot dogs

Sometimes a paragraph compares and contrasts more than one topic. In the following paragraph, one topic being compared and contrasted is underlined. Find a second topic being compared and contrasted.

<u>Kurt and Barry both eat a healthful breakfast every morning. However, Kurt has milk and cereal, and Barry has eggs and juice.</u> Every day, Barry and Kurt leave for school at the same time. Barry rides his bike and gets there early. Kurt walks and gets there just before the bell rings.

Skill Practice

Read the following paragraph. Use the Tips for Comparing and Contrasting to answer the questions.

Justin and Amanda are both sick. Justin has an allergy to something in the air, unlike Amanda, who has pinkeye. Justin has itchy eyes. He sneezes many times a day. Amanda's eyes are itchy, too. Justin knows that he cannot pass his allergy to another person. Amanda, however, must be careful not to pass her pinkeye pathogens to anyone else.

1 What are two ways Justin and Amanda are alike?

2 What are two differences between their illnesses?

3 What are two signal words that helped you identify likenesses and differences in this paragraph?

Draw Conclusions

Draw conclusions by using information from the text and your own experience. This can help you understand what you read. You can use a graphic organizer like this one to help you draw conclusions.

What I Read
Use facts from the text to help you understand.

+

What I Know
Use your own experience to help you understand.

=

Conclusion:
Combine facts and details in the text with prior knowledge or personal experience.

Tips for Drawing Conclusions

- To draw conclusions, ask—*What information do I need to think about?*
- Then ask—*What do I know from my own experience that could help me draw a conclusion?*
- Pay close attention to the information the author gives, as well as to your experience, to be sure the conclusion is valid, or makes sense.

Here is an example.

> Latrisha wanted to go for a bike ride with her friends. Her mom was concerned about the dark storm clouds outside. A clap of thunder shook the room and Latrisha's mom shook her head. Latrisha picked up her book and went to her bedroom.

Story information

Your own experience

Here is what you could record in the graphic organizer.

What I Read
Latrisha wanted to go for a bike ride, but there were storm clouds outside.

+

What I Know
Loud thunder usually signals a bad storm.

=

Conclusion:
Latrisha could not go for a bike ride.

More About Drawing Conclusions

Sensible conclusions based on your experience and the facts you read are valid. For example, suppose the paragraph on page 332 included a sentence that said the sun came out and Latrisha had a smile on her face. You could then draw a different conclusion about Latrisha's bike ride.

What I Read		What I Know		Conclusion:
It looked as if the bike ride would not happen, but the sun came out.	+	People smile when they are happy.	=	Since the sun came out and Latrisha was smiling, she must have gone for the bike ride.

Sometimes a paragraph might not contain enough information to draw a valid conclusion. Read the following paragraph. Think of one valid conclusion you could draw. Then, think of one conclusion that would be invalid.

Allie knows that lightning usually hits the tallest object above ground. She decides to stay low to the ground. She wheels her bicycle into a nearby ditch and climbs in next to it. Then Allie looks up. She sees something she has never seen before.

Skill Practice

Read the following paragraph. Use the Tips for Drawing Conclusions to answer the questions.

Paul could not wait to go swimming, fishing, and boating. As soon as he arrived at the lake, he ran down to the shore. Confused, he looked down at the water as he bent to pick up an old trash bag. Paul saw algae covering the water's surface. He ran back up to the house to talk to his mom.

1 What conclusion did you draw about Paul's trip to the lake?

2 What information did you use from your personal experience that helped you draw the conclusion?

3 What story information did you use to draw the conclusion?

Identify Cause and Effect

Learning how to identify cause and effect can help you understand why things happen. You can use a graphic organizer like this one to show cause and effect.

Cause:
A cause is an action or event that makes something happen.

Effect:
An effect is what happens as a result of an action or event.

Tips for Identifying Cause and Effect

- To find an effect, ask—*What happened?*
- To find a cause, ask—*Why did this happen?*
- Remember that events can have more than one cause or effect.
- Look for signal words and phrases, such as *because* and *as a result* to help you identify causes and effects.

Here is an example.

> Cause
>
> Effect

Eddie roller-skated for 30 minutes. Because of this, his heart beat faster. Eddie exercises at least three times a week. He knows that it is good for his health.

Here is what you could record in the graphic organizer.

Cause:
Eddie roller-skated for 30 minutes.

Effect:
Eddie's heart beat faster.

More About Cause and Effect

   Events can have more than one cause or effect. For example, suppose the paragraph on page 334 included a sentence that said Eddie's lungs took in more air while he was roller-skating. You could then identify two effects of Eddie's roller-skating.

Cause:

Eddie roller-skated for 30 minutes.

➡ Effect:

Eddie's heart beat faster.

➡ Effect:

Eddie's lungs took in more air.

   Some paragraphs contain more than one cause and effect. In the following paragraph, one cause and its effect are underlined. Find a second cause and its effect.

   The next day Eddie ran for 30 minutes after school. <u>Because he forgot to stretch first, he pulled a muscle in his leg.</u> Eddie's mom gave him first aid. As a result, Eddie's leg soon felt better. Eddie now understands the importance of stretching before exercising.

Skill Practice

   Read the following paragraph. Use the Tips for Identifying Cause and Effect to help you answer the questions.

   Sarah Smith's mom smokes two packs of cigarettes every day. Because of this, Mrs. Smith has bad breath. Her clothes smell like smoke. Even her hair smells like smoke. As a result of smoking, Mrs. Smith's teeth have turned yellow. Sarah wants her mom to stop smoking.

1 What has caused Mrs. Smith's teeth to turn yellow?

2 What are three other effects her smoking has caused?

3 What two signal phrases helped you identify the causes and effects in this paragraph?

Identify Main Idea and Details

Being able to identify the main idea and details can help you understand what you read. You can use a graphic organizer like this one to show the main idea and details.

Main Idea: The most important idea of a paragraph, several paragraphs, or a selection

Detail: Information that tells more about the main idea	Detail: Information that tells more about the main idea	Detail: Information that tells more about the main idea

Tips for Identifying Main Idea and Details

- To find the main idea, ask—*What is this mostly about?*
- Remember that the main idea is not always stated in the first sentence.
- Look for details that answer questions such as *who, what, where, when, why,* and *how.*
- Use pictures as clues to help you figure out the main idea.

Here is an example.

> Main Idea
>
> Your skin is the largest organ of your body. It has two layers that enclose and protect the rest of your body. The epidermis is the top layer. It holds moisture in and keeps germs out. The dermis is the bottom layer. It contains blood vessels and nerve endings.
>
> Detail

Here is what you could record in the graphic organizer.

Main Idea: Your skin is your body's largest organ.

Detail: Skin has two layers.	Detail: The first layer is the epidermis.	Detail: The second layer is the dermis.

More About Main Idea and Details

Sometimes the main idea is not at the beginning of a passage. If the main idea is not given, it can be understood from the details. Look below at the graphic organizer. What do you think the main idea is?

Main Idea: ?

Detail:	Detail:	Detail:
Sweat reaches the skin's surface through pores.	You sweat the most when you are hot.	Sweat changes from a liquid to a gas.

Sometimes a paragraph's main idea might contain details of different types. In this paragraph, identify whether the details give reasons, examples, facts, steps, or descriptions.

Wash your hands thoroughly to rid them of germs. First, *be sure to use soap and warm water.* Next, wash the skin on your knuckles and under your fingernails. Dirt tends to build up there. Finally, rinse your hands well and dry them.

Skill Practice

Read the following paragraph. Use the Tips for Identifying the Main Idea and Details to answer the questions.

We all have traits that make us special. Your physical traits determine the length of your toes. If you are a good artist with a kind heart, you can thank your mental and emotional traits. If your stomach feels queasy when you meet new people, your social traits are the reason. Your personal traits make you uniquely you!

1 What is the main idea of the paragraph?

2 What supporting details give more information about the main idea?

3 What details answer any of the questions—*who, what, where, when, why,* and *how*?

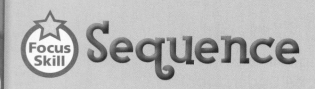

Paying attention to the sequence of events, or the order in which things happen, can help you understand what you read. You can use a graphic organizer like this one to show sequence.

1. The first thing that happened 2. The next thing that happened 3. The last thing that happened

Tips for Understanding Sequence

- Pay attention to the order in which events happen.
- Recall dates and times to help you understand the sequence.
- Look for signal words such as *first*, *next*, *then*, *last*, and *finally*.
- Sometimes it is helpful to add your own time-order words to help you understand sequence.

Here is an example.

> Time-order word

> What happens to the food you eat? First, food enters your body through your mouth and travels down the esophagus. Next, the food is broken down in your stomach, and the nutrients are absorbed in the small intestine. Finally, the undigested waste goes into your large intestine.

Here is what you could record in the graphic organizer.

1. Food goes into the mouth and down the esophagus. 2. Food goes into the stomach and the small intestine. 3. Undigested waste goes into the large intestine.

More About Sequence

Sometimes information is sequenced by dates. For example, on what date did you learn to walk? Kick a soccer ball? Play in your first soccer game? Use the graphic organizer to sequence some things that happened as your body was growing and changing.

| 1. I started walking on July 15, 1998. | | 2. I first kicked a soccer ball on February 10, 1999. | | 3. I played in my first soccer game on June 24, 2003. |

When time-order words are not given, add your own words to help you understand the sequence. In the paragraph below, one time-order word has been included and underlined. How many more time-order words can you add to understand the paragraph's sequence?

Eating a cracker will start the process of digestion. <u>First,</u> your teeth will break the cracker into smaller parts. Your tongue will push the cracker around in your mouth. Saliva will begin to break down the nutrients in the cracker. Off it goes down the esophagus.

Skill Practice

Read the following paragraph. Use the Tips for Understanding Sequence to answer the questions.

When you call 911 in an emergency, first, tell the operator your name. Next, give the phone number and address from which you are calling. Then, tell the operator what the problem is. Last, give the operator a family member's name and phone number.

1 What is the first thing you should do when you call 911 in an emergency?

2 What might happen if you did not follow the right sequence or left out a step?

3 What four signal words helped you identify the sequence of instructions in this paragraph?

Summarize

Learning how to summarize helps you to identify the most important parts in a passage. This can help you understand what you read. You can use a graphic organizer like this one to show how to summarize.

Main Idea:		Details:		Summary:
Tell about the most important information you have read.	+	Add details that answer important questions like who, what, where, when, why, and how.	=	Retell what you have just read and include only the most important details.

Tips for Summarizing

- To write a summary, ask—*What is the most important idea of the paragraph?*
- To add details to your summary, ask—*who*, *what*, *when*, *where*, *why*, and *how*.
- Remember to use fewer words when retelling the information.
- Tell the information in your own words.

Here is an example.

Main Idea

    Every member of a family has an important role. The main role of a school-age child is to go to school and be responsible. A parent's job is to support and care for the children. Over time, roles change as family members get older.

Details

Main Idea:		Details:		Summary:
Every member of a family has an important role.	+	Children go to school, and parents provide children with care and support. Roles change.	=	In a family, both children and parents have important roles which can change.

More About Summarizing

Sometimes a paragraph has details that are not important enough to be included in a summary. For example, suppose the paragraph on page 340 included a sentence that told what it meant to be a responsible child. The graphic organizer would remain the same because that detail is not important to understanding the paragraph's main idea.

Main Idea:		Details:		Summary:
Every member of a family has an important role.	+	Children go to school, and parents provide children with care and support. Roles change.	=	In a family, both children and parents have important roles which can change.

Sometimes the main idea of a paragraph is not in the first sentence. In the following paragraph, two important details are underlined. What is the main idea?

Ann's grandmother sews all her own clothes. <u>Ann's dad is an artist.</u> He loves drawing cartoons. <u>Ann's mom works every day in a restaurant.</u> She is an excellent cook. Ann respects every member of her family. Each person has a unique talent or skill.

Skill Practice

Read the following paragraph. Use the Tips for Summarizing to answer the questions.

Susan Scott has a headache. When Susan's sister, Pam, gets a headache, Mr. Scott gives her a pain reliever. However, Mr. Scott does not let Susan take a pain reliever. He reminds Susan that she does not like the side effects. Instead, he has Susan lie down until she feels better.

1 If a friend asked you what this paragraph was about, what information would you include? What would you leave out?

2 What is the main idea of the paragraph?

3 What two details would you include in a summary of the paragraph?

First Aid

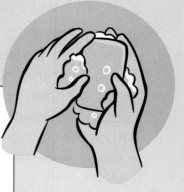

342

Health and Safety

For Bleeding–Universal Precautions

You can get some diseases from another person's blood. Avoid touching anyone's blood. To treat a wound, follow the steps below.

If someone else is bleeding

1

Wash your hands with soap if possible.

2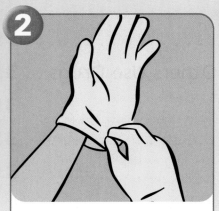

Put on protective gloves, if available.

3

Wash small wounds with water. Do *not* wash serious wounds.

4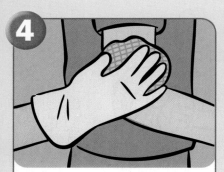

Place a clean gauze pad or cloth over the wound. Press firmly for ten minutes. Don't lift the gauze during this time.

5

If you don't have gloves, have the injured person hold the gauze or cloth in place with his or her hand.

6

If after ten minutes the bleeding has stopped, bandage the wound. If the bleeding has not stopped, continue pressing on the wound and get help.

If you are bleeding, you do not need to avoid your own blood.

For Choking

If someone else is choking

1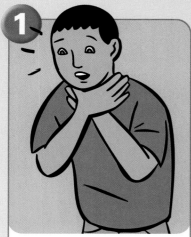

Recognize the Universal Choking Sign—grasping the throat with both hands. This sign means a person is choking and needs help.

2

Stand behind the choking person, and put your arms around his or her waist. Place your fist above the person's navel. Grab your fist with your other hand.

3

Pull your hands toward yourself, and give five quick, hard, upward thrusts on the person's stomach.

If you are choking when alone

1 Make a fist, and place it above your navel. Grab your fist with your other hand. Pull your hands up with a quick, hard thrust.

2 Or, keep your hands on your belly, lean your body over the back of a chair or over a counter, and shove your fist in and up.

For Burns

- Minor burns are called first-degree burns and involve only the top layer of skin. The skin is red and dry, and the burn is painful.

- Second-degree burns cause deeper damage. The burns cause blisters, redness, swelling, and pain.

- Third-degree burns are the most serious. They damage all layers of the skin. The skin is usually white or charred black. The area may feel numb because nerve endings have been destroyed.

All burns need immediate first aid.

Minor Burns

- Run cool water over the burn or soak it for at least five minutes.

- Cover the burn with a clean dry bandage.

- Do *not* put lotion or ointment on the burn.

More Serious Burns

- Cover the burn with a cool, wet bandage or cloth.

- Do *not* break any blisters.

- Do *not* put lotion or ointment on the burn.

- Get help from an adult right away.

For Nosebleeds

- Sit down, and tilt your head forward. Pinch your nostrils together for at least ten minutes.

- You can also put a cloth-covered cold pack on the bridge of your nose.

- If your nose continues to bleed, get help from an adult.

For Insect Bites and Stings

- Always tell an adult about bites and stings.

- Scrape out the stinger with your fingernail.

- Wash the area with soap and water.

- A covered ice cube or cold pack will usually take away the pain from insect bites. A paste made from baking soda and water also helps.

- If the bite or sting is more serious and is on an arm or leg, keep the leg or arm dangling down. Apply a cold, wet cloth. Get help immediately.

- If you find a tick on your skin, remove it. Protect your fingers with a tissue or cloth to prevent contact with infectious tick fluids. If you must use your bare hands, wash them right away.

- If the tick has already bitten you, ask an adult to remove it. Using tweezers, an adult should grab the tick as close to your skin as possible and pull the tick out in one steady motion. Do not use petroleum jelly because it may cause the tick to struggle releasing its infectious fluids. Wash the bite site.

For Skin Rashes from Plants

Many poisonous plants have three leaves. Remember, "Leaves of three, let them be." If you touch a poisonous plant, wash the area and your hands. Put on clean clothes and wash the dirty ones. If a rash develops, follow these tips.

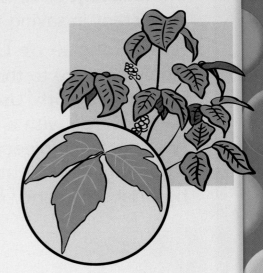

- Apply calamine lotion or a baking soda and water paste. Try not to scratch. Tell an adult.

- If you get blisters, do not pop them. If they burst, keep the area clean and dry. If your rash does not go away in two weeks, or if the rash is on your face or in your eyes, see your doctor.

For Dental Emergencies

You should know what to do if you have a dental emergency.

Broken Tooth

- Rinse your mouth with warm water. Wrap a cold pack with a cloth. Place it on the injured area. Save any parts of the broken tooth. Call your dentist immediately.

Knocked-Out Permanent Tooth

- Find the tooth and clean it carefully. Handle it by the top (crown), not the root. Put it back into the socket if you can. Hold it in place by biting on clean cloth. If the tooth cannot be put back in, place it in a cup with milk or water. See a dentist immediately. Time is very important in saving the tooth.

Bitten Tongue or Lip

- Apply pressure to the bleeding area with a cloth. Use a cold pack covered with a cloth to stop swelling. If the bleeding doesn't stop within 15 minutes, go to a hospital emergency room.

Food/Objects Caught Between Teeth

- Use dental floss to gently take out the object. Never use anything sharp to take out an object that is stuck between your teeth. If it cannot be removed, call your dentist.

Estimating Serving Size

Choosing a variety of foods is only half the story. You also need to choose the right amounts. The table below can help you estimate the number of servings you are eating of your favorite foods.

Estimating Serving Size

Food Group	Amount of Food in One Serving	Some Easy Ways to Estimate Serving Size
Bread, Cereal, Rice, and Pasta Group	$\frac{1}{2}$ cup cooked cereal, rice, or pasta 1 slice bread, $\frac{1}{2}$ medium bagel 1 cup ready-to-eat (dry) cereal	ice cream scoop
Vegetable Group	1 cup raw leafy vegetables $\frac{1}{2}$ cup other vegetables, cooked or chopped raw $\frac{1}{2}$ cup tomato sauce	about the size of a tennis ball
Fruit Group	1 medium apple, pear, or orange 1 medium banana $\frac{1}{2}$ cup chopped or cooked fruit 1 cup fresh fruit 4 oz cup fruit juice	about the size of a baseball
Milk, Yogurt, and Cheese Group	$1\frac{1}{2}$ oz natural cheese 8 oz yogurt 8 oz milk	about the size of three dominoes
Meat, Poultry, Fish, Dried Beans, Eggs, and Nuts Group	2–3 oz lean meat, chicken, or fish 2 tablespoons peanut butter $\frac{1}{2}$ cup cooked, dry beans	about the size of a computer mouse
Fats, Oils, and Sweets Group	1 teaspoon margarine or butter	about the size of the end of your thumb

Fight Bacteria

You probably already know to throw away food that smells bad or looks moldy. But food doesn't have to look or smell bad to make you ill. To keep your food safe and yourself from becoming ill, follow the steps outlined in the picture below. And remember—when in doubt, throw it out!

FIGHT BAC!

Keep Food Safe From Bacteria ®

CLEAN
Wash hands and surfaces often.

SEPARATE
Don't cross-contaminate.

CHILL
Refrigerate promptly.

COOK
Cook to proper temperatures.

Copyright 2003 Partnership for Food Safety Education

Food Safety Tips

Tips for Preparing Food

- Wash hands with hot, soapy water before preparing food. Also wash hands after preparing each dish.

- Defrost meat in a microwave or the refrigerator—not on the kitchen counter.

- Keep raw meat, poultry, fish, and their juices away from other foods.

- Wash cutting boards, knives, and countertops immediately after cutting up meat, poultry, or fish. Never use the same cutting board for meats and vegetables without thoroughly washing the board first.

Tips For Cooking

- Cook all food thoroughly, especially meat. Cooking food completely kills bacteria that can make you ill.

- Red meats should be cooked to a temperature of 160°F. Poultry should be cooked to 180°F. When done, fish flakes easily with a fork.

- Eggs should be cooked until the yolks are firm. Never eat food that contains raw eggs such as uncooked cookie dough.

Tips for Cleaning Up the Kitchen

- Wash all dishes, utensils, and countertops with hot, soapy water.

- Store leftovers in small containers that will cool quickly in the refrigerator.

Bike Safety Check

A safe bike should be the right size for you.

- You should be able to rest your heel on the pedal when you sit on your bike with the pedal in the lowest position.

- When you are standing astride your bike with both feet flat on the ground, your body should be 2 inches (about 5 cm) above the bar that goes from the handlebar to the seat.

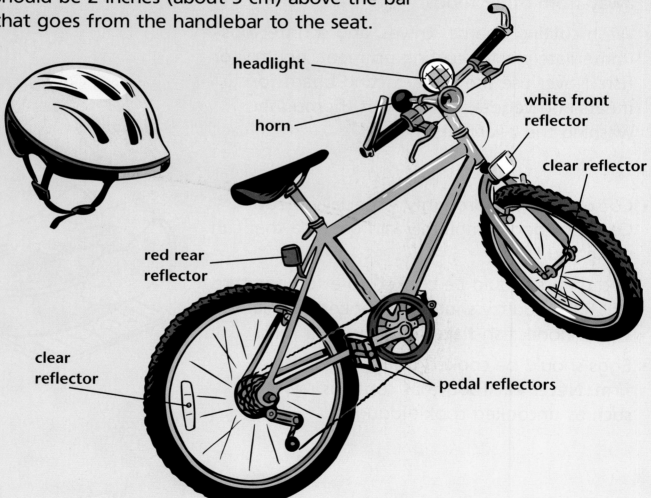

headlight

horn

white front reflector

clear reflector

red rear reflector

clear reflector

pedal reflectors

A bike should have all the safety equipment shown above. Does *your* bike pass the test?

Safety While Riding

Here are some tips for safe bicycle riding.

- Always wear your bike helmet, even for short distances.

- Check your bike every time you ride it. Is it in safe working condition?

- Ride in single file in the same direction as traffic. Never weave in and out of parked cars.

- Before you enter a street, **STOP**. **Look** left, right, and then left again. **Listen** for any traffic. **Think** before you go.

- Walk your bike across an intersection. **Look** left, right, and then left again. Wait for traffic to pass.

- Obey all traffic signs and signals.

- Do not ride your bike at night without an adult. If you do ride at night, be sure to wear light-colored clothing, use reflectors, and front and rear lights.

Your Bike Helmet

- About 500,000 children are involved in bike-related crashes every year. That's why it's important to always wear your bike helmet.

- Wear your helmet properly. It should lie flat on your head. The straps should be snug so it will stay in place if you fall.

- If you do fall and your helmet hits the ground, replace it—even if it doesn't look damaged. The inner foam lining may be crushed. It might not protect you if you fell again.

What to Do When Others Use Drugs

You should make a personal commitment to not use alcohol, tobacco, or other drugs. But you may be around other students or adults who make unhealthful choices about drugs. Here is what you can do.

Know the Signs

Someone who has a problem with drugs may be sad or angry all the time, skip school or work, or forget events often.

Talk to a Trusted Adult

Do not keep someone's drug use a secret. Ask a trusted adult for help. You can also get support from adults to help you resist pressure to use drugs.

Be Supportive

If a person decides to stop using drugs, help them quit. Suggest healthful activities you can do together. Tell them you are happy they have quit.

Stay Healthy

Do not stay anywhere that drugs are being used. If you cannot leave, stay as far away from the drugs as possible.

Where to get help
- Hospitals
- Alateen
- Alcoholics Anonymous
- Narcotics Anonymous
- Al-Anon
- Drug treatment centers

A Drug-Free School

Many schools make rules and sponsor activities to encourage people to say *no* to drugs. This makes the schools a more healthful environment for everyone.

School Rules

Many schools decide to be drug free. They often have strict penalties for anyone found with drugs. For example, a person found with drugs may be expelled or suspended from school.

Positive Peer Pressure

Peer pressure can be bad or good. *Positive peer pressure* is the effect of people the same age encouraging each other to make healthful choices. For example, students may make posters or hold rallies to encourage others to choose not to use drugs.

When Home Alone

Everyone stays home alone sometimes. When you stay home alone, it's important to know how to take care of yourself. Here are some easy rules to follow that will help keep you safe when you are home by yourself.

Do These Things

- Lock all the doors and windows. Be sure you know how to lock and unlock all the locks.

- If someone who is nasty or mean calls, hang up immediately. Tell an adult about the call when he or she gets home. Your parents may not want you to answer the phone at all.

- If you have an emergency, call 911. Be prepared to describe the problem and to give your full name, address, and telephone number. Follow all instructions given to you. Do not hang up the phone until you are told to do so.

- If you see anyone hanging around outside your home, call a neighbor or the police.

- If you see or smell smoke, go outside right away. If you live in an apartment, do not take the elevator. Go to a neighbor's house, and call 911 immediately.

- Entertain yourself. Time will pass more quickly if you are not bored. Work on a hobby, read a book or magazine, do your homework, or clean your room. Before you know it, an adult will be home.

Do Not Do These Things

- Do NOT use the stove, microwave, or oven unless an adult family member has given you permission, and you know how to use these appliances.

- Do NOT open the door for anyone you don't know or for anyone who is not supposed to be in your home.

- Do NOT talk to strangers on the telephone. Do not tell anyone that you are home alone. If the call is for an adult family member, say that he or she can't come to the phone right now and take a message.

- Do NOT have friends over unless you have permission from your parents or other adult family members.

A telephone with caller ID display can help you decide whether to answer the phone.

Backpack Safety

Carrying a backpack that is too heavy can injure your back. Carrying one incorrectly also can hurt you.

Safe Weight

A full backpack should weigh no more than 10 to 15 percent of your body weight. Less is better. To find 10 percent, divide your body weight by 10. Here are some examples:

Your Weight (pounds)	Maximum Backpack Weight (pounds)
60	6
65	$6\frac{1}{2}$
70	7

This is the right way to carry a backpack.

Safe Use

- Use a pack with wide shoulder straps and a padded back.

- Lighten your load. Leave unnecessary items at home.

- Pack heavier items inside the pack so that they will be closest to your back.

- Always use both shoulder straps to carry the pack.

- Never wear a backpack while riding a bicycle. The weight makes it harder to stay balanced. Use the bicycle basket or saddlebags instead.

This is the wrong way to carry a backpack.

Glossary

Numbers in parentheses indicate the pages
on which the words are defined in context.

PRONUNCIATION RESPELLING KEY

Sound	As in	Phonetic Respelling	Sound	As in	Phonetic Respelling	Sound	As in	Phonetic Respelling
a	bat	(BAT)	eye	idea	(eye•DEE•uh)	th	thin	(THIN)
ah	lock	(LAHK)	i	bit	(BIT)	u	pull	(PUL)
air	rare	(RAIR)	ing	going	(GOH•ing)	uh	medal	(MED•uhl)
ar	argue	(AR•gyoo)	k	card	(KARD)		talent	(TAL•uhnt)
aw	law	(LAW)		kite	(KYT)		pencil	(PEN•suhl)
ay	face	(FAYS)	ngk	bank	(BANGK)		onion	(UHN•yuhn)
ch	chapel	(CHAP•uhl)	oh	over	(OH•ver)		playful	(play•fuhl)
e	test	(TEST)	oo	pool	(POOL)		dull	(DUHL)
	metric	(MEH•trik)	ow	out	(OWT)	y	yes	(YES)
ee	eat	(EET)	oy	foil	(FOYL)		ripe	(RYP)
	feet	(FEET)	s	cell	(SEL)	z	bags	(BAGZ)
	ski	(SKEE)		sit	(SIT)	zh	treasure	(TREZH•er)
er	paper	(PAY•per)	sh	sheep	(SHEEP)			
	fern	(FERN)	th	that	(THAT)			

A

abstinence (AB•stuh•nuhns)
Avoiding a behavior that can harm your health *(182)*

Activity Pyramid (ak•TIV•uh•tee PIR•uh•mid)
A guide to physical activity *(106)*

addiction (uh•DIK•shuhn)
A craving that makes a person keep using a drug even when he or she knows
it is harmful *(195)*

advertising (AD•ver•tyz•ing)
A way businesses give people information about their products *(48)*

aerobic exercise (air•OH•bik EK•ser•syz)
Physical activity that makes your heart and lungs work harder, improving the
health of your cardiovascular system *(100)*

air bag (AIR BAG)
In a car, van, or truck, a bag that inflates during a collision to protect the
people in the front seat *(144)*

alcohol (AL•kuh•hawl)
A drug found in beer, wine, and liquor *(224)*

alcoholism (AL•kuh•hawl•iz•uhm)
A disease in which people cannot control their use of alcohol *(229)*

allergy (AL•er•jee)
A noncommunicable disease in which a person's body reacts to a certain substance *(176)*

anaerobic exercise (an•air•OH•bik EK•ser•syz)
Physical activity that makes your muscles stronger and bigger *(100)*

antibodies (AN•tih•bahd•eez)
Chemicals the body makes to fight disease *(167)*

arteries (AR•ter•eez)
Blood vessels that carry blood away from the heart *(22)*

arthritis (ar•THRYT•is)
A noncommunicable disease in which the body's joints become damaged and are painful *(179)*

asthma (AZ•muh)
A noncommunicable disease of the respiratory system; it causes breathing problems *(177)*

bacteria (bak•TIR•ee•uh)
One-celled living things; most are harmless, but some can cause disease *(162)*

balanced diet (BAL•uhnst DY•uht)
A diet made up of healthful amounts of foods from each of the food groups *(69)*

basic needs (BAY•sik NEEDZ)
The physical, mental, emotional, and social needs that all people have *(252)*

blended family (BLEND•uhd FAM•uh•lee)
A family that is formed when two single parents with children marry *(283)*

brain (BRAYN)
The organ that controls the nervous system *(12)*

bronchi (BRAHNG•ky)
The two tubes that carry air from the trachea to the lungs *(20)*

bully (BUL•ee)
A person who hurts or frightens others, especially those who are smaller, weaker, different, or alone *(149)*

caffeine (ka•FEEN)
A drug found in coffee, tea, chocolate, and certain soft drinks *(196)*

cancer (KAN•ser)
A disease in which body cells that are not normal grow out of control *(175)*

capillaries (KAP•uh•lair•eez)
The tiny blood vessels that deliver blood to the tissues *(22)*

carbohydrates (kar•boh•HY•drayts)
The starches and sugars that are the body's main source of energy *(60)*

cavity (KAV•ih•tee)
A hole in a tooth *(36)*

cell (SEL)
The smallest working part of the body *(4)*

cocaine (koh•KAYN)
A powerful drug made from the leaves of the coca plant *(202)*

communicable disease (kuh•MYOO•nih•kuh•buhl dih•ZEEZ)
An illness that can spread from person to person *(158)*

compassion (kuhm•PASH•uhn)
An understanding of the needs and feelings of others *(268)*

compromise (KAHM•pruh•myz)
A solution in which each side in a conflict gives up part of what it wants *(263)*

conflict (KAHN•flikt)
A disagreement between people who have different needs or wishes *(262)*

conflict resolution (KAHN•flikt rez•uh•LOO•shuhn)
The resolving of a problem between people *(262)*

conservation (kahn•ser•VAY•shuhn)
The careful use of resources to make them last longer *(324)*

consumer (kuhn•SOOM•er)
A person who buys a product *(48)*

cooperate (koh•AHP•er•ayt)
To work helpfully with others *(296)*

dermis (DER•muhs)
The thick bottom layer of skin; it contains blood vessels and nerves *(33)*

diabetes (dy•uh•BEET•eez)
A noncommunicable disease in which the body stops making insulin or stops using it properly and so cannot use sugar properly *(178)*

diaphragm (DY•uh•fram)
The muscle beneath your lungs that helps move air into and out of the lungs *(21)*

disease (dih•ZEEZ)
A condition that damages or weakens part of the body *(158)*

dose (DOHS)
The amount of medicine you should take each time you use it *(191)*

drug (DRUHG)
A substance other than food that changes the way the body works *(188)*

drug dependence (DRUHG dih•PEN•duhns)
The need to take a drug just to feel normal *(201)*

emergency (ee•MER•juhn•see)
A situation in which help is needed right away *(116)*

environment (en•VY•ruhn•muhnt)
All of the living and nonliving things that surround you, including plants, animals, air, water, soil, buildings, and roads *(304)*

epidermis (ep•uh•DER•mis)
The top layer of the skin *(32)*

esophagus (ih•SAHF•uh•guhs)
A tubelike organ that pushes food from your mouth to your stomach *(16)*

expiration date (eks•puh•RAY•shuhn DAYT)
A date on a medicine container that tells you when the medicine will no longer be safe to take *(192)*

extended family (ek•STEN•duhd FAM•uh•lee)
A family that includes more than just parents and children; it may include grandparents or other relatives *(283)*

family emergency plan (FAM•uh•lee ee•MER•juhn•see PLAN)
Steps your family takes to stay safe during an emergency *(118)*

fats (FATS)
Nutrients that give your body more energy than any other kind of nutrient *(61)*

flood (FLUHD)
An overflow of water onto normally dry land *(139)*

food guide pyramid (FOOD GYD PIR•uh•mid)
A diagram that helps people choose foods for a healthful diet *(69)*

food poisoning (FOOD POY•zuhn•ing)
An illness caused by eating food that contains germs *(84)*

fungi (FUN•jy)
Simple living things, such as molds, yeasts, and mushrooms; some fungi can cause disease *(163)*

gang (GANG)
A group of people who often use and sell drugs, carry weapons, and use violence to commit crimes *(150)*

goal (GOHL)
Something you are willing to work for *(255)*

graffiti (gruh•FEET•ee)
Writing or drawing done on public property without permission *(308)*

habit (HAB•it)
Something you do so often that you don't even think about it *(72)*

hazard (HAZ•erd)
An object or condition that makes a place unsafe *(122)*

heart (HART)
The organ that pumps blood through the body *(22)*

hurricane (HER•ih•kayn)
A storm that forms over an ocean; it has strong winds and heavy rain, and it can cause flooding *(139)*

illegal drug (ih•LEE•guhl DRUHG)
A drug that is not a medicine and that is against the law to sell, buy, have, or use *(200)*

immune system (ih•MYOON SIS•tuhm)
The body system that fights off disease *(166)*

immunity (ih•MYOON•ih•tee)
The body's ability to fight off pathogens *(167)*

infection (in•FEK•shuhn)
The growth of pathogens in the body *(163)*

ingredients (in•GREE•dee•uhnts)
All the things used to make a food, medicine, health-care product, or household product *(81)*

inhalants (in•HAYL•uhnts)
Substances that have fumes some people use as drugs *(197)*

intoxicated (in•TAHK•suh•kay•tuhd)
A condition in which a person is strongly affected by too much alcohol *(228)*

large intestine (LARJ in•TES•tuhn)
The last organ of the digestive system; it removes water to form solid waste *(16)*

lens (LENZ)
In the eye, the clear, curved part that bends light to form an image on the back of the eye *(42)*

lifeguard (LYF•gard)
A person who is trained to rescue people who are in danger of drowning *(128)*

lightning (LYT•ning)
A large release of electricity between clouds and the ground; it can injure or kill people, cause fires, and damage property *(139)*

lungs (LUHNGZ)
Organs that allow oxygen from the air to pass into the body *(20)*

marijuana (mair•uh•WAHN•uh)
An illegal drug made from the hemp plant *(200)*

medicine (MED•uh•suhn)
A drug used to prevent, treat, or cure a health problem *(188)*

minerals (MIN•er•uhlz)
Nutrients that help your body grow and work and are not made by living things *(62)*

muscle (MUHS•uhl)
An organ that contracts and relaxes to produce movement *(25)*

muscular system (MUHS•kyoo•ler SIS•tuhm)
The body system that allows your body to move *(25)*

natural resources (NACH•er•uhl REE•sawrs•uhz)
Materials from nature that people use to meet their needs; they include rocks, minerals, plants, animals, air, sunlight, water, and soil *(312)*

negotiate (nih•GOH•shee•ayt)
To work together to resolve a conflict *(263)*

nerves (NERVZ)
Bundles of fibers that carry messages *(12)*

nervous system (NERV•uhs SIS•tuhm)
The body system that coordinates all of the body's activities *(12)*

nicotine (NIK•uh•teen)
A very addictive chemical in tobacco; it speeds up the nervous system *(219)*

noncommunicable disease (nahn•kuh•MYOO•nih•kuh•buhl dih•ZEEZ)
An illness that does not spread from person to person *(159)*

nonrenewable resources (nahn•rih•NOO•uh•buhl REE•sawrs•uhz)
Resources that take a very long time to replace or that cannot be replaced at all *(313)*

nuclear family (NOO•klee•er FAM•uh•lee)
A family consisting of a mother, father, and one or more children *(282)*

nucleus (NOO•klee•uhs)
The control center of a cell *(6)*

nutrients (NOO•tree•uhnts)
Substances the body can use *(18)*

nutritious (noo•TRISH•uhs)
Having value as a food *(80)*

organs (AWR•guhnz)
Groups of tissues that work together to perform a certain job *(7)*

over-the-counter medicines (OH•ver•thuh•kown•ter MED•uh•suhnz)
Medicines that can be bought without a prescription *(191)*

pathogens (PATH•uh•juhnz)
Organisms, such as bacteria or viruses, that cause communicable diseases *(162)*

peer pressure (PIR PRESH•er)
The strong influence people your own age can have on you *(207)*

plaque (PLAK)
A sticky film that forms on the teeth *(36)*

pollution (puh•LOO•shuhn)
Harmful materials that make the air, water, and land unsafe *(316)*

portion (POR•shuhn)
The amount of food you want to eat or the amount you may be served *(70)*

posture (PAHS•cher)
The position of the body in standing or sitting *(92)*

prescription (prih•SKRIP•shuhn)
A doctor's order for medicine *(190)*

prescription medicine (prih•SKRIP•shun MED•uh•suhn)
Medicine that only an adult can buy and then only with a doctor's order *(190)*

privacy (PRY•vuh•see)
Time by yourself *(254)*

proteins (PROH•teenz)
A kind of nutrient that gives you energy and helps build and repair your cells *(61)*

pupil (PYOO•puhl)
In the eye, the opening through which light enters *(42)*

R

renewable resources (rih•NOO•uh•buhl REE•sawrs•uhz)
Resources that can be replaced by nature—for example, trees *(313)*

resistance (rih•ZIS•tuhns)
The body's natural ability to fight off disease *(180)*

rest (REST)
Quiet time to relax and give your heart, muscles, and mind a chance to slow down *(102)*

retina (RET•uh•nuh)
In the eye, the part on which an image forms; the image is carried by nerve signals to the brain *(42)*

role model (ROHL mahd•uhl)
A person who sets a good example *(272)*

self-concept (self•KAHN•sept)
The way you think about yourself *(248)*

self-confidence (self•KAHN•fih•duhns)
A good feeling you have about what you are able to do *(248)*

self-control (self•kuhn•TROHL)
Your ability to express your feelings responsibly *(258)*

self-respect (self•rih•SPEKT)
The feeling that you have about yourself when you like yourself and are proud of what you do *(206)*

serving (SER•ving)
The measured amount of a food a person should eat at one time *(69)*

side effects (SYD ih•FEKTS)
Unwanted changes a medicine may cause in the body *(189)*

single-parent family (SING•guhl PAIR•uhnt FAM•uh•lee)
A family made up of one parent and his or her children *(282)*

skeletal system (SKEL•uh•tuhl SIS•tuhm)
The body system made up of all your bones; it supports your body, protects your organs, and allows you to move *(24)*

skull (SKUHL)
The bones of your head that protect your brain *(24)*

small intestine (SMAWL in•TES•tuhn)
A tubelike organ just below the stomach; nutrients are absorbed into the body through its walls *(16)*

solid waste (SAHL•id WAYST)
Garbage and litter *(317)*

spine (SPYN)
The backbone; it is made up of small bones that protect the spinal cord *(24)*

stomach (STUHM•uhk)
The organ that mixes digestive juices with food *(16)*

system (SIS•tuhm)
A group of organs that work together *(7)*

tar (TAR)
A dark, sticky material that coats the lungs and air passages of smokers *(219)*

tissue (TISH•OO)
A group of cells that work together to do a job *(7)*

tornado (tawr•NAY•doh)
A violent windstorm that spins in a funnel shape *(139)*

trachea (TRAY•kee•uh)
The tube that carries air to the bronchi; the air then passes into the lungs *(20)*

traditions (truh•DISH•uhnz)
Customs that family members follow *(282)*

trait (TRAYT)
A characteristic, or quality, that a person has *(4)*

vaccine (vak•SEEN)
A medicine that can prevent a certain disease *(170)*

values (VAL•yooz)
Strong beliefs about how people should behave and live *(294)*

veins (VAYNZ)
Blood vessels that carry blood back to the heart *(22)*

virus (VY•ruhs)
The smallest kind of pathogen *(162)*

vitamins (VYT•uh•minz)
Nutrients that help your body do certain jobs and are made by living things *(62)*

water (WAW•ter)
A nutrient necessary for life; it helps your body break down foods and carries nutrients to your cells *(63)*

weapon (WEP•uhn)
An object that can be used to kill, injure, or threaten someone *(151)*

Index

CREDITS

Cover Design: Bill Smith Studio

Photographs:

KEY: (t) top, (b) bottom, (l) left, (r) right, (c) center, (bg) background, (fg) foreground

Cover Photographer: Brian Fraunfelter

viii (b) Ronnie Kaufman/Corbis, ix (t) Bob Daemmrich Photography; 5 (t) Getty Images; 7 (t) G.W. Willis, M.D./Visuals Unlimited; 7 (tc) Science Vu/Visuals Unlimited; 7 (bc) Dr. Mary Notter/Phototake; 7 (b) Fred Hossler/Visuals Unlimited; 13 (tl) Chris Lowe/Index Stock Imagery; 13 (tc) Tim Davis/Photo Researchers; 13 (cl) Mark Richards/PhotoEdit; 13 (cr) Index Stock Imagery; 13 (bl) Myrleen Ferguson Cate/PhotoEdit; 13 (bc) David Young-Wolff/PhotoEdit; 22 Frank Siteman/Mira.com; 23 Dennis Kunkel/Phototake; 27 Warren Morgan/Corbis; 37 (t) E.R. Degginger/Color-Pic; 37 (b) Science Photo Library/Photo Researchers; 39 Royalty-Free/Corbis; 52 Stephen Simpson/Getty Images; 55 Tom Stewart/Corbis; 60 David Brooks/Corbis; 64 (l) Christie's Images; 64 (r) The Art Archive/Musee Bouilhet-Christofle Paris/Dagli Orti; 70 (tr) Michael Newman/PhotoEdit; 87 Jeff Zaruba/Corbis; 88 (tl) Michael Pohuski/FoodPix; 88 (br) Jim Scherer Photography/StockFood; 99 Craig Hammell/Corbis; 100 (l) Jeffry W. Myers/Corbis; 100 (r) Diaphor Agency/Index Stock Imagery; 106 (tl) Richard Hutchings/Corbis; 106 (cr) Ty Allison/Getty Images; 106 (bc) Michael Newman/PhotoEdit; 106 (br) Tom & Dee Ann McCarthy/Corbis; 108 (l) Tony Freeman/PhotoEdit; 108 (r) David Young-Wolff/PhotoEdit; 109 (b) Bill O'Connor/Peter Arnold, Inc.; 109 (inset) David Young-Wolff/PhotoEdit; 112 (tr) Tom & Dee Ann McCarthy/Corbis; 112 (br) Richard Hutchings/Corbis; 117 (tl) David R. Frazier; 117 (tr) Tony Freeman/PhotoEdit; 117 (b) Pat LaCroix/Getty Images; 129 Robert Harding Picture Library/Alamy Images; 130 Mark E. Gibson Photography; 131 PA1 Harry C. Craft, III/U.S. Coast Guard Digital; 137 (t) Roy Morsch/ Bruce Coleman, Inc.; 137 (c) Jeri Gleiter/Getty Images; 137 (b) E.R. Degginger/Color-Pic; 139 (l) Charles A. Doswell, III/Visuals Unlimited; 139 (r) Marc Epstein/Visuals Unlimited; 139 (b) Aaron Horowitz/Corbis; 143 (r) Myrleen Ferguson Cate/PhotoEdit; 153 Andrea Booher/FEMA ; 160 Dennis MacDonald/PhotoEdit; 162 (inset) Dr. Dennis Kunkel/Visuals Unlimited; 162 (l) Bettmann/Corbis; 163 (tl) Network Productions/Index Stock Imagery; 163 (tr) Gopal Murti/Phototake; 163 (cr) Dr. David Phillips/Visuals Unlimited; 163 (br) Dr. Dennis Kunkel/Visuals Unlimited; 164 Custom Medical Stock Photo; 165 (inset) Science VU/CDC/Visuals Unlimited; 165 George H.H. Huey/Corbis; 166 Dennis Kunkel/Phototake; 169 (tr) Chris Lowe/Phototake; 169 (br) Spencer Grant/PhotoEdit; 170 Tony Freeman/PhotoEdit; 174 (inset) Lester Lefkowitz/Corbis; 174 (l) Brand X/Creatas Royalty Free Stock Resources; 176 (inset) BIOS (Klein/Hubert)/Peter Arnold, Inc.; 180 (l) Creatas Royalty Free Stock Resources; 180 (r) David Young-Wolff/PhotoEdit; 183 Creatas Royalty Free Stock Resources; 185 (tl) Custom Medical Stock Photos; 185 (tr) Chris Lowe/Phototake; 185 (bl) Science VU/CDC/Visuals Unlimited; 185 (br) BIOS (Klein/Hubert)/Peter Arnold, Inc.; 188 (l) Rob and Ann Simpson/Visuals Unlimited; 195 Mark E. Gibson Photography; 200 (l) D. Lyons/Bruce Coleman, Inc.; 200 (r) Bob Child/AP/Wide World Photos; 201 (t) Andrew Lichtenstein/The Image Works; 201 (b) Royalty-Free/Corbis; 202 (l) Ivan Polunin/Bruce Coleman, Inc.; 202 (c) Mick Rock/Bruce Coleman, Inc.; 202 (r) brt Photo/Mira.com; 204 Royalty-free/Corbis; 206 (t) Tony Freeman/PhotoEdit; 207 (t) Tony Freeman/PhotoEdit; 207 (b) Bob Daemmrich Photography; 213 Bob Daemmrich Photography; 218 (r) Michael Newman/PhotoEdit; 219 (t) Phototake; 219 (b) Clark Overton/Phototake; 223 Dennis MacDonald/PhotoEdit; 228 (t) Tom Carter/PhotoEdit; 241 (b) Custom Medical Stock Photos; 243 Tony Freeman/PhotoEdit; 249 (t) Jonathan Nourok/PhotoEdit; 249 (b) Lawrence Migdale; 250 (r) Tom & Dee Ann McCarthy/Corbis; 254 (b) Larry Dale Gordon/Getty Images; 256 (l) Lucidio Studio/Corbis; 256 (r) Amos Morgan/Getty Images; 257 (l), (r) Getty Images; 258 (t) Jim Cummins/Getty Images; 260 Tom & Dee Ann McCarthy/Corbis; 264 (bg) Getty Images; 264 (r) Russell Burden/Index Stock Imagery; 269 Omni-Photo Communications/Index Stock Imagery; 270 (t) Lawrence Migdale; 282 (l), (r) Creatas Royalty Free Stock Resources; 283 (l) SW Productions/Brand X Pictures; 283 (r) Creatas Royalty Free Stock Resources; 285 Ronnie Kaufman/Corbis; 296 (l) Ariel Skelley/Corbis; 296 (r) SW Productions/Brand X Pictures; 297 (l) Royalty-free/Corbis; 297 (r) Creatas Royalty Free Stock Resources; 304 (b) Greg Probst/Panoramic Images/NGS Images.com; 306 (cl) Andre Gallant/Getty Images; 306 (cr) Syracuse Newspapers/John Berry/The Image Works; 306 (bl) Jack Affleck/Superstock; 306 (br) Renee Lynn/Photo Researchers; 307 (t) Fred Bruemmer/Peter Arnold, Inc.; 307 (b) Jim Olive/Peter Arnold, Inc.; 308 (l) Karl Weatherly/Corbis; 308 (r) Mark E. Gibson Photography; 309 (t) Royalty-Free/Corbis; 309 (b) Laima Druskis/Photo Researchers; 310 Ted Horowitz/Corbis; 312 (l) Jeff Greenberg/Peter Arnold, Inc.; 312 (c) Matt Meadows/Peter Arnold, Inc.; 312 (r) Paul A. Souders/Corbis; 312 (bg) Harvey Lloyd/Peter Arnold, Inc.; 313 (l) David R. Frazier/Photo Researchers; 313 (c) Scott Barrow, Inc.; 313 (r) Bill Ross/Corbis; 314 (t) V.C.L./Getty Images; 314 (b) Grapes.Michaud/Photo Researchers; 316 (b) Robert Landau/Corbis; 316 (inset) Judyth Olatt; Ecoscene/Corbis; 317 (b) Bill Ross/Corbis; 318 (bl) Michael St. Maur Sheil/Corbis; 318 (br) P. Plisson/Explorer/Photo Researchers; 318 (tl) Jeff Greenberg/Photo Researchers; 318 (tr) Garry D. McMichael/Photo Researchers; 319 (inset) The Cleveland Press Collection, Cleveland State University Library; 319 (r) Mark E. Gibson Photography; 320 (b) Michael P. Gadomski/Photo Researchers; 320 (t) Mark Joseph/Getty Images; 321 Bob Daemmrich Photography; 324 Mark E. Gibson Photography; 327 Tim Thompson/Getty Images.

All other photos © Harcourt School Publishers. Harcourt photos provided by the Harcourt Index, Harcourt IPR, and Harcourt photographers; Weronica Ankarorn, Victoria Bowen, Eric Camden, Annette Coolidge, Doug Dukane, Ken Kinzie, Brian Minnich, and Steve Williams.

Illustrations:

Lisa Blackshear, x, xi, xii, xiii, 10, 11, 48-49, 76, 77, 84-85, 93, 104, 105, 122-123, 126, 127, 128, 136-137, 142-143, 146, 147, 152, 172, 173, 198, 220, 221, 232, 234, 235, 252-253, 266, 267, 275, 282-283, 294, 295; David Brooks, ix, 330, 332, 334, 336, 338, 340; Denny Butts, 118, 119; Jean Calder, iv, 12, 17, 18, 21, 22, 24-25; Mark Collins, 56, 132, 154, 244, 278, 300, 328; Mike Dammer, vi, 87, 118; John Karapelou, vii, 6, 7, 13, 28, 33, 37, 43, 44, 167, 171, 184, 203, 222, 227; Ed Shems, 62, 86, 176, 196, 212, 224, 229, 231, 240, 241, 299, 325; Martin Shovel, 12, 16, 24, 27, 37, 38, 44, 55, 63, 92, 99, 111, 120, 124, 131, 140, 153, 167, 168, 177, 183, 213, 243, 257, 265, 269, 277, 288, 324, 327; Carl Wiens, ix, 342, 343, 344, 345, 346, 347, 348, 349, 350, 351, 352, 353, 354, 355, 356, 357, 358.